D1560920

THE ART OF
OGATA KENZAN

THE ART OF
OGATA KENZAN

*Persona and Production
in Japanese Ceramics*

BY RICHARD L. WILSON

New York   WEATHERHILL   Tokyo

First edition, 1991

Published by Weatherhill, Inc., 420 Madison Avenue, 15th
Floor, New York, New York, 10017, and Tanko-Weatherhill, 8-3
Nibancho, Chiyoda-ku, Tokyo 102. Protected by copyright
under terms of the International Copyright Union; all rights
reserved. Printed in the United States.

Publication of this book was assisted by a grant from the
Japan Foundation

Library of Congress Cataloging in Publication Data:

Wilson, Richard L., 1949–
The art of Ogata Kenzan: persona and production in Japanese
ceramics / by Richard Wilson. — 1st ed.
p.   cm.
Includes bibliographical references and index.
ISBN 0-8348-0240-6 : $49.95
1. Ogata, Kenzan, 1663–1743.   2. Potters — Japan — Biography.
3. Pottery, Japanese — Edo period, 1600–1868.   I. Ogata
Kenzan, 1663–1743.   II. Title.
NK4210.039W55   1991
738'.092 — dc20
[B]   91-3957
                                                  CIP

For Tomi-chan

CONTENTS

FOREWORD

Yamane Yūzō
Professor Emeritus, Tokyo University

Richard Wilson has been studying Kenzan — the man and his tradition — with a singular intensity for some ten years. I first met him in 1982 through the late Satō Masahiko, who at that time was president of the Kyoto City University of Fine Arts. Satō, himself a ceramics specialist, had written on Kenzan some years back, and had made both the studio and academic facilities of his university available for Richard's dissertation research. Richard knew of my work on the Rimpa-school painters Tawaraya Sōtatsu and Kenzan's older brother Kōrin, and whenever he was in Tokyo he would call for an appointment. We began to visit collections of Kenzan ware together, and with each new meeting, I was increasingly impressed with Richard's character and the sharpness of his questions about Kenzan and Kōrin. Here was someone determined to make a genuine study of Kenzan. I would be remiss in not mentioning here the selfless dedication of Saeko, his wife.

Americans have been studying Japanese art for over a century, and given the important place that ceramics occupies in Japanese culture, it seems only natural that someone would want to study one of our greatest potters. As our own recent experience has shown, however, Kenzan can be something of a demon who devours art historians instead of yielding to their inquiries. There are so many facets to this artist — questions of design, painting, calligraphy, and ceramics technique — that studying him becomes a formidable challenge. Just as he clothed his pots in thick slips and rich enamels, Kenzan has, it seems, pulled a thick cloak of obscurity around himself.

All of this has failed to deter Richard. In his recent article "Searching for Style in Kenzan Ware," written for the Japanese-language ceramics journal *Tōyō Tōji*, Richard undertook a rigorous stylistic analysis of Kenzan ware — a project hitherto avoided by Kenzan specialists in this country. The results were impressive. In a subsequent roundtable discussion that was carried in our art magazine *Me no Me*, Richard demonstrated a knowledge and judgment that surpassed the Japanese panelists, Gotoh Museum curator Takeuchi Jun'ichi and Tokyo National University professor Kōno Motoaki. This is remarkable given the fact that Takeuchi and Kōno are the foremost Kenzan specialists in our country.

In the present study, Richard has brought many years of research to fruition; it is clear that he has overtaken Kobayashi Taichiro's *Kyoto Kenzan*, the authoritative work on Kenzan since its publication in Japan some forty years ago. Richard's exposition of Kenzan's background should restore the context that has been lacking in the field, and his exhaustive survey of Kenzan's art — documents, ceramics, and painting outside as well as inside Japan — will provide dramatic new insights. His componental approach to Kenzan design will establish the correct method for studying the artist's works. He deserves the highest respect for challenging these thorny problems. As for his consideration of the Kenzan succession and later imitators, based on an extensive survey of collections here and abroad, we can be assured that it will clearly surpass anything ever attempted. His treatment of the history of Kenzan scholarship, especially his exposition of the reception of Kenzan in the West, will also be a first. Finally, we all await his opinion on the infamous Sano Kenzan scandal, since he can claim to be a dispassionate observer of an affair that shocked the Japanese art world at that time.

In my travels outside Japan I have always been impressed by the admiration that artists like Kenzan and Kōrin receive. In our country, these figures are loved so much that it is difficult at times to treat them objectively. But Richard has found a place for both sharpness and sympathy. Without a doubt, this book is the first full-scale, serious study of Kenzan and his work of the post-Kobayashi era. I know it will captivate Western readers and boost Kenzan studies everywhere.

PREFACE

I was afraid of Zen monks. They always seemed to know what you were, or weren't. But here was a kind-looking man, inviting me inside his temple; he had something to show me. Hoping that his treasure was something other than the stick that the great monks used against their charges, I walked in.

I had known something of Ogata Kenzan, a famous potter who had worked in these parts some two centuries ago. News that his kiln was up here in the northwest hills of Kyoto had brought me to the Hōzōji temple gate. As it turned out, the temple was built on the very site of Kenzan's workshop, and the monk's treasure was potshards — dozens of them in the temple collection and many more still in the ground. The range of techniques and decorative styles was astounding. One didn't have to know the Kenzan legend to sense a strong vision behind the workshop that created these objects. It was 1978, and I had started on the Kenzan road.

Dreaming of writing a scholarly thesis on Kenzan, I returned home and enrolled in graduate school. From the beginning, and in every subsequent stage of research, I had the immense good fortune to be assisted by my wife Saeko, who contributed her expertise in calligraphy, tea ceremony, and Japanese culture in general. From 1980 to 1982 I read as much of the Japanese writing on Kenzan as I could. Then came the much-hoped-for opportunity to return to Kyoto. Sponsored by a Fulbright Fellowship and later a Japan Foundation Fellowship, I enrolled at the Kyoto City University of Fine Arts, where I pursued Kenzan from the perspective of art historian and potter. In addition to the standard archival work, I translated Kenzan's original pottery notes, searched for his materials in the hills and construction sites around Kyoto, and ran tests out of my studio. The famous potter Tomimoto Kenkichi had conducted similar tests at the same university some three decades earlier, and now I was fortunate enough to be advised by his students. I also received much encouragement from my academic advisor in Japan, Satō Masahiko. Notorious for his dour character, he nevertheless welcomed me into a field that for all practical purposes was taboo; on his deathbed he shed tears of happiness over my first Kenzan publication. My sense of loss — and gratitude — continues.

Before leaving Japan I received from the cooperative Hōzōji monks a dozen shards from the Kenzan kiln site on the promise that I would analyze them. A postdoctoral fellowship from the Smithsonian Institution in 1985 afforded a year at the Freer Gallery, where I undertook scientific studies of the shards and compared them with the many Kenzan pieces in the Freer collection. Director Thomas Lawton and his staff, especially Marty Amt, Tom Chase, Louise Cort, Fu Shen, and Ann Yonemura offered much assistance in that year — and thereafter. In the summer of 1986, through a grant from the Asian Cultural Council, I excavated a hundred more pieces at Hōzōji, and have just begun a second round of tests at Rice University. The results will form part of a future scientific and archaeological study on Kenzan and his equally famous predecessor Ninsei.

During the year at the Smithsonian I also began an extensive collection tour, this time not only to Japan but to the "attic" collections in North America and Europe. I discovered hundreds of Kenzan pieces, often neglected and always of variable quality. Among the many kind people I met in those travels I must mention Rose Hempel, then curator at the Museum für Kunst und Gewerbe, Hamburg. Another trip to Japan, sponsored by the Metropolitan Center for Far Eastern Studies, yielded still more materials. In Japan, Yamane Yūzō, an emeritus professor of Tokyo University and now an advisor to the Idemitsu Museum, has offered continuing good advice and assistance and has graciously contributed a foreword to this book. Takeuchi Jun'ichi of the Gotoh Museum and Yabe Yoshiaki at Tokyo National Museum have generously shared their time and resources, as has Tachi Kokuryū, abbot of the Zen'yōji temple, the site of Kenzan's grave. Yoshida Hiroshi, Yanagi Takashi, Sakakibara Satoru, and Kuroda Taizō provided much help in locating illustrations.

From collection visits and from earlier publications, I assembled a group of photographs and statistics on Kenzan pieces — mostly pots but some paintings and calligraphies as well. By the end of 1988 I had surveyed a total of over three thousand works. I then tried to divide the works into every conceivable category — vessel shape, technique, decor style, secondary pattern, subject and style of inscription, signature style, and types of monogram and seal. After months of cutting, matching, and pasting — and searching for demonstrable kinships across these categories — I arrived at about twenty clusters, representing phases of Kenzan-style production from the master's day to the present. To see these clusters emerge from the jumble of materials that had been passed off as Kenzan was my most exciting experience as an art historian. Not only was a chronology of the total Kenzan tradition becoming apparent, but by reading back through that chronology I could isolate work of the original Kenzan workshop — the authentic pots. Encouraged by this breakthrough, I turned again to primary sources on Kenzan and his day, this time finding significant connections between his career and various cultural contexts. It was time to write.

In the course of preparing the manuscript I received much help from Marla Wells and Ann Arnett in my university department. Allen Matusow, Dean of Humanities at Rice University, has made it possible for me to return to Japan to obtain additional material. The Metropolitan Center of Far Eastern Art Studies provided a generous subvention for the illustrations. Critical reading of the manuscript was generously accomplished by two professor-mentors: J. Edward Kidder at International Christian University, and Stephen Addiss at the University of Kansas. Steve has been supportive at every stage of the project. Professor Fumiko Yamamoto, also at the University of Kansas, made helpful suggestions on my poetry translations. Jack Greene, with an eye for Kenzan as sharp as anyone's, has been a constructive critic. At Weatherhill, editor Kim Schuefftan welcomed my initial proposal, and Editor-in-Chief Jeffrey Hunter has provided a steady and clear organizational vision throughout the manuscript stages. Liz Preston capably edited the text, and Liz Trovato provided the design. Thanks to these people and many more, the book will be ready in time for the 250th Kenzan commemorative, to be held in 1992.

In order to bring Kenzan to the broadest possible audience, his personal letters, period documents, and interpretive details are included in an annotated appendix. Readers interested in Kenzan scholarship are urged to consult this. Potters will find a wealth of technical details in a translation of Kenzan's pottery manual, which is also appended to the text proper. Points on connoisseurship — the real vs. fake — are enumerated in a visual appendix.

Macrons have been omitted for Japanese words in common English use like Kyoto and shogun. Temple names are given with their *ji* and *dera* suffixes without separation by hyphens. Japanese personal names are given in traditional order, with family name first; premodern artists are referred to by their pseudonyms alone after first mention (e.g., Ogata Kōrin becomes "Kōrin"). Ages for historical persons are given according to Japanese count, which assigns a year at birth. All translations are by the author unless otherwise noted.

Chapter One

BETWEEN FIGURE AND GROUND

The distance between raw clay and finished pot is measured in human inspiration. What kind of messages might be embedded in a single vessel? The roughly ten thousand years of ceramics production in Japan offers a panoply of answers. Prehistoric earthenwares appear to speak of a seamless world, one in which immediate survival needs and magic were indivisible. After exposure to Chinese and Korean models in the common era, the Japanese potter became preoccupied with an external standard, one of advanced technologies and dignified forms. At the same time, however, many rural potters maintained the simplest of methods. Their artless vessels awaited the discerning eye of the sixteenth-century tea master, who made the circumstances of manufacture — forming marks, glaze imperfections, and kiln accidents — into elements of style.

Since the debut of the tea master, the expressive possibilities of ceramics have been a concern of both makers and users in Japan. Pottery production is, however, an incremental and corporate enterprise, one that tends to obliterate the personal mark. In comparison, the art of the brush is naked and immediate. It is hardly surprising, then, that Japan's first "individual" potters emerged just as brush met clay. The breakthrough occurred in Kyoto, the imperial capital of Japan, where the local pottery lore is replete with celebrities: Ninsei, who brought elegant, courtly designs into his tea-ceremony wares; Eisen, the first independent potter to decorate porcelain; and Eisen's student, Mokubei, famed for his powerful work in Chinese-style blue-and-white and overglaze-enamel decor.

But it was Ogata Kenzan (1663–1743) who burst upon the

Japanese ceramics scene with a force that can only be described as alchemical. To a world still dominated by the astringent canons of the tea ceremony, Kenzan brought a revolutionary approach to form, color, and design. In his kilns, the first of which opened in 1699 in the northwest (*ken*) mountains (*zan*) of Kyoto, one might find pots that looked like paintings, and pots that resembled antiques; pots whose surfaces recalled cloth, paper, or flowers; pots that were dazzlingly bright, and pots that evoked the dark of night. In a world obsessed with self-effacement, Kenzan seemed to delight in self-expression. Idiosyncrasy sings in his pots. In high-collar Japanese museums and galleries, Kenzan ware is subversive — a cheerful, babbling child amid morbid monks. When used as tableware, his exuberant designs all but consume the food within them. Plainly, Kenzan redefined the balance between what a pot "said," and what a pot "did." Japanese ceramics would never be the same.

Despite his expressive range and occasional beastly force, Kenzan was no mere primitive. The cultivated scion of a wealthy family of textile designers, Kenzan brought extensive cultural credentials to the world of ceramics. His wares were rich in high-culture images, especially the scholar's arts of painting, poetry, and calligraphy, but the pot never disappeared; retaining something of the elemental sense so strongly articulated in the tea-ceremony wares, Kenzan wares managed to be at once poetic and potlike. This captured not only the fancy of eighteenth-century potters and patrons, but the attention of each generation that followed. If the aristocratic images evoked in his work are considered "high" and the clay medium "low," Ogata Kenzan effected a meeting of heaven and earth.

In terms of historical judgment, Kenzan the man has acquired an aura only slightly less than celestial. His popular biography is long on appeal: a wealthy Kyoto dilettante aspires to the life of a scholar-recluse, and begins ceramics as a cultured hobby under the tutelage of the most famous potter of the day, Nonomura Ninsei. After a decade of work at his own kiln, for reasons seemingly inexplicable, Kenzan is pressed into mass production at an urban workshop. Artistic decline inevitably follows. At the end of his life he flees to an unknown city (Edo) where, despite obscurity and poverty, he finds artistic vindication.

This synthesis of East Asian literary and religious ethos with Western artistic angst found enormous favor in the art boom following World War II. As for the ceramics, painting, and calligraphy attributed to Kenzan, they have come to light not through systematic investigation, but through a system of interlocking obligations that has traditionally confined art dealers and art scholars in Japan to a chorus of soft acceptances. A loosening of standards in the burgeoning postwar antiquities trade encouraged imitators to try their hands at the Kenzan style, setting the stage for the notorious Sano Kenzan scandal of 1962. In that year, the sudden introduction of dozens and later hundreds of pots and documents said to be made by Kenzan in his seventy-fifth year in the rural village of Sano polarized the Japanese art community and eventually discredited some of the world's most prominent experts. From Japan's foremost potter, Kenzan had become Japan's foremost art scandal.

In the rush to deify Kenzan, the nature of his enterprise has been all but forgotten. To be sure, Ogata Kenzan endowed ceramics with a new level of associative power, infusing pots with images ranging from literary classicism to contemporary urban fashion. But precedent was also important. Kenzan was the beneficiary of a highly developed urban craft system, one characterized by broad access to materials, technical maturity, task specialization, and quick responsiveness to fashion trends. By the late sixteenth century, that system had come to be exploited by non-specialists, beginning with tea masters and soon expanding to amateurs of all persuasions. Some of them included Kenzan's own ancestors, and there is every indication that Kenzan too was a mediator rather than maker. The story of Kenzan ware, then, is not that of a lone artist's production, but of the relationship of a designer to a workshop tradition, both in his lifetime and afterward. Therein we see the meeting of Japanese ceramics, which before Kenzan focused almost entirely on technical expression, with the broader world of design. The urban craft system and the design tradition that it helped to spawn are the subjects of this chapter.

Kenzan's triumph in design was equally dependent on developments outside the craft world. In Chapter 2 we will examine how the Ogata family's social position and affluence gave Kenzan access to the most exciting centers of the day: the academy of Itō Jinsai (1627–1705), then the most prominent

Confucianist in Kyoto; the temples of the Ōbaku Zen sect, where new life was being injected into Buddhism; and the salons of Naba Yūei, the most celebrated amateur scholar in the city. A common thread was the revival of Chinese-inspired literary culture, which had languished with the decline of the great Kyoto Zen temples in the chaotic fifteenth and sixteenth centuries. Kenzan even opened his own salon, the Shūseidō, where he pursued the classics, composed poetry, and studied calligraphy — a particular forte of his ancestors. The world of the gentleman-scholar, with calligraphy as its most visible manifestation, would constitute the new, non-ceramic element in Kenzan ware.

The Kenzan design story unfolds in three successive locations, and a chapter is devoted to each. Narutaki, Kenzan's first workshop located in the hills outside Kyoto, was the site for his exposition of *shōko*, or veneration of the ancient, a theme that governed his designs (and even became one of his pseudonyms). Kenzan's pots are examined as an outgrowth of the new sinophile culture, as well as an attempt to turn those images into merchandise.

At a second kiln in Chōjiyamachi, in downtown Kyoto, Kenzan refitted his workshop to the metropolitan ceramics industry. He aimed his product at a growing urban bourgeoisie sophisticated enough to demand not only luxury but irony and wit in their vessels. In his attempts to satisfy this clientele, Kenzan was amply assisted by his older brother, the celebrated painter Ogata Kōrin (1658–1716). A series of simple but stunning designs suggest new relationships between painting and pot.

In the last decade of his life, Kenzan moved to Edo and returned to salon culture and amateurism. Patronized by an imperial prince, he joined the circle of haiku enthusiasts at Fukagawa, the former residence of the master poet Matsuo Bashō (1644–94). Kenzan's Edo ceramics, and a new interest in painting proper, are seen not as commercial production, but as part of *ozashiki*, a kind of art-as-entertainment done for and with a circle of intimates.

In the sense that much of what we know about Kenzan was crafted posthumously, we must acknowledge his followers. There are two distinct Kenzan traditions: one in Kyoto, which is manifested in stoneware design, and one in Edo, which attracted mostly amateur earthenware potters and antiquari-

ans. The scope of this Kenzan tradition also includes scholarship in the field, which not only produced information but
unwittingly encouraged certain kinds of forgeries. These
movements will be discussed in Chapter 6. My conclusions,
in the final chapter, are framed against the notorious Sano
Kenzan scandal. Here I suggest that the problems in the field,
while undoubtedly multiplied by self-serving arbiters of the
tradition, are inextricably linked to gestures made by Kenzan
himself.

Kenzan fakes abound. A proverb familiar to enthusiasts of
Japanese art even warns that the two things one will never
encounter are a ghost and an authentic work of Kenzan. Of the
approximately five thousand pots (and a lesser number of
paintings and writings) that bear the Kenzan signature, only a
small percentage were made by him or under his supervision.
Authenticity is therefore a major problem, and one that
authorities have assiduously avoided. But the interpretive project proposed here is possible only because of authentication — devising correct methods to classify the wares and then
separating Kenzan's own products from those of his legitimate
followers, and those of his imitators. Since a detailed exposition of this process would overwhelm the equally important
issues of design and cultural context, criteria for attribution are
summarized in the text; an extensive visual appendix, organized into seventeen groups beginning with the master's
workshop and covering up to the present day, treats them in
detail.

Our guide through the Kenzan tradition will be an operational principle that the master himself abided by: design in its
widest sense. For a person as educated and resourceful as
Kenzan, the world was an inventory of design components. He
was capable of incorporating ceramic techniques, painting,
calligraphy, poetry, and textile patterns into a single object.
Kenzan's masterpieces may be examined as summations of
these elements — unified, yes, but also carefully assembled to
produce visions of aristocratic grace, lofty seclusion, or urban
chic. Kenzan's purported last words were that he had done
what he wanted, in his own way — and that he had consumed
the whole world in a mouthful. Indeed, his creative appetite
seemed to engulf all of East Asian culture. Through careful
sifting of the artistic and documentary evidence, Ogata
Kenzan emerges from the prism of dreams and deceptions as a

competent kiln manager, a highly focused technician, and a master of ceramic design.

AN URBAN CRAFT TRADITION

For many twentieth-century observers, ceramics are objects made in limited editions by potters working alone or in small groups. This studio- or artist-potter concept is a recent notion, however, rooted in a romantic protest against industrialization that commenced in the West of the mid-nineteenth century. From that time, critics began to identify those who combined the creativity of the artist with the productivity of the artisan. The lifestyle and work of these figures were seen as providing an alternative to machine-age alienation. The small-scale pottery, often located in an idyllic rural setting, was offered as one appropriate site for this revolution. Since Ogata Kenzan himself had begun work at a secluded spot in the Kyoto hills, he seemed a suitable model.

But Kenzan was not a rural potter. In pre-modern Japan, rural villages were self-supporting and mostly self-sufficient. Makers and users of pottery were part of that system. Materials were gathered, processed, and formed, and the products were sold locally. A single potter might dig the clay, make the pots, and fire the kiln. A family member might even be responsible for marketing the wares. This tight socio-economic nexus guaranteed limited and predictable consumption, permitting cultivators to double as potters. Needless to say, the rural potter could not be concerned with subtle nuances of form and decoration.

The urban system in which Kenzan worked was quite different. Clients living in large towns and cities, the centers of political, economic, and social activity, made complex demands. The potter had to address functions ranging from ritual to mundane, and had to build into the wares a sense of exclusiveness, usually in the form of technical sophistication. That called for highly skilled and specialized labor. Clay was ordered from suppliers, and vessels were fabricated by full-time formers, then fired by a separate group of specialists. Decoration in underglaze or overglaze pigments was the responsibility of yet another unit. In many cases these groups lived and worked in separate quarters and had little mutual contact. When I lived in the Kyoto potter's quarter of Go-jōzaka, the overglaze enamel specialists next door to me knew nothing about other aspects of the potter's craft.

Coordinating the work of urban specialists was traditionally the province of wholesale agents, who for the most part were concerned only with sales. In the early decades of the seventeenth century, however, urban merchants began to take a more immediate interest in craft manufacture. They brought their personal cultivation into considerations of materials, fabrication, and formal style — in short, they became designers. This might be described in terms of three stages. The first was the establishment in the eleventh century of a vocabulary of motifs and surface treatments that functioned in the same allusive manner as poetry. The second was the emergence of personal design as a means of self-expression, which occurred in the tearooms of the sixteenth century. In the third stage, which took place in seventeenth-century Kyoto salons, the individual designer infused that allusive vocabulary into a wide variety of materials. This would set the stage for Kenzan's bridging the gulf between "taste" and "touch" in ceramics.

Kyoto was the setting for the infusion of poetic allusion into material culture. By no means the only traditional urban crafts center in Japan, Kyoto has nonetheless occupied the lead in technical skill and design since its founding as Heian-kyō — the Capital of Peace and Tranquility — at the end of the eighth century. Modeled after the great metropolises of north China, Kyoto was the imperial capital and the geographical hub of the country, and before long it became a center for religion, learning, and the arts. The demand for crafts in such a place was as large as it was multifold: objects were needed for ritual and governmental functions as well as for the private lives of court nobles and bureaucrats. Government-operated ateliers were opened to address these needs, and private workshops met the demands of temples, shrines, and commoners. Tenth-century records on the official workshops cite guidelines for material processing and manufacture that are staggering even by contemporary standards. This type of technical sophistication vaulted Kyoto crafts into national prominence.

Technique alone, however, could not sustain the urban crafts. What also evolved was a pattern of symbols that drew consumers into familiar but exclusive systems of value — or, put another way, the crafts developed a voice. In early Kyoto production, two principal modes may be observed. One was

1. Page from the *Nishiyama Gire* (Fragments from Ishiyama). Poem by Ki no Tsurayuki.

centered around Chinese poetry and prose literature, knowledge of which signified cultivation in a formal, official sense; the other was the world of Japanese narratives and verse, evoking feelings that could not be expressed in the fundamentally alien Chinese medium. Especially from the time of Japan's decision to break diplomatic ties with China in the late ninth century, the literary and visual arts began to display a distinctive and evocative vision of nature, love, and other human affairs. An intimacy with and respect for nature had been part of early Japanese spiritual life. In courtly culture, nature was linked with feelings of love. In its deeply familiar yet transitory way, nature was a metaphor for the passing — and hence the poignancy — of love as well as life.

The allusive voice first sounded in the small world of the Kyoto court. In this circle of cognoscenti, even the most fragmentary poetic suggestion — to seasonal flowers and grasses, a famous place, or a passage from a novel — could summon a world of associations. This would have particular importance for the urban craft tradition. Poetic condensation could now empower simple visual motifs. In the eleventh century, poetically charged signs such as plovers and waves, beach pines, and cartwheels in water began to appear on lacquerwares, mirrors, and calligraphy papers. For example, a stationery box decorated with plovers might summon feelings close to those expressed in the tenth-century diary, *Tosa Nikki:*

As I go to her,
my longing unbearable,
a plover's lament
rises in the winter night,
so cold blows the river wind.[1]

But allusion and abbreviation are not the same. Simple signs need an atmosphere to propel them beyond their minimal forms. This is achieved through a sensitive orchestration of shapes, materials, techniques of fabrication, and surface motifs. This zone of intervention, which is neither the ground of the vessel nor the figures that decorate its surface, is of supreme importance in the history of Japanese urban craft. It is the element that distinguishes the Japanese products from "decorative arts" whose painted signs merely derive from high arts such as painting. Its successful application can be seen in calligraphy papers from the eleventh century (fig. 1). These sheets, frequently created from a paper collage with accents of metallic grains and leafs, are a sumptuous backdrop for the calligraphy on one hand and quasi-pictures on the other; and yet they would never be confused with paintings. The juxtaposition of torn pieces of paper — some solidly colored and others filled with small repeat patterns such as waves or reeds — is evocative on one hand while militating against strict pictorial recognition on the other. In this ambiguous atmosphere, where simple but highly inferential motifs are interpenetrated with the stuff of their fabrication, a Japanese way of design emerges. Here is where the designer works — *between* figure and ground. The allusive voice is not found in the vessel or motifs proper; rather, the coherence and suggestiveness of the total composition produces atmosphere. This was the space in which Kenzan would make his greatest contribution.

Despite the rise of the warrior class and its relocation of the capital to Kamakura in eastern Japan in 1185, the sophistication of urban craft production hardly changed. Even in the turmoil that accompanied the return of the warrior government to Kyoto in the mid-fourteenth century, high-quality craft production continued. Since those in power (as well as aspirants to power) created ample demand for fine goods, they not only protected Kyoto crafts but urged the industry on to higher standards. The warriors, especially upstart chieftains of the late sixteenth century like Oda Nobunaga (1532–82) and Toyotomi Hideyoshi (1536–98), also had their own preferences — for exotic subjects, luxurious materials, or monumental scale (fig. 2). In the struggle for supremacy and legitimacy, art had to assume a public function, and this too would do much to empower crafts and their designers.

2. Cabinet with design of pampas grass and paulownia crests.

THE ADVENT OF THE DESIGNER

Courtly pathos and warrior flamboyance provided Japanese crafts with theme and style, but neither courtier nor samurai took a personal role in transforming their tastes into tangible objects. They depended on petty bureaucrats or wholesale agents. Circumstances in the sixteenth century, however, made it possible for some of the upper-class merchants — *machishū* — to add something of their own to the products, and thus become designers.

The *machishū* were originally petty traders, artisans, and

provincial samurai lured to a growing Kyoto in the fourteenth and fifteenth centuries. They formed guilds that were patronized and protected by the court and religious institutions, and in return they paid taxes for permission to sell specific products. As trade — especially in sake — began to flourish, brewers invested their excess capital in pawnbroking and moneylending; their ability to supply funds for commercial expansion gave them an influence and prestige that belied their nominal occupations. When Kyoto was devastated by the Ōnin Wars (1467–77), the merchants financed the rebuilding. As hapless priests and courtiers straggled back to the capital in the postwar years, they forged alliances with the merchants, exchanging cultural prestige for financial support. This assimilation of aristocratic culture with civil reconstruction encouraged the *machishū* to represent themselves as guarantors of the city's ancient traditions.

The first site for *machishū* initiatives in design was in *chanoyu*, the tea ceremony. Tea drinking was one of the many Chinese practices imported to Japan in the eighth century; shavings from a brick of spiced tea were boiled into an amber-colored liquid and served at court ceremonies. A tea that was infused and whisked, rather than boiled, was introduced to Japan from China by the Zen monk Eisai (1141–1215). Despite Eisai's advocacy of tea as a medicinal beverage, from the fourteenth century tea consumption became an important part of lavish warrior-class entertainments which centered on gambling; the prizes were the precious Chinese vessels from which the brew was imbibed. So vast were the acquisitions of the ruling Ashikaga family that by the mid-fifteenth century a class of professional handlers, or *dōbōshū,* was formed to catalogue and display them. In their connoisseurship and tea-service activities, these men were the forerunners of the tea masters. Their formulations of "correct" Chinese utensils, properly displayed, not only became part of late medieval military etiquette; ownership of those utensils constituted a badge of legitimacy for the military usurpers — Nobunaga, Hideyoshi, and Tokugawa Ieyasu (1542–1616) — who followed.

From the late fifteenth century some of these handlers began to offer alternatives to the crassness and exoticism then governing the world of tea. The first appears to have been Murata Shukō (1422-1502), a priest from Nara who served the warriors but also sought to instill some spiritual content into the tea gathering. Shukō's teachings are said to have been transmitted to Takeno Jōō (1502–55), a merchant from Sakai, a bustling port city whose culture was spared the ravages of the Ōnin Wars. In the course of their foreign-trade activities, Sakai merchants had the opportunity to buy, sell, and use tea utensils, thereby acquiring a level of cultural prestige previously associated with the military aristocracy. Inspired by new aesthetic standards that expressed beauty in terms of sobriety rather than opulence, and by the detachment espoused in Zen Buddhism, Jōō moved toward simplification. In place of the large formal reception rooms used by the warrior class, Jōō convened tea gatherings in a small detached hut. Tea was prepared on the floor mat, in front of the guest, from a kettle set in a rustic sunken hearth. Architectural elements and tea utensils accentuated severity and restraint, as if to remove a veneer of preciousness. Spiritual reform was coupled with design reform.

The final breakthrough is traditionally attributed to another Sakai merchant, Sen no Rikyū (1522–91). Rikyū attained contemporary prominence in official service to warlords Nobunaga and Hideyoshi, but he is known to posterity for his style of quiet restraint, or *wabi*. This term had been used previously to describe feelings of alienation and loneliness, but for Rikyū it became an aesthetic standard. Humility and poverty were not merely to be admired in a vague poetic way but were goals to be cultivated in every element of the ceremony, including the environment. Rikyū and his colleagues from Sakai began to design new tea rooms, tea procedures, and tea utensils, and in some cases, made objects themselves.

Production and supply are the usual areas of interest to merchants, but in the course of employment with powerful warriors the line between professional activity and personal expression was frequently crossed. There are earlier instances of amateur pursuits in the Japanese visual arts — for example, the monochrome painting by monks in urban temples of the fourteenth and fifteenth centuries — but those activities were informed by an older Chinese notion of painting and calligraphy, which conceived them as a byproduct of the gentleman's search for virtue rather than the perfection of art for its own sake. Amateurism, then, was a state of high-mindedness, not the random efforts of the dilettante that the word evokes today. According to Chinese decorum, however, gentlemen did not involve themselves in the crafts, which were the province of the lower classes. In late sixteenth-century Japan the stakes were different. The merchants and the new rulers had risen to prominence through personal effort, not pedigree. The entire notion of legitimacy simply had to change — in a sense the new became legitimate. The ability to produce the new was called *sakui*, which might be translated as "creativity" or "creative mind." Tea master Yamanoue Sōji (1544–90), an important chronicler of this era in tea history, summed up this sentiment in comments about fellow tea master Tsuji Gensai: "Tsuji is not sharp-eyed, and very poor at *chanoyu*. Even if he becomes the pupil of a great master, a man without *sakui* remains inept."[2]

As obvious as it may seem to the Western reader, this decoupling of artistic inspiration from programmatic study and correct pedigree was revolutionary in the Japanese context. The true artist, in this case the tea master, brought all creative facilities to bear on the exigencies of the moment. And since the role of host and artist were, at least in this instance, inseparable, creative efforts had to expand in every direction. This took the tea master beyond identifying appropriate objects for tea into commissioning and even making them. The tea diaries from this period begin to exhibit an open fascination with the contemporary and experimental, including a kind of designed ceramics fittingly entitled "Now Ware." In this manner, the merchant tea masters, implicitly supported by warriors (who felt much better within the still-flexible space of the tea room than they did at pompous court or temple rituals), ignited a tradition of personal design.

Political developments in the early seventeenth century shifted the site of *sakui* from the battlefield tearoom to the urban salon. With decisive victories over the Toyotomi faction in 1600 and 1615, the Tokugawa clan gained uncontested leadership of the nation. Their pacification program stimulated cultural activities and fostered alliances that would have a great influence on urban crafts production. As the center of lingering Toyotomi allegiances, Kyoto was a particular target of Tokugawa policy. In 1615, the shogunate promulgated a series of ordinances regulating the court, military, and religious institutions. In place of political involvement, the sovereign was to pursue learning; the court was obliged to follow a rigid system of rank and protocol. A political marriage was arranged: in 1620, a fourteen-year-old Tokugawa daughter, Masako (1607–78), was sent to Kyoto to marry Emperor Gomizunoo. For a short time, relations between court and military appeared cordial; the monarch quickly fathered two children with Masako, and in 1626 made a celebrated official visit to the warriors in their own Nijō Castle. Then, in 1629, Gomizunoo suddenly resigned, and in the following year placed his eight-year-old daughter Ichinomiya Okiko on the throne, where she reigned for fourteen years as Empress Meishō (1623–96). The source of the crisis was the so-called Purple Robe Incident, wherein the shogunate withdrew a final privilege of the court — that of high ecclesiastical appointment. This was widely perceived as a forced abdication of Gomizunoo.

The upper merchant class also had reason for discontent. The sixteenth century hegemons Nobunaga and Hideyoshi had oppressed the *machishū* by abolishing guilds, shifting monopoly privileges, and establishing direct military administration of key cities. After the Tokugawa had unification in 1600, there was no need for quartermaster services, and a series of isolation edicts passed over the ensuing decades eliminated merchants' prospects in foreign trade. In their disenfranchisement, the *machishū* and court were natural allies.

Alienation, when well funded, may often turn to mere nostalgia. The Tokugawa pacification program poured huge amounts of money into Kyoto; from the time that Masako was moved to Kyoto, the imperial stipend was tripled, along with a raise in courtier allowances. Masako's brother, third-generation shogun Iemitsu (1604–51), provided funds for rebuilding court-affiliated temples and shrines such as Ninnaji, Kiyomizudera, and Yasaka Shrine. Ample funds for cultural activities and the onset of construction thus encouraged a revival mood. The *Gomizunoin Tōji Nenchū Gyōji*, a record of affairs during the Emperor's retirement, relates his desire to revive court ceremonies from the era of Emperor Daigo. The era was not idly selected: the reigns of Emperors Daigo (r. 896–930) and Murakami (r. 946–967) were perceived as a period of splendor, marked by seminal developments in culture such as Ki no Tsurayuki's literary masterpiece *Tosa Nikki* and the imperially authorized poetry anthology, *Kokinshū*. Moreover, that court was free of Fujiwara (parallel: Tokugawa) meddling. In suggesting the imperial heyday as ordered and normal, and the military-controlled present as disordered and abnormal (in his famous abdication poem, Gomizunoo describes the world as having grown "rank and wild"), the court was instigating a classical revival.

Gomizunoo's retirement salon, the Sentō Gosho, was the center of activities in flower arrangement, tea ceremony, Noh drama, kabuki theater, and poetry competition. Salon activities also spread through the numerous Kyoto temples presided over by imperial kin. A well-known example is Rokuonji (Kinkakuji), where Hōrin Shōshō (1592–1668), a relative of Emperor Goyōzei (1571–1617), was installed as abbot. Between 1635 and his death in 1668, Hōrin kept a diary called *Kakumei Ki* (Record of the Gap Between Auspicious Omens), which documents a manifold involvement in the literary, visual, and performing arts. Guests included courtiers, prominent Zen priests, warriors such as the military governor of Kyoto, Noh performers, painters, potters, art dealers, and tea masters. Many guests on Hōrin's list, irrespective of rank, maintained their own salons as well.[3]

For the salon-goers, there were serious negotiations behind the frivolity — each group was staking out territory in the new polity, in which Kyoto became a powerful symbol. For the courtiers, Kyoto represented their traditional seat of power and an era of bygone splendor; for the merchants, Kyoto was the place that they had built out of the ashes of the Ōnin War; for the samurai, it was a city they now administered but, as ill-bred rustics, could never really possess. As the locus for all these interests, Kyoto's heritage was a prime subject for representation in works of art.

Although the salons patronized artists of many persuasions, only one school of painting and design managed to bring the classical imagery into a unified corpus of two- and three-dimensional objects: Rimpa. The style was inaugurated principally by Kenzan's great uncle, Hon'ami Kōetsu (1558–1637), and a painter, Tawaraya Sōtatsu. Together they reconfigured ancient literary themes and subjects from nature in bold compositions and vibrant colors. As we shall see, Ogata Kōrin and his brother Kenzan, working a century later, harmonized the style with the luxury-loving tastes of the Genroku era (1688–1704). The Ogata brothers also transmitted Rimpa to Edo, where it was given new life in the early nineteenth century by Sakai Hōitsu. The art and design of Rimpa would even spread beyond Japan to subtly influence Western design movements like Art Nouveau. In Japanese art, Rimpa is broadly held to be the zenith of visual and tactile sumptuousness.

Hon'ami Kōetsu, descended from specialists who served the military aristocracy in the fourteenth and fifteenth centuries, was well positioned to expand the role of the urban designer beyond the confines of the tea room. Through his family profession of sword connoisseurship, which entailed not only authenticating and maintaining blades but outfitting them with decorative hilts and scabbards, Kōetsu knew Kyoto craftsmen and their materials. As a participant in the urban salon network, where he maintained good relations with merchants, warriors, and the court, Kōetsu was close to the centers of patronage and taste. Finally, Kōetsu himself was a person of cultivation. As a youth he is said to have practiced the Kanze-style Noh drama, and he pursued calligraphy under an imperial prince, Sonchō (1552–97). Evidence suggests that he studied tea with warriors Furuta Oribe (1544–1615) and Oda Uraku (1547–1621). With fellow merchants and with artisans, Kōetsu brought the classical revival into publishing, lacquerware, and calligraphy.

Kōetsu's design involvement can be traced in three of his letters. One, addressed to an Imaeda Naiki, states that if Imaeda found it difficult to execute the metal decoration for a hand drum in Kanazawa (present Ishikawa Prefecture), Kōetsu would have it done in Kyoto. A second, addressed to an otherwise unknown Shimbei, mentions options for a near-finished lacquer object, including choices of materials and critical comments about the shape of certain decor elements. In a third and recently discovered letter, Kōetsu writes that he had shown two writing boxes to an artisan, and that in turn he would bring them to the unnamed addressee, probably a client.[4] These documents seem to portray Kōetsu not as a lacquerer or even a regular designer, but as an intermediary confident, knowledgeable, and respected enough to intervene in certain stages of production.

A map of Takagamine village, thought to have been founded by Kōetsu in north Kyoto in 1615, suggests that Kōetsu surrounded himself with some of the most prominent merchants and artisans of the day, including Chaya Shirōjirō (trader), Ogata Sōhaku (clothier and calligrapher), Tsuchida

Sōtaku (lacquerer), Fudeya Myōki (mounter and brush maker), and numerous relatives. This constituency has fueled speculation that Takagamine was an art colony, but there is no evidence of its products or any indication that the landowners named on the map inhabited their plots. The "colony" theory emerged in the 1930s, just when influential aesthetes such as Mushanokōji Saneatsu (1885–1976) and Yanagi Sōetsu (1889–1961) were formulating art-utopias of their own. There is also some indication that the village functioned as a religious commune; at least three Nichiren Buddhist temples were established there during or shortly after Kōetsu's lifetime. Contrary to popular speculation, then, Takagamine was probably not a precedent to Kenzan's decision to establish his own workshop in the secluded mountains outside Kyoto.

Kōetsu's suggestions about form and surface imagery notwithstanding, it was still the artisans who were responsible for transforming those ideas into objects. In lacquerware Kōetsu worked with the Tsuchida and Igarashi ateliers, and for decoration of poem card and scroll surfaces his preference seems to have been the Tawaraya atelier headed by Sōtatsu. The little we know about Sōtatsu suggests that he was a merchant of some cultivation, and quite possibly a relative of Kōetsu through marriage; he and Kōetsu are said to have married sisters. Contemporary references portray the Tawaraya as a shop specializing in the decoration of folding screens, fans, poem sheets, and possibly even textiles. These decorative painters were heirs to an ongoing indigenous tradition — one rooted in picture scrolls of the Heian period (794–1185) but increasingly characterized by enlargement of form and emphatic, almost tactile surface effects. Sōtatsu and his staff refined that style through compositional rigor, further abbreviation, and careful attention to the methods and materials of painting. Their *mokkotsu* ("boneless" painting without outlines) style, especially when carried out on non-absorbent paper and metallic leaf surfaces, imparts a strong sense of the tangible. The *tarashikomi* (pigment or water added to an undried wash to create blurred and pooled effects) technique also provides a rich sense of surface. Like Italian Renaissance masters, Sōtatsu may have been stimulated by access to a "classical" past; in 1602 he is said to have been employed to repair the richly illuminated frontispieces of the twelfth-century handscrolls known as the *Taira Family Sutras*. That allusive atmosphere, first witnessed in those eleventh-century calligraphy papers, had become in itself a genre of monumental painting.

The restoration of the past assayed by Kōetsu and Sōtatsu was also invested with urgencies of the present. Their designs were aimed not only at the imperial aristocracy, but at recently risen merchants and samurai. Thus in their decisions about shape, size, material, fabrication, color, and finish of forms and surface decorations, they had to incorporate additional allusions — to cultural images that had meaning for the new elites. Accordingly, classical themes are augmented by displays of

3. Att. Hon'ami Kōetsu: Stationery box with design of boat bridge (*funabashi*).

4. Att. Hon'ami Kōetsu and Tawaraya Sōtatsu: Sheet from an album of poem cards (*shikishi*).

ELEMENTS OF RIMPA DESIGN:

1) Simplification. Constituent elements are reduced to their essentials. Floral elements, for example, frequently appear in silhouette, without inner markings or outlines; clay looks clay-like; lacquer looks like lacquer. 2) Selective formal exaggeration, governed by geometry. This occurs in individual painted elements, such as the rounding of Sōtatsu's hills, or in the shapes of three-dimensional objects, like the swelling lids of Kōetsu lacquer boxes. Pattern elements like water undergo further distillation. 3) Serial repetition of elements like flowers, trees, hills, and animals are animated by irregular changes. 4) Flat fields. The compositions include elements like bridges, hillocks, sandbars, and clouds depicted as broad, flattened planes, with little interior detail. 5) Explicit interest in materials. New materials and techniques are used, and circumstances of manufacture are incorporated into visual style. Examples include the use of plain lead sheets in Kōetsu lacquerware or the deliberately pooled pigments (*tarashikomi*) in Sōtatsu's painting.

5. Att. Tawaraya Sōtatsu: Detail from a screen decorated with fans.

6. Att. Hon'ami Kōetsu: Flute case with design of deer.

warrior flamboyance on one hand and the humility of Rikyū's merchant tearoom on the other. These thematics combine with technique in five prominent traits of Rimpa design (figs. 3–6).

The notion of amateur designer in the manner of Kōetsu, and the particular subjects and formal strategies for objects made in concert with artisans like Sōtatsu, was to have an enormous impact on Kōrin and Kenzan. And although Rimpa style was most suitable for mass-produced items like ceramics, it would take another hundred years for that to happen. Why?

KYOTO CERAMICS AND DESIGN

The medium of ceramics was one of the last to be taken up by urban workshops in Japan. The late entry is all the more conspicuous, given the longevity of the Japanese ceramics tradition. Yet the fact is that over the early centuries of development, most ceramics production consisted of unglazed ware for the most humble utilitarian applications. The more technically sophisticated wares emulated, for the most part, models from China and to some extent Korea. In wealthy households, fine ceramics were imported, and utilitarian wares came from outlying areas as part of a well-established tribute system. Other food service demands were filled by wood and lacquerware vessels.

This ceramic "gap" is particularly obvious in Heiankyō (Kyoto), which had become the imperial capital at the end of the eighth century. High-fired ceramics had been made in the Kyoto basin from the sixth century, and green-glazed tile and earthenware vessels were produced shortly after the city's founding. By the eleventh century, however, all fine ceramics production ceased, not to resume until five centuries later. The catalyst for renewed production was the tea ceremony, and the presence of tea master-designers who could build distinction into the wares. Their impact was felt at such earthenware workshops as Raku and Oshikōji, and at the stoneware kilns, particularly that of Nonomura Ninsei. These workshops helped to bring ceramics techniques to the level of other Kyoto urban craft traditions. In their own respective ways, they also provided inspiration for Ogata Kenzan.

The Raku style emerged as a collaboration between tea master Sen no Rikyū and Chōjirō, son of a foreign-born tilemaker. In 1574, Chōjirō executed and signed a roof ornament in the shape of the mythical lion-dog, or *shishi*. Rikyū's activity in ceramic design is suggested in a 1586 entry in the tea ceremony diary *Matsuya Kaiki*, mentioning a "Sōeki [Rikyū]-shape" teabowl. The earliest Raku kiln may have been located in Kyoto on the grounds of Hideyoshi's Jūraku mansion, where Rikyū was in official attendance. The few works from the first Raku generation were handmade, coated with black or transparent lead glazes, and fired to a quick maturation in a small updraft muffle kiln (fig. 7). The black Raku glaze, composed of the ferro-manganic Kamogawa stone and fritted lead, was fired to the comparatively high temperature of 1100–1200 degrees C. The lower-firing transparent glaze (often used over a high-iron or ochre-slipped body to make red Raku) was made of lead and siliceous rock powder — the same ingredients used in earlier lead-glazed products. These artless wares seemed an inversion of all the values invested in the precious celadons and porcelains from China. For that reason alone, Raku ware spoke.

Although Rikyū is thought not to have fashioned the ware himself, the simplicity and immediacy of the Raku technique, as well as its associations with *sakui*, would also tempt non-specialists in the generation that followed Rikyū. The first seems to have been Kōetsu. In the *Hon'ami Gyōjō Ki* (Annals of the Hon'ami Family), Kōetsu describes his own work in ceramics as *tesusabi* — a hobby. In keeping with his amateur status, Kōetsu adapted the Raku methods to a more spontaneous and personalized approach to forming and glazing. The brusquely formed cylinders and inflated spheroids that make up Kōetsu tea bowls are the first hints of self-expression on the part of a maker of ceramics. The question of whether or not Kenzan studied Raku will be taken up in the next chapter, but its appropriation by amateurs like Kōetsu opened a wide conceptual door — one that Kenzan would brazenly enter.

Kenzan is quite explicit in acknowledging his debt to Oshikōji, the other glazed earthenware tradition in Kyoto. In his 1737 pottery manual, *Tōkō Hitsuyō*, he states that near the intersection of Oshikōji and Yanagi no Baba streets a potter named Ichimonjiya Sukezaemon had started making low-fired ceramics with techniques learned from a foreigner, and that the tradition may have predated that of Chōjirō. Kenzan further relates that he hired an Oshikōji veteran named Magobei, and from him learned the secret earthenware tech-

7. Chōjirō: Red Raku ware tea bowl, named *Yugure*.

8. Oshikōji-style ware (att. to Chōjirō): Bowl with design of melons and vines.

niques of the workshop. In his second pottery manual, entitled *Tōji Seihō*, Kenzan mentions Oshikōji vessels with figures of birds, trees, and animals carved into the surface and painted in yellow, green and purple. A polychrome-glazed dish with a melon pattern in the Tokyo National Museum (fig. 8) is an early example of this kind of work.

Kenzan's testimony about the history of this kiln has taken on new meaning with the recent discovery, in Kyoto, of a variety of lead-glazed earthenware fragments bearing Oshikōji-type polychrome lead glazes. The burial contexts suggest a date of late sixteenth to early seventeenth century.[5] These objects, made in the form of tea ceremony bowls, refute the assumption that the Raku workshop was the pioneer in glazed wares for tea; the Oshikōji workshop now seems to have competed for patronage in the nascent teaware market. Unfortunately, there is little further evidence about the Oshikōji kiln. *Yōshū Fushi*, a gazetteer published in Kyoto between 1673 and 1684, states that among the ceramic enterprises in the city there is "Oshikōji south of Nijō [street]; it uses an *uchigama* [muffle kiln] whereby the ceramics are fired in a kiln set inside the workshop." When the Tosa potter Morita Kyūemon (1641–1715) visited Kyoto in 1678, he mentioned in his diary that preliminary bisque-firing was done at the Oshikōji workshop, and that the high-temperature firing took place at Kiyomizu Shirodani. Finally, *Wakan Sho Dōgu*, an inventory of tea utensils published in 1694, mentions: "Oshikōji ware: later becomes Kyoto ware."

Ceramics historian Mitsuoka Chūsei has speculated that the Oshikōji involvement in borrowed kiln space at Kiyomizu may signify the transition from small glazed-earthenware workshops to larger workshops that fired stonewares decorated with overglaze enamels — a move generally acknowledged to have taken place in the second half of the seventeenth century.[6] As for Oshikōji itself, it completely disappeared from records at the end of the seventeenth century — perhaps absorbed, as the *Wakan Sho Dōgu* and Mitsuoka suggest, into a more all-encompassing Kyoto-ware industry. Probably the early Oshikōji products have been mistakenly attributed as Raku wares or as the polychrome-glazed wares from Ming-dynasty China called Kōchi. Despite the possible extinction of the Oshikōji product, we shall see that Kenzan made good use of its stable of recipes — the Oshikōji glazes became his painting palette.

Earthenwares like Raku and Oshikōji may have attracted the innovative hobbyist, but high-fired stonewares had artistic and industrial importance. According to Japanese ceramics lore, the high-temperature ceramics enterprise in Kyoto was begun in 1624 at Awataguchi, in the eastern hills of the city, by a Seto potter named Sammonjiya Kyūemon. Diary references, such as that of Rikyū's tea associate Kamiya Sōtan (1551–1635) to a "Kyoto-ware" square-shouldered tea caddy in 1605, suggest a somewhat earlier origin. Regardless of the date, it can safely be assumed that the Kyoto stoneware industry was founded by skilled artisans from the Seto-Mino district who were lured to Kyoto by the burgeoning salon culture and its practice of the tea ceremony. Seto had a long tradition of producing iron-glazed tea bowls and tea caddies, and from the mid-sixteenth century the neighboring Mino potters had produced a succession of innovative styles prized by tea masters: Yellow Seto, Black Seto, Shino, and Oribe wares.

The most comprehensive record of Kyoto patronage is the *Kakumei Ki,* the aforementioned diary of priest-aesthete Hōrin Shōshō. Hōrin documents the particular fascination of Kyoto patrons for Chinese-style tea caddies and Korean-style tea bowls coming out of the Awataguchi, Otowa, Kiyomizu, and Yasaka kilns on the eastern slopes of the city. At the hands of these patrons, the wares were subject to various forms of personalization. Hōrin made paper-pattern designs (*kirigata*) for his custom orders, invited potters to display their skills at his salon, and even contrived to build his own kiln on temple grounds. The most systematic manipulations seem to have originated with Kobori Enshū, official tea master to the third Tokugawa shogun and a Kyoto salon habitué. Enshū had Kyoto and other Japanese kilns make reproductions of the orthodox continental styles and provided the pots with an antique veneer through poetic naming and box inscription. Yet remarks in the *Kakumei Ki* hint at a major change in preference around the time of Enshū's death at mid-century. The interest in subdued and elegant tea-ware styles began to give way to decorated ceramics, beginning with Ming porcelains, then domestic porcelains from Arita, and finally decorated stonewares from Kyoto — especially those from the Ninsei kiln at Omuro, northwest Kyoto.

Ninsei ware represents on one hand the final creative phase in ceramics for the tea ceremony — and a movement toward the surface effects so admired by Kenzan on the other. In 1648 the *Kakumei Ki* mentions an "Omuro-ware" tea caddy; the same year the diary of teaman Matsuya Hisashige describes a "Ninnaji-ware tea caddy." Additional references over subsequent years to "potter Seiemon," "Tamba-ware Seiemon," and "jar-maker Seiemon," coupled with information in Kenzan's diaries, suggest that Ninsei, whose personal name was Seiemon, hailed from Nonomura village in the Tamba district, where he presumably mastered the large-ware techniques associated with the local tradition. After a period of further training at the Seto ceramics center, he opened his kiln in Omuro, in the precinct of the Ninnaji temple, which had been rebuilt with funds from the shogunate in 1647. As Kenzan relates in his pottery manual *Tōkō Hitsuyō*, the Ninsei title came from combining the *Nin* of Ninnaji and the *Sei* of Seiemon.

Ninsei ware has two faces. Based on the kind of objects mentioned in diaries and ledgers, it is now believed that Ninsei's early products consisted of clever variations of the teaware classics (fig. 9). What distinguished them from earlier products were the novel shapes and glaze pours devised by tea master Kanamori Sōwa (1584–1656), whose name was associated with the kiln from its inception. The elegant Seto-style iron glazes found on those wares — and on fragments excavated from the Ninsei kiln site — are described in detail in pottery notes that Kenzan would inherit. The elegant overglaze-enameled stonewares commonly associated with Ninsei, however, are not in evidence until 1660, when the *Kakumei Ki* records an "enameled Omuro Ninsei tea bowl." Overglaze enamels — colored glasses that could be painted on top of high-fired glazes and fused to them in an additional low-temperature firing — permitted decor in a range of colors approaching the painter's palette. The technique appeared in the 1640s at the Arita porcelain kilns in Kyushu, where initially it was used in imitation of Chinese export styles. The Ninsei decorators tied the technique in with the Kyoto environment by painting Japanese-style motifs — landscapes, trees, and flowers — on vessels formed from the local white stoneware from Kurodani (fig. 10). The painting was of a quality hitherto unseen in Japanese ceramics. The gazetteer *Yōshū Fushi* even states that the famous Kanō-school painters Tan'yū and Yasunobu decorated Ninsei products.

Ninsei wares endowed Japanese ceramics with a new stan-

9. Ninsei ware: Faceted tea caddy.

dard of elegance, and brought Kyoto ceramics to the level of technical maturity and elegance that the name "Kyoto ware" evokes today. Ninsei's success was made possible by its urban situation. First, the workshop took advantage of the access to materials that a metropolis like Kyoto could offer: the notes compiled by the Ninsei workshop (and preserved by Kenzan in his own pottery manual) mention clays and glaze materials from a variety of locations. Second, the influx of master potters from rural kilns (Ninsei himself was an example) provided technical expertise, and many professional painters were on hand to decorate the wares. In its heyday, through the efforts of designer-promoter Sōwa, the kiln seemed to capture the fascination with classical culture that had been nurtured in Kyoto's early seventeenth-century salons.

The success was short-lived. Promissory notes written in 1674 and 1677 show that "Nonomura Seiemon," with "Ninsei" as the guarantor, borrowed a sum of money from one Kayama, a samurai quartered at Ninnaji. Apparently the original Nonomura Seiemon Ninsei had retired, leaving the workshop in the hands of his first son, who had inherited his common name. This is supported by a description of the workshop in the 1678 diary of Morita Kyūemon, which reads, "Now the owner is Nonomura Seiemon," suggesting a change in generation. The transfer of title is at last confirmed in a 1695 entry in the *Maeda Sadachika Oboegaki,* a diary kept by an official of the powerful Maeda family of the Kaga domain (Ishikawa Prefecture). An order of incense boxes from the Ninsei kiln was returned and eventually canceled because the "second-generation Ninsei" was unskillful; the order was sent instead to the Arita porcelain kilns. This mention of a second-generation title holder may well signify the founder's death.

A revolution had begun. How could Ninsei wares, potted in dull stoneware clays and decorated with conservative themes, ever compete with porcelain's hardness, whiteness, translucency, and compatibility with painting? Arita ware was flooding the Kyoto market at reasonable prices. At the same time, tea-ceremony wares, the original staple of the Ninsei workshop, were becoming available as ordinary merchandise in urban markets. In a world increasingly moved by fashion, Ninsei wares had become out of date.

As a skilled artisan, Ninsei had blossomed magnificently. He could couple skillful forms with fine decoration, but he

10. Ninsei ware: Tea-storage jar with design of poppies.

could not manufacture allusiveness — that atmosphere so critical to the Kyoto craft tradition. But his withering left a fertile ground for a completely different kind of flower. Kenzan had something besides technique to put on a pot. He would appropriate the artisan's methods to produce images of the amateur scholar — images accumulated over three decades of immersion in Kyoto high culture. It is to that period that we now turn.

1. Poem no. 339 in the *Tosa Diary*, trans., Helen Craig McCullough, *Brocade by Night: Kokin Wakashū and the Court Style in Japanese Classical Poetry* (Stanford: Stanford University Press, 1985), 359. With the permission of the publishers, © 1985 by the Board of Trustees of the Leland Stanford Junior University.

2. In the tea diary *Yamanoue Sōji Ki,* published in typeset transcription in Sen Sōshitsu, ed., *Chanoyu Koten Zenshū* 6 (1967), 98.

3. The early seventeenth-century salons are inventoried in Kumakura Isao, "Kan'ei no Fūkei" [View of the Kan'ei Era], *Tankō* 37 (1983), 8–18.

4. These three letters are published in Arakawa Hirokazu, "Kōetsu Makie toshite no Shōsoku" [Letters Concerning Kōetsu Makie], *Shikō Shi* 2 (1979), 70–72.

5. See Komori Shunkan, "Shoki Kyoyaki" [Early Kyoto Ware], *Tōsetsu* 433 (1989), 43–49.

6. Yamato Bunkakan 1963, 98.

Chapter Two
OF SILK AND LETTERS

I
n his 1684 novel *Kōshoku Nidai Otoko* (Son of a Man Who
Loved Love) Ihara Saikaku (1642–93) described three
types of urban merchants. One was independently
wealthy, possessing the finest art objects that money could buy.
Oblivious to worldly affairs, he would retreat to his tea hut at
the first sign of snow; spring flowers would move him to write
poetry. A second had achieved wealth, but was unable to
renounce his business concerns totally. He would, however,
entrust the details to shop clerks and devote his spare time to
culture. A third was nouveau riche, wealthy through rice
speculation. This merchant consumed wildly, lent out money
at high interest, and kept a nervous watch over the rise and fall
of prices.[1]

Saikaku's profiles are not without relevance for Kenzan's
family, the Ogata. Successive masters of the house had kept
one hand in the affairs of their profitable dry-goods business,
which had attracted some of the most powerful patrons in the
land; in their leisure time, they immersed themselves in culture. As second and third sons, heirs to extensive family
property but not the trade, Kōrin and Kenzan were raised to
be dilettantes. Yet Kōrin quickly exhausted his fortune and had
to engage in the kind of get-rich-quick schemes familiar to
Saikaku's nouveau riche. Kenzan, on the other hand, seems to
have conserved his resources, enjoying such cultured pursuits
as tea and poetry amid the splendors of nature. This chapter
introduces evidence linking Kenzan to those pursuits, especially to a wave of intellectual and artistic fashion for things
Chinese that swept Kyoto in the second half of the 1600s.
Kenzan became particularly enamored of Chinese modes of
poetry and calligraphy and the reclusive environment that was
believed to spur their production. He frequented the sinophile
salons, and even opened one of his own in the hills outside the

city. Kenzan's world of the gentleman-recluse found concrete form through the quintessential scholar's art: calligraphy. And despite the apparent distance between cultivation and pottery production, Kenzan parlayed his background in silk and letters into a revolutionary style of ceramics.

MASTERS OF THE KARIGANEYA

Historian Ōishi Shinzaburō has suggested that seventeenth-century Japanese culture revolved around silk.[2] Raw silk was so significant an import that the new Tokugawa shogunate assumed a total monopoly over it in 1604. The huge consumption of silk caused a serious trade deficit that drained a good share of Japan's metallic reserves. The hunger for silk naturally reflected a renewed stability and prosperity at home, primarily due to expanded agricultural production. A 1642 law restricting all peasants to cotton garments also suggests that at least a few of them had become sufficiently wealthy to afford silk. That townspeople were compulsive consumers of the material is seen in a series of edicts — nine between 1683 and 1693 — prohibiting the use of luxurious fabrics. For members of the military class, the need to compete for prestige during periods of mandatory residence in the capital guaranteed indulgence. Lacking cash to pay for silk, the warriors borrowed irresponsibly, eventually bankrupting many of the prominent merchant houses in Kyoto. Silk touched the lives of many people, and one of them was Kenzan.

In the seventeenth century, production of linen, cotton, and even silk was beginning to flourish in the Japanese islands. The capital of the textile trade was, however, Kyoto, celebrated for its high technical standards and the sophistication of its designs. At the very center of this booming and ultrafashionable craft was the house of Ogata. Their rise to prominence through silk is charted in the *Konishi Ke Monjo* — an archive of genealogies, sketches, and other documentary material passed down in the Konishi, the descendants of Kenzan's brother Kōrin. The earliest dated Konishi document, a 1602 business ledger, lists the shop title Kariganeya (Golden Goose), followed by orders for first Tokugawa shogun Ieyasu, his successor Hidetada, Hidetada's wife Oeyo, Toyotomi Hideyoshi's wife Nene, Hideyoshi's favorite consort Yodogimi, and Hideyoshi's heir Hideyori. Patronage for the Kariganeya obviously came from the very top — the Toyotomi and Tokugawa, two warrior clans locked in what would be a climactic struggle for national supremacy.

A transfer of the Konishi archive from the family to politically prominent businessman Mutō Yamaji (1867–1934) was thrown into confusion when Mutō was assassinated at a railway station in Tokyo. No one seemed to know where the papers were, or who was the rightful owner. In the decades that followed, the papers were distributed among the governmental Agency for Cultural Affairs, the Osaka Municipal Museum, and various private collections. The Osaka holdings, which include Kariganeya design books, Kōrin sketches, and four Kenzan letters, are the most comprehensive. Still other papers have been lost, including three genealogies which account for most of the early Ogata history: *Genealogy of the Saeki Family; Successive Generations and Necrology of the Ogata Family; Genealogy Covering from Kōrin's Father Sōken to Kōrin's Son Saijirō.* Fortunately, scholars made an inventory of their contents before they disappeared.

These documents place Kenzan's ancestors close to the most tumultuous events in medieval Japanese history. The Ogata lineage is first established in the war chronicle *Gempei Seisuiki* (Rise and Fall of the Genji and Heike Clans), written in the Kamakura period (1185–1333). The earliest ancestor, a resident of Ogata village in northern Kyushu, was Ōgami Tarō Koremoto, product of an unlikely union between a Shinto tutelary deity and the daughter of a local gentleman. Five generations later came Ogata Saburō Koreyoshi, who figured in the late Kamakura-period history *Azuma Kagami* (Mirror of the East) as a skilled archer who picked off warriors from the defeated Taira clan as they straggled into Kyushu after their defeat to another band of warriors, the Minamoto. Because of his alliance with Minamoto Yoshitsune (1159–89), who had incurred the wrath of his older brother and supreme commander Yoritomo (1147–99), Koreyoshi was exiled to Agano. Even though he was later pardoned, Koreyoshi was forbidden to return to his native village of Ogata, so he moved to nearby Saeki, taking the latter name as his own. This explains the title of the earliest genealogy. Koreyoshi and a dozen generations of his descendants served the Ōtomo clan in Kyushu.

In the sixteenth century, the Ogata story shifts to Kyoto, where several warlords were contending for the seat of power only nominally occupied by the Ashikaga family (see geneal-

GENEALOGY OF THE
OGATA FAMILY

━━━ family headship

- - - - marriage

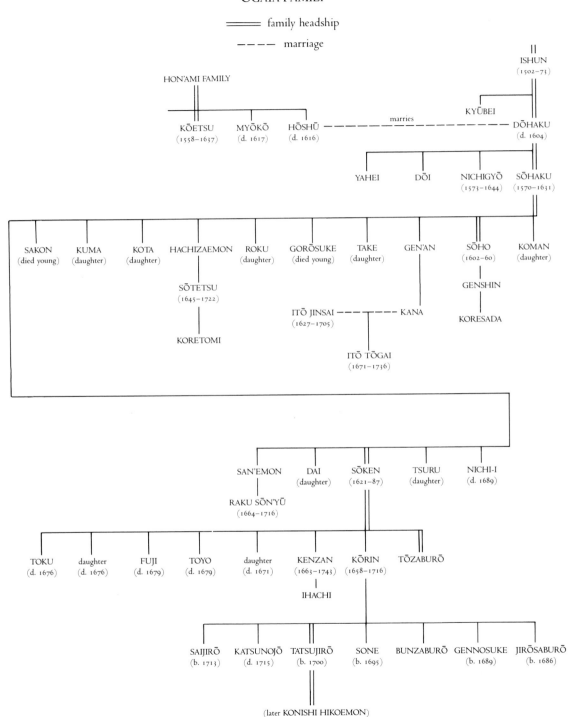

ogy). Five generations before Kenzan, Saeki Ishun (1502–73) left his native Kyushu for Kyoto, where he was employed by the last of the Ashikaga shoguns, Yoshiaki (1537–97). Ishun changed his name back to Ogata and the Saeki genealogy maintains that under Yoshiaki, "Ogata Shinzaburō Ishun" was assigned the estimable (although perhaps never realized) salary of five thousand rice shares. Yoshiaki was looking for allies to help overturn his most powerful adversary, Oda Nobunaga, and apparently used Ishun in secret entreaties to warlord Asai Nagamasa (1545–73), quartered in nearby Ōmi. In 1573, however, Yoshiaki was pushed into exile by Nobunaga, and the Asai were vanquished at their stronghold at Odani. The Saeki genealogy maintains that Ishun remained in Kyoto.

The three daughters of Asai Nagamasa survived the Odani debacle. Like many women of consequence, however, they became pawns in political alliances: oldest sister Chacha became a consort of Toyotomi Hideyoshi under the name of Yodogimi; the middle sister, Ohatsu, wed the Echizen (Fukui Prefecture) warlord Kyōgoku Takatsugu (1563–1609); after one short marriage Ogō (Oeyo), the youngest, married Tokugawa Hidetada (1579–1632) in 1595. The women of the Asai would nevertheless remember a former retainer: the Saeki document maintains that Ishun's son Dōhaku became chief clothier to Hideyoshi. This must have been at Yodogimi's insistence. She and her son Hideyori were annihilated in the final Tokugawa victory in 1615, but that would have little effect on Dōhaku, who in the intervening years seems to have changed sides. His son, Sōhaku (1570–1631), is listed as a part of the retinue in Oeyo's wedding to Hidetada, and Oeyo's daughter Masako, better known by her imperial title Tōfukumon'in, lavishly patronized three generations of Kariganeya masters.

Dōhaku was also discriminating in his choice of a mate. The *Hon'ami Gyōjō Ki,* or Hon'ami Family Annals, states that Ogata Dōhaku married Hōshū, the older sister of the merchant-aesthete Kōetsu. Here was a cultural entrée. Sōhaku, the first son of this union, built the family dry-goods business into one of the most prosperous in the nation, and was also known as a man of cultivation. His name appears as owner of a plot of land at Kōetsu's Takagamine village in north Kyoto. A 1675 calligraphy copybook called *Kōetsu Shiboku* (Four Kōetsu-school Calligraphers) identifies Sōhaku (along with Kōetsu,

Akiba Kōan, and Suminokura Yōichi [Sōan]) as one of the most able exponents of the highly regarded Hon'ami script style.

Sōhaku fathered fifteen children, many of whom achieved distinction. His first wife, identified only by her maiden name Inoue and posthumous Buddhist name Myōsen, bore four sons and four daughters. The Saeki genealogy praises the character of first-born son and heir Sōho (1602–60), who in difficult times took in the poor and gave them employment; in 1634, when Shogun Iemitsu distributed cash gifts to all Kyoto households, Sōho was honest enough to return an excess allotted him on the basis of the four houses he owned. Sōho's younger brothers Gen'an and Sōchū pursued medicine and Confucianism, respectively; Gen'an received the honorary court title hokkyō for his efforts. There is also evidence of scholarly achievement in both Sōho's and his siblings' children.

When Myōsen died in the second decade of the seventeenth century, Sōhaku married Akiba (maiden) Ichijūin (posthumous), and they produced four sons and three daughters. Eldest son Nichii became the thirteenth-generation head of Kyoto's Chōmyōji temple, of the Nichiren sect; the second son was Kenzan's father Sōken, who eventually succeeded Sōho as master of the Kariganeya. The youngest son San'emon is thought to be the father of Sōn'yū, the fifth-generation head of the Raku pottery workshop. Sōhaku's parental legacy is thus remarkable in its richness and diversity; with Myōsen, he produced an eminent group of learners, and with Ichijūin, a line of distinguished artists.

Adroitly balancing business and cultural affairs, Kenzan's father, Ogata Sōken (1621–87), embodied the second type of Saikaku merchant. As a youth he was called Shume, and later Kōsai. He was only eleven years old when his father died in 1631, but his mother skillfully advanced him as next master of the Kariganeya. Business ledgers preserved in the Konishi archive show that as early as 1646 Sōken had acquired a number of important clients; with Sōho's death in 1660, he became titular head of the family. Backed by the strong support of his mother until her death in 1671 (which coincided with the premature death of Sōho's son and rightful Kariganeya heir Genshin), Sōken brought the Kariganeya to new heights of prosperity. In 1678, the year of Tōfukumon'in's death, income from the palace alone was triple that in Sōhaku's heyday. Additional patronage from rich merchant houses enhanced that success.

Sōken was an amateur artist, devoted to calligraphy, painting, and the Noh drama. It is certainly possible that Sōken studied calligraphy from his father, though the mid-nineteenth century painting history *Koga Bikō* alleges that his teacher was Kōetsu. But Sōken was only seventeen when Kōetsu, perhaps already infirm from a stroke suffered several decades earlier, died in 1637. A passage in an 1892 sequel to the picture book *Ogata Ryū Hyakuzu* identifies Sōken's teacher as Kojima Sōshin, another skillful Hon'ami-style calligrapher. Sōshin was born in 1580, and as one of his dated poem scrolls demonstrates, he was still active in 1655. The Konishi archive has an abundance of materials from his hand. The contents of twenty-one letters portray Sōshin and Sōken as intimates — there are notes of appreciation, discussion of paper types, and regards to the latter's mother. Two albums of Japanese poetry and one album of Chinese verse — a total of 208 sheets in all — are formally executed by Sōshin as calligraphy models. Even today it is difficult to distinguish between the elegant handwriting of the two men.

Only a few examples of Ogata Sōken's painting style survive. A depiction of the auspicious deity Ebisu attributed to Sōken and reproduced in the 1889 *Ogata Ryū Hyakuzu* displays in its heavy, modulated outlines a style associated with the Kanō school, which was heavily patronized by the military class; a hanging scroll depicting the Shinto god of Sumiyoshi, now in the collection of the Tokyo University of Fine Arts, reveals the thin outlines associated with the Tosa style, which had developed under the patronage of the imperial court. Other Sōken paintings include a bird-and-flower theme inspired by poems by fourteenth-century master Fujiwara no Teika (1162–1241); a portrait of a Korean gentleman; a pair of decorated poem cards; and a painting of puppies. Sōken's involvement with brushwork seems to have been eclectic and casual.

His devotion to the Noh drama is better documented. Of such value was his collection of costumes, props, and musical instruments for Noh that they were given special mention in his will. The Konishi archive includes a copy of *Kadensho,* the treatise by Noh pioneer Zeami, copied out in 1672 by Sōken's second son Ichinojō (Kōrin); an inscription on the back of the document testifies that in the tenth month of that year Sōken and his two elder sons Tōzaburō and "Ichi" (Ichinojō) put on a four-day Noh performance. Neighbors were invited, and it is not unreasonable to envision an awed Kenzan, then ten years old, in the audience. Here is firsthand evidence of how Sōken transmitted cultured hobbies to his children.

Sōken also surrounded his children with silk. Patterns used by the Kariganeya are preserved in three sketchbooks from the early 1660s, Sōken's heyday. They show patterns in what is known as the Kambun style — simple, large-scale motifs orchestrated in a sweep from hem to shoulder, leaving large parts of the cloth undecorated. The decorations were sumptuous, executed in embroidery, tie-dyeing, and metallic leaf. The fluid, asymmetrical approach to surface, deliberate treatment of negative space, and large scale patterns — all calculated to make a strong impression, even from a distance — that would characterize much of Kōrin's painting and Kenzan's ceramics have their roots here. The younger Ogata brothers may have been raised as dilettantes, but they were no strangers to the process and products of design. Through their aristocratic hobbies and the family business environment, they were unwittingly prepared for careers in the plastic arts.

Sōken seems to have been less successful in transmitting a prosperous business to the next generation. The Konishi archive reveals that the Ogata, like other wealthy Kyoto merchants, had large outstanding loans to military families. From the mid-seventeenth century, periods of mandatory attendance in Edo and occasional public works levies required most daimyo to make expenditures in excess of their fiefs' productivity. For cash they turned to the merchants, who were initially attracted by the prestige of the borrowers and the prospect of high interest income. From the 1680s, when it became clear that most of these loans would never be repaid, the largest merchant houses in Kyoto began to go bankrupt. There was also a dwindling market for the kind of personal draper's services provided by the Ogata. *Chōnin Kōken Roku* (Observations on Merchants), a critique of seventeenth-century Kyoto merchant families compiled in the 1720s by Mitsui Takafusa (1684–1748), states that "Whereas they [drapers in official service] once got all the daimyo drapery business, nowadays the daimyo mansions are scrutinizing prices and either buy in Edo or get commercial establishments in the appropriate line of business to put in tenders."[3] These changes haunted Sōken's first son and successor Tōzaburō, who was probably born around 1650.

Tōzaburō's early adulthood was marked by misfortune, for nearly all family members and important patrons perished: Ogata matriarch Ichijūin and Tōzaburō's sister in 1671; his own daughter in 1672; his mother Okatsu and two more sisters in 1676; patron Tōfukumon'in in 1678; his two remaining sisters in 1679; and his father in 1687. Sometime between 1683 and 1687, Tōzaburō had been expelled from the family and then reinstated. A genealogy copied out in 1714 by Kōrin's son reveals that Tōzaburō eventually moved to Edo, where he took employment under samurai Kawaguchi Genzaburō with the new name of Sukemon. Perhaps an obscure grave marked "Ogata Sukemon" may someday be found in Tokyo; it surely would have been visited by younger brother Kenzan during his own late-life sojourn in that city.

The Kariganeya business was in decline as the two younger brothers, Ichinojō (Kōrin) and Gompei (Kenzan), came of age. The family resources were nevertheless vast enough to ensure their cultivation and a large inheritance upon Sōken's death on the ninth day of the sixth month, 1687. Receipts in the Konishi archive permit this reconstruction:

Tōzaburō

Two houses on Nakatachiuri
Business capital and furnishings
Palace accounts
Inventory of textiles

Ichinojō (Kōrin)

Jūraku Yamazatomachi house
West Kyoto house
Set of costumes and props for the Noh drama
Half of family cash and art collection
Half of accounts receivable from daimyo loans

Gompei (Kenzan)

Muromachi Hanatatechō house
Jōkaimmachi house

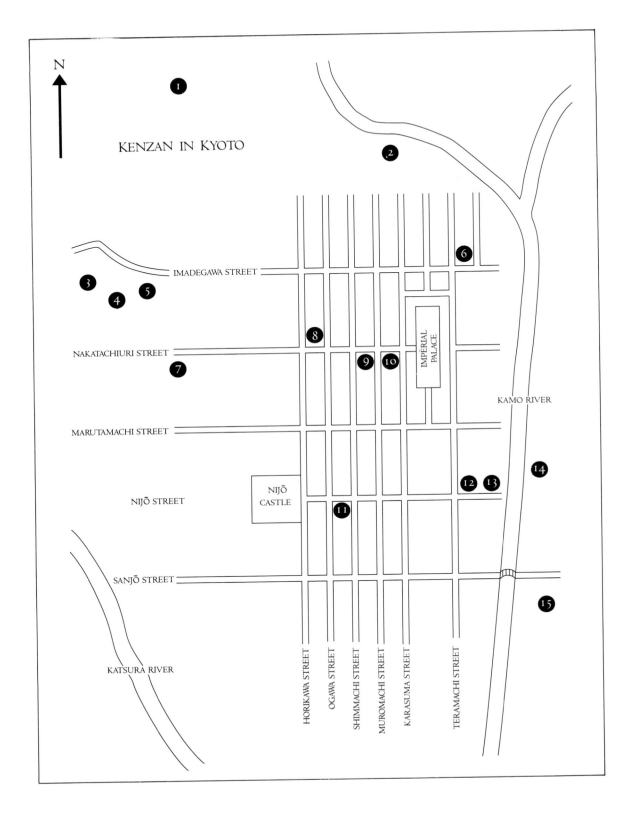

N

KENZAN IN KYOTO

IMADEGAWA STREET

NAKATACHIURI STREET

IMPERIAL
PALACE

MARUTAMACHI STREET

KAMO RIVER

NIJŌ
CASTLE

NIJŌ STREET

SANJŌ STREET

KATSURA RIVER

HORIKAWA STREET

OGAWA STREET

SHIMMACHI STREET

MUROMACHI STREET

KARASUMA STREET

TERAMACHI STREET

Takagamine house
Calligraphy scroll by Yin Yuejiang
Family library
Half of family cash and art collection
Half of accounts receivable from daimyo loans

Sōken's legacy thus consisted of seven houses (see map), cash, business and personal property, and large outstanding loans to daimyo (which were never repaid). Given the custom of the times, the settlement was particularly generous. Novelist Saikaku wrote in his 1692 *Seken Munazan'yō* (Worldly Mental Calculations) that in a wealthy family it was usual for the first son to inherit the family house and about half the family assets; the second son would receive the resort house and about thirty percent of the assets; the third son would receive the smallest share of the assets and would be adopted into another family.[4] Kōrin and Kenzan obviously received more than the conventional shares upon Sōken's death.

With his large inheritance, Ogata Kōrin was free to pursue a life of pleasure. His dalliances (he fathered seven children, all illegitimate, with six different women), which emerge in the Konishi papers, combine with legend to place him as a dandy moving in the fast world of urban pleasures. That image has been reinforced by his superstitious consultations with onomantic diviners, his speculative lending to samurai, and his extensive pawning and borrowing. Indeed, Kōrin is often said to embody the spirit of the Genroku era, a period associated with a free-spending and self-indulgent urban middle class. The unusually good documentation of Kōrin's affairs may place him in an unflattering light — doubtless other wealthy merchants were similarly indulgent — but from an artistic point of view, Kōrin's proximity to the world of urban fashion would prove to be one of the rich sources for Kenzan wares.

CONFUCIANISM, ZEN, AND SECLUSION

Nakatachiuri, north Kyoto: late seventeenth-century maps show that the neighborhood was populated by merchants in service to the court, and even today the street runs into the west gate of the imperial palace (fig. 11). Just further to the west were the textile quarters at Nishijin, still a center for weaving, dyeing, and decorating fine silks. In 1663 Kenzan was born at the Kariganeya, located at the intersection of Na-

11. Nakatachiuri, Kyoto: site of the Kariganeya.

katachiuri and the Ogawa, a small stream that wound through these affluent suburbs. His father, Ogata Sōken, was forty-three; Sōken gave his third son the common name of Gompei and formal name of Koremitsu.

What happens to a fourteen-year-old boy when he loses his mother? And, within a few years of that, the last of his five sisters? We can provide only an indirect answer. His two older brothers, spared the impact of the tragedy by virtue of their adulthood, were undeterred pleasure-seekers. For Kenzan, the solitude was far more poignant. He immersed himself in study, as suggested by his inheritance of the family library and especially of a calligraphy scroll by Chinese monk Yin Yuejiang (1267–ca. 1350), whose writing was highly esteemed in Zen Buddhist and tea-ceremony circles. Kenzan's scholarly inclinations were to be nurtured further by the newest wave in seventeenth-century urban culture: an interest in Chinese studies. This encompassed Confucian philosophy, a new sect of Buddhism from the continent called Ōbaku, and literature. We shall see that merchant-class aspirants, including Kenzan, would be particularly attracted by the poetic images of seclusion so prevalent in the imported Chinese literature.

At the middle of the seventeenth century, Kyoto was a thriving peacetime city of about 600,000 people, an increasing number of whom had the means to pursue the liberal arts. Zen Buddhism, which had dominated cultural discourse over the previous centuries, now seemed inadequate to address the social, economic, and educational issues in a prosperous urban society. The new military government also sought a set of historical and ethical justifications for their regime outside of the old Buddhist framework. Confucianism, an ancient Chinese moral system that advocated loyalty and responsibility in family, society, and state, addressed these needs. For the rulers headquartered in Edo, Confucianism (particularly a revised form called Neo-Confucianism) provided an instrument of legitimacy, regulation, and control; in the comparatively free merchant-class milieu of Kyoto, it was interpreted in such a way as to buttress an increasingly pragmatic world view. The chief architect of the latter was the most famous Kyoto philosopher of his day, Itō Jinsai, Kenzan's cousin through marriage.

Jinsai was something of a rebel. He began to pursue philosophy from his mid-teens and by his early thirties he had written several essays in the Neo-Confucian persuasion. But during a period of self-imposed isolation starting in 1655, he underwent a dramatic change of heart. Returning to the ancient texts of Confucius and Mencius, he found an emphasis on benevolence as the highest moral value. Jinsai began to insist that external morality, the principle so beloved by his adversaries in the Neo-Confucian school, was empty. Morality had to have a local, internal disposition, or it was simply not morality. This was best observed in everyday life, in the common activities of human beings and in ordinary things. Jinsai emerged from seclusion to found the Kogidō (Hall of Ancient Veneration), located just south of Shimotachiuri on Horikawa street, north Kyoto. This was just around the corner from Kenzan's Kariganeya.

Jinsai's commonsense teachings, coupled with his own lack of interest in worldly gain, won him a wide following. Kogidō students numbered in the hundreds, and included samurai, courtiers, wealthy merchants, doctors, and artists — representing all but three provinces in the entire nation. Evidence that one of these students may have been Kenzan is found in a diary kept by Jinsai, which mentions that on the second day in the first month, 1683, "Ogata Gompei [Kenzan] and Shinzaburō" visited with New Year's greetings (Shinzaburō was probably Kenzan's second cousin, a grandson and heir of Kenzan's deceased uncle, Sōho). Kenzan stood to gain much from Jinsai, who enjoyed a general reputation as an authority on China. He was esteemed for his correct Chinese prose and for his skill in calligraphy; and in Jinsai's equation of the highest principle with mundane activities, Kenzan might later envision a world in which one could be both a gentleman-scholar and potter.

Ogata Sōken's death in 1687 was clearly a turning point for Kenzan. With his inheritance of real estate, cash, and art objects he could have continued a comfortable life in urban Kyoto, but he elected neither to stay at Kariganeya nor move to one of his inherited properties. The kind of lifestyle his brothers were leading held little allure. A name change in 1688 from the boyhood "Gompei" to "Shinsei" (composed of characters signifying "deep meditation") seems to signal a new direction. Within a year, Kenzan was living in the hills outside the city. An early 1689 entry in the official diary of the Ninnaji temple mentions "Ogata Shinsei" as a local resident paying respects to the prince-abbot. As this was Kenzan's first appearance in the record, we may infer that he was a recent arrival in Omuro, the village that spread out before the temple gate.

Had Kenzan become a hermit? Period literature suggests that for a merchant with means, a secluded villa was quite fashionable. According to Mitsui Takafusa's *Chōnin Kōken Roku*, a chronicle of the rise and fall of the great merchant families of seventeenth-century Kyoto, ". . . in recent years, after their fathers die, young persons seclude themselves on the pretext of illness and behave as though in retirement. As they give themselves over to idleness, they lose their sense of respon-·sibility."[5] This trend to early "retirement" was encouraged by a growing exposure to the eremetic ideal long celebrated in East Asian religion, literature, and art. In Japan, the notion of the recluse was first nurtured in the apocalyptic visions spread by Buddhists between the twelfth and fifteenth centuries. For famous monk-recluses like Saigyō (1118–90), Kamo no Chōmei (1153–1216), and Yoshida Kenkō (1283–1350), escape from the world was an acknowledgement of its corruption and ultimately its impermanence. The new wave of Chinese studies in Kenzan's youth introduced a Daoist model, in which the world was regarded as neither impermanent nor evil, but uncomfortable. Nature was the proper environment for spiritual regeneration. This was realized in the reclusive activities of seventeenth-century men of letters such as Kinoshita Chōshōshi (1569–1649) and Ishikawa Jōzan (1583–1672). Eremeticism was further depoliticized and domesticated in publications like Motomasa Shōnin's 1644 *Fusō In'itsu Den* (Biographies of Japanese Recluses), which included Chōshōshi and Jōzan, and Saikaku's fictional account, *Fusō Kindai Yasa Inja* (Modern Japanese Recluses).

Kenzan's chosen place of retreat was hardly a remote wilderness but an address that evoked various political and literary figures. Ninnaji had been the retreat of the "classical" Emperor Uda (867–931) and had functioned as a salon from its rebuilding in 1647. The nearby twin hills of Narabigaoka were linked with the aforementioned Kenkō, author of the cherished fourteenth-century masterpiece *Tzurezuregusa* (Essays in Idleness). For Kenzan, was the reclusive life just another cultural cachet or a real commitment? His predicament seems to have been detected by a pair of priests who visited him at his new villa, the Shūseidō (Hall of Mastering Tranquility), in autumn 1690:

Shūseidō Ki

At the foot of Narabigaoka, there lives a certain gentleman; his personal name is Reikai and his surname is Ogata. His father's name was Sōken, and he used the pseudonym Kōsai. The Ogata have lived in Kyoto for generations, where they have enjoyed the lavish favor of Tōfukumon'in, and are held in high esteem. Sōken was an extremely fine calligrapher whose writing compares favorably with that of the Jin-dynasty masters; he was also known as a man of taste. After Sōken's death, the young master lost his interest in worldly affairs; a desire came over him to escape the world and seclude himself. He purchased a small plot of land, built a humble cottage, and has set up a home. In the ninth month of 1690, we were invited for a day's visit.

Strolling outside after our meal in the fresh, crystal-clear air, we felt as if we had left the ordinary world behind. The serene environment did not compare unfavorably to the hermitage of [poet-hermit] Wei Ye [960–1019] of the Song dynasty or to Tao Yuanming's village of Lu Li in Pengze xian [Jiangxi Province]. To the southwest, the luxuriously green summit of Narabigaoka jutted into the sky, somehow resembling a huge green snail. Turning to the southeast, the famous Myōshinji could be vaguely seen, shielded throughout the forest; the sound of its bell, however, tolling the morning and evening hour, made us feel as if we were near. In the northwest, the multi-storied pagoda of the Ninnaji stood serenely, its high eaves and lofty spire protruding though the mist-enshrouded landscape. Turning to the northeast, the peaks of Mount Kinugasa towered loftily above us; with the serenity and brilliance of the lotus leaf, it was a scene to be admired. This was the setting of the Shūseidō.

The house itself was a building of just a few rooms, with plain earthen walls and no ornamentation. The doors were of woven bamboo and the narrow winding paths were paved with stones. Pine and bamboo shimmered in the sun, and plum trees and willows cast cool shadows. We could hear the sound of water trickling into a pool, and saw steam from a tea kettle wafting out a window. Chinese and Japanese classics were stacked carelessly on shelves; the furnishings were spartan but showed extraordinary taste.

Looking out a little to the south, we could see a small detached room with a sign entitled Kin Sen [The Enlightened One]. The shrine was not more than ten feet square and had a thatched roof. Inside was a small statue of the Buddha, over which were suspended precious stones. These jewels were arranged as if in a net, their delicacy pleasing to the eye.

In front of this shrine an irregularly shaped pond was dug out, spanned by a wooden bridge. Many trees and shrubs of various shapes and sizes cast their reflections into the water. Beyond the shrine was a bath with enough room for four or five people to bathe at once. In the garden to the back of the house, chrysanthemums bloomed triumphantly in the frost, along with a rough bamboo hedge. Coxcombs were drenched with dew, and eggplants and potatoes grew profusely, overflowing from the furrows. This is where the young master strolled when tired of reading or writing, lost in high-minded thoughts.

Such a situation is suitable to the spirit and pleasant to live in, for one can easily forget about the affairs of the world and about the rise and fall of prices. As for the people whose hearts become captivated by desire for fame or profit, they can find pleasure only in hunting, music, or womanizing. Here is someone, however, who in the prime of his life has turned his back on the world. A person like the young master should be praised.

Then I put a question to the young master. Earlier he asked me to inscribe a signboard with the word *shūsei,* but I asked him whether or not he could grasp its meaning. He paused, silent in thought. At that point I told him the following: "To put it broadly, in this world the most prized thing of all is tranquility — water so still that it reflects the hair on one's head; ground so firm that anything would stand secure on it. By its very permanence a stone bluff is stable; because a mountain range never moves it appears to have existed forever. Among the sages and saints of old, and even among Confucianists and famous lay persons, there were many who found tranquility as the basis of their pursuits.

If one is going to search for life's treasure the waves of life must be quieted; when the water is turbulent it is impossible to see into it. If the water is calm, clean, and pure, the radiance of a jewel-like heart will naturally appear. If you do not devote yourself wholeheartedly to the way of Zen through meditation, every purpose will become confused, your relationship with others will lose direction, and the three evil passions of greed, anger, and foolishness will obscure your heart. The six senses will blur and mix in your mind. For you to arrive at the stillness of heart which is at the root of all things is still difficult, is it not? Please, young master, try hard to study this; always strive to learn tranquility. Study quietly, widely, and tacitly, and after a long period of maturation enlightenment will occur naturally. When that happens, for the first time you will be really worthy of being called a wise man who has abandoned the world to learn the way of the Buddha."

Nodding in agreement, the young master rose to his feet and bowed in thanks. Saying that these words were truly inspirational, he asked me to write them down so he could study them as a precept. I therefore copied this down for him.

This account portrays Kenzan as a wealthy person who had set up a dwelling where he could quietly enjoy nature and cultured hobbies. The salon-like nature of the place is suggested by Kenzan's purported activities in reading, writing, and the tea ceremony — and indeed by the visit itself. That the Shūseidō was far more than a recluse's hut is shown in a plan of the compound passed down in the Kaji family, which later seems to have inherited the place (fig. 12). The central building, now called Ryōkakutei, is preserved as a tea house at the nearby Ninnaji temple, where it was moved in the 1830s. It may well be the same room in which Kenzan and his visitors communed in 1690.

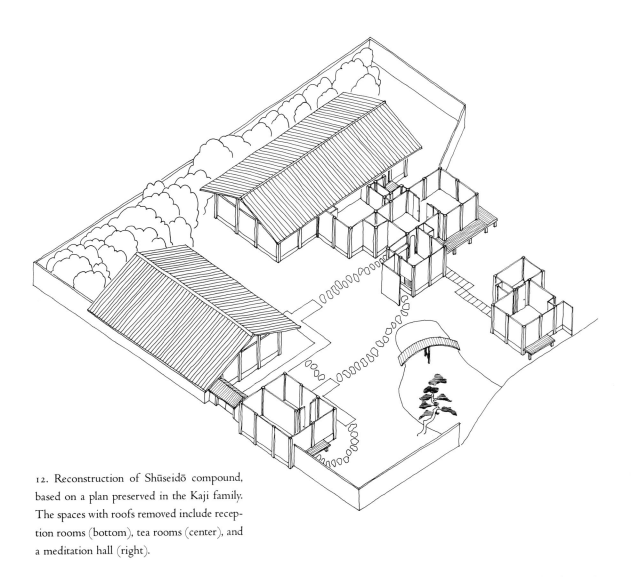

12. Reconstruction of Shūseidō compound, based on a plan preserved in the Kaji family. The spaces with roofs removed include reception rooms (bottom), tea rooms (center), and a meditation hall (right).

But if the "carrot" in the *Shūseidō Ki* is praise for Kenzan's well-appointed abode, the "stick" is one of Zen. Kenzan's decision to leave the city was admirable, but that was only the beginning. Now he had to search out the jewel. That could be found only beneath the restless waves of human desire and attachment, which might be quieted by meditation and deep study. After enlightenment those scholarly pastimes would take on true meaning. How serious were these exhortations, and how far did they penetrate into the heart of their recipient? Something of an answer emerges in Kenzan's affiliation with Ōbaku Zen, a Buddhist sect new to Japan.

Kenzan's visitors to the Shūseidō on that day in 1690 were Dokushō Shōen (1617–94), an older monk, and Gettan Dōchō (1635–1713), the author of the text. Dokushō was one of the most lauded disciples of Ingen (Chinese: Yinyuan; 1592–1673), the Chinese priest who brought the Ōbaku (Chinese: Huangpo) sect of Zen Buddhism to Japan in 1654. The timing was fortuitous, for the old Zen establishment in Japan was flagging. Ōbaku was also exotic; its unusual liturgy, art, and architecture represented China during a period in which government seclusion edicts put the esteemed continental neighbor out of reach. Saikaku, whose writings were never far from the irony in contemporary life, wrote, "In today's world, where daily survival is no longer a concern, the foreign priest Ingen has merely to wave his wand, and the success of his Buddhism will be automatically assured!"[6] Prominent doctors, Confucian scholars, and wealthy merchants became followers, as did priests from other sects. In 1659, Ingen was invited to Dokushō's Saga retreat, bestowing upon it the new name of Jikishian — Direct Perception Hermitage. Dokushō and Gettan thereupon became Ōbaku converts, and were successful in garnering support among the Kyoto elite. Gettan, in fact, was so prolific an author that he was referred to by the half-facetious title *Moji* Zen (literary Zen); a good deal of his work survives in block-printed form.

Kenzan seems to have been closest to Dokushō. Dokushō's journal *Jikishi Dokushō Zenji Kōroku,* published in block-printed form in 1704, mentions that 1690 visit to Kenzan, and an undated entry on an adjacent page discusses the meaning of "Reikai," one of Kenzan's favorite pseudonyms. The juxtaposition of these entries suggests that Dokushō granted the name during that autumn visit, or that the visit was in celebration of Kenzan's receiving the name. In the ninth month of 1692, just two years before his death, Dokushō made another visit to Kenzan, composing a spontaneous poem likening the young master to the Chinese recluse-poet Tao Yuanming. We might imagine that Kenzan's training consisted of periodic visits to Jikishian, where he would hear Zen lectures and practice meditation. I was surprised to find this tradition of lay instruction still intact on a trip in 1983 to Mampukuji, the Ōbaku-sect headquarters outside of Kyoto. A group of young salaried employees from Osaka bashfully admitted that they enjoyed weekend retreats to the temple. That Dokushō took on only serious lay students is suggested by their small number; besides Kenzan's "Reikai" only two other names, "Gizan" and "Kohō," emerge in his records. Gizan was the fabulously wealthy moneychanger Naba Sōjun (1633–97), and Kohō was his son, Naba Kurozaemon Yūei (1652–99). Of special significance is Kenzan's relationship with the latter, for at the time of his death in 1699 Yūei reigned as the doyen of amateur scholars in Kyoto.

As one of the wealthiest merchant houses in Kyoto, the Naba epitomized Saikaku's "oblivious" merchant introduced at the beginning of this chapter. Their saga emerges in *Chōnin Kōken Roku*. Founder Naba Jōyū (d. 1664) came from his native Banshū (Hiroshima Prefecture) to build a quick fortune in Edo and then Kyoto. Son Sōjun must have spent a good deal of his time squandering the family wealth, for the military government censured him for frivolous conduct. His punishment was to rebuild the Uji Bridge, a project that took three years; the *Chōnin Kōken Roku* nevertheless relates that it cost Sōjun but a month's income. Some of his expenditures suggest more serious intentions: his funding of repairs at the Zen temple Daitokuji and at Dokushō's Jikishian; his building of a meditation hall called Kōgendō at the family residence on Nijō Ogawa; and his invitation to the Ōbaku monks to a villa at Takagamine called Chikandō. These interests were continued by the third-generation scion, Naba Kurozaemon Yūei.

Like his father Sōjun, Yūei received a Zen name from Dokushō. The *Chōnin Kōken Roku* maintains that Yūei was the most formidable merchant-scholar of Genroku-era Kyoto, skilled in Chinese and Japanese poetry as well as Confucianism. His circle of friends included Kōetsu's grandson Kōho (1601–62); Kenzan's cousin Genshin; Jinsai's son Itō Tōgai; and Uda Kōki (1664–1721), son of another wealthy Kyoto merchant. Despite his range of activities and associations, bad health (his journals contain moving passages about his illnesses) and personal disposition drew him toward the reclusive life. Such a person would have held great attraction for a young aspirant like Kenzan.

Thanks to a recent find, the relationship between Kenzan and Yūei is no longer speculation. *Shōsō Yōgin* (Continued Recitations of Shōsō), a ten-volume diary of Naba Yūei, was recently discovered by Kawasaki Hiroshi in the storerooms of the Rakutō Ihōkan, a collection of heirlooms of the Kashiwabara and Naba families. The diary, covering from 1686 to 1699, includes three references to our subject. The first records a 1692 gathering at the Myōkōji temple located in the hills about a mile northwest of the Shūseidō. Besides Yūei and the aforementioned Uda Kōki, there were merchant scholars Kitamura Tokusho (1647–1718); Maeda Shōu (born ca. 1665); a priest named Rinshō; and "Shinsei the gentleman recluse from Ninnaji," or Kenzan. Yūei described the day as first clear, then clouding over with a wintry feeling. The group collected the prized *matsutake* mushrooms, and spent the evening composing poems. Kenzan's is recorded:

> Like Xie Lingyun [of ancient China],
> Leaving my hut in mindless haste
> For a mountain temple, barren with fallen leaves.
> While still lost in high-minded amusements,
> The temple bell tolls the day's end.

Kenzan played the *shō,* a kind of panpipe, in an impromptu concert that followed — and according to Yūei, the party broke up at midnight. The second reference occurs at the time of Sōjun's death in 1697. A condolence gift of fruits and tea from "Shūseidō Shinsei, the gentleman-recluse of the western hills" is cited. Kenzan was thus still living at the Shūseidō, but the third and final *Shōsō Yōgin* reference hints at a move. In 1698, Yūei and a priest named Keigaku visited Gettan at Jikishian; on the way home they stopped at the "humble cottage or hermit's cell (*iori*) of Shinsei the gentleman-recluse from Narutaki mountain."

Every indication from the Ōbaku and Naba records portrays Kenzan as enjoying the life of scholar-gentleman in the Chinese mode. Another side to Kenzan's activities in the 1690s is revealed in the records of the house of Nijō, where the names of Kenzan and Kōrin begin to appear in 1689. The Nijō were one of the five noble houses (*gosekke*) that traditionally provided candidates for the imperial posts of regent (*sesshō*) and civil dictator (*kampaku*). The real benefits of such rank were of course highly circumscribed in Kenzan's day, but courtly prestige was still a powerful lure for merchants who had wealth but no franchise. It was probably through Kariganeya business contacts that the Ogata brothers met Nijō family head Tsunahira (1670–1732), recently adopted from another noble house, the Kujō. The Nijō diaries depict a thriving salon, with wealthy merchants, painters, and Noh dramatists in frequent attendance; from the mid-1690s Kōrin himself seems to have undertaken some painting at the behest of the noble family. Here was a center dedicated to the plastic and performing arts.

The relationship with Nijō quickly escalated: After single visits in the years 1689 and 1692, in 1693 Kenzan visited a total of nineteen times. In 1694, the same year that his Zen teacher Dokushō died, Kenzan obtained from Nijō Tsunahira a plot of land at Narutaki, about a mile northwest of the Shūseidō. A deed for the transaction is preserved in the Hōzōji, the temple that now occupies the site. Was this acquisition the first stage toward the ceramics enterprise that opened there five years later? The traditional consensus is yes — Kenzan was considering a livelihood in light of a declining inheritance. A letter to Kōrin in 1696 is usually offered as evidence. The older brother had borrowed a substantial sum of money from Kenzan, and the loan was secured only by promissory notes from military men — notes that were now acknowledged to be worthless. Kenzan chided Kōrin for placing so many of his possessions in hock, although he admitted to having visited the pawnbroker himself.

The total picture is not, however, one of desperation. Kōrin, for all his troubles, managed to purchase a large house at Nakamachi Yabunouchichō in the late 1690s. As for Kenzan, he must have had enough cash to purchase the Narutaki land. The deed preserved at Hōzōji states that Nijō granted Kenzan the land, but in those times courtiers survived by "granting" real estate, calligraphy, and court awards to wealthy commoners. The deed was necessitated by a government policy forbidding commoners to initiate purchases of real estate. The brothers unquestionably had cash flow problems, but they were hardly bankrupt. After his land acquisition, Kenzan let five leisurely years pass before opening his Narutaki kiln. Surely, if he had had a strong personal and financial urgency to begin ceramics, he would want to realize his ambitions sooner than later — or at least make some pots.

Did Kenzan dabble in ceramics before opening his own kiln in 1699? Most authorities maintain that Kenzan's receipt of a pottery manual from Kōetsu's grandson Kōho, and his statement in his 1737 pottery manual *Tōji Seihō* that he had been on intimate terms with fourth-generation Raku master

Ichinyū (1640–96) are proof of an early interest in the potter's craft. But I suspect the opposite. The Ogata family's intimacy with the Raku was not based on an interest in making ceramics; the Ogata were patrons of the Raku, and they may well have saved these potters from extinction.

The Raku family had fallen on hard times from the period of third-generation master Dōn'yū, who is mentioned in the annals of the Hon'ami family as being poor. A document called *Sōn'yū Monjo* (Archive of Sōn'yū), preserved in the Raku family collection, relates that Ichinyū had to work out of his wife's house at Inokuma Ichijō. Ichinyū's successor-to-be Sōn'yū was born in 1664, and was adopted into the Raku at the age of two. After replacing Ichinyū's natural son Yahei as the heir, Sōn'yū moved the family to new quarters at Aburakōji Nijō Agaru. According to a nineteenth-century document entitled *Raku Daidai* (Generations of the Raku), this property had been in the possession of Sōn'yū's natural father (and Kenzan's uncle), Ogata San'emon. Obviously the Ogata had rescued the Raku family from unpromising circumstances. The present-day wealth and prestige of the Raku family has encouraged an inversion of the true relationship between these two houses. Ichinyū was not a mentor for Kenzan, and Kenzan's later work in ceramics displays little technical debt to the Raku tradition.

Sōn'yū typifies the necessity of the declining merchant families to seek new trades, and Kenzan would eventually follow. But in the 1680s and 1690s, Kenzan was not interested in pots. It is more plausible that, as the 1698 entry in the Naba diary suggests, Kenzan first bought the Narutaki mountain land as a resort place. Until some very sudden circumstances at the end of the decade, Kenzan was a gentleman-scholar. His first artistic forays were not carried out in clay, but in characters.

CALLIGRAPHY

Ogata Kenzan created a new world of ceramics — or perhaps we should say a new kind of potter. Kenzan was certainly not an artisan. There is no proof that he ever made pots on the wheel or in molds, and the circumstantial evidence — the advanced age at which he started his workshop (thirty-seven), class notions that weighed against extensive participation in manual chores, and the complete absence of comments on fabrication or kiln firing in his writings — also suggests that he

13. Chang Jizhih: The Diamond Sutra (detail).

had little interest in potting proper. But Kenzan was more than a kiln manager. His two pottery manuals demonstrate a keen interest in techniques, especially in strategies for modifying surfaces through slips and glazes, and for decorating in underglaze pigments or overglaze enamels. His personal forte, however, was calligraphy. It was his first art, and the one that he applied with confidence and versatility throughout his career. Kenzan was the first to produce ceramics whose artistic focus was handwritten script, and in doing so he vastly increased the range of associations that a pot might have. This triumph is unthinkable without those years of cultivation at the salons — and many quiet hours with brush and paper at the Shūseidō.

"When the heart is right, the brush will be right." This old Chinese adage captures the fascination that calligraphy has had for literate East Asian audiences from the early centuries of the common era. The tradition developed in China first as a form of communication, and then, when it was realized that calligraphy showed most nakedly the spirit of its maker — the "right heart" — it became a treasured form of art. In Japan, calligraphy carried the status of continental learning and later, with the development of a native script style, a strong sense of national identity. Westerners have found still other significance in East Asian calligraphy. For those uninitiated in the literal meanings of the characters it has invited comparisons with twentieth-century abstract expressionist painting.

In China and Japan, however, calligraphy was not conceived of as pure graphic energy, but rather as a play between the creative powers of the artist and well-understood formal conventions such as stroke order and balance of parts. The zone of delectation is the space between these two poles — the line may dance but it never breaks the basic rules. With that kind of dialectic in mind, the informed viewer of calligraphy may follow stroke by stroke the entire process leading to the finished work. One further dimension is historical style; one could, for example, evoke some bygone era just by writing in the style of a famous scribe from that period.

By the time Ogata Kenzan took up the brush, historical associations were substantial indeed. The Chinese script tradition, now over three thousand years old, was subsumed under the term *karayō* — Chinese ideographic characters (*kanji*) executed in modes known as clerical, formal, semicursive, or cursive. Kenzan would have known this world through *bokuseki* (ink traces), the writing of prominent Zen monks displayed in the tea ceremony. The Zen-inspired preference for direct expression over technical precision meant that a diversity of Song- and Yuan-dynasty individualists ranging from court favorites Huang Shangu (1050–1110) and Zhang Jizhi (1186–1286) (fig. 13) to monk Yin Yuejiang — as well as their admirers in Kamakura- and Muromachi-period Zen centers in Japan — could be held up as models.

In Kenzan's day there was also a growing concern for authentic (i.e., contemporary) continental script styles, but the means of transmission was less than perfect. In Kyoto the Daishi school of calligraphy teachers claimed roots in the work of the tenth-century Japanese monk and renowned calligrapher Kūkai (774–835; also known as Kōbō Daishi), but in fact drew many of their script models from Chinese Ming-dynasty copybooks. The monks of the Ōbaku sect, including founder Ingen and his followers Mokuan (Chinese: Muan; 1611–84) and Sokuhi (Chinese: Chifei; 1616–71), encouraged their devotees to execute non-Japanized script styles, but the Ōbaku manner was, in light of contemporary metropolitan practice in China, itself highly idiosyncratic. The multiplicity and intermingling of sources preclude in Kenzan's *karayō* calligraphy the succinct reference to historical models that we might expect in the work of master calligraphers in China.

Faced with the problem of adapting Chinese to their native language, the Japanese had gradually devised new script types of their own. Japanese-style calligraphy, or *wayō*, was written in Chinese characters borrowed for their phonetic values (*man'yō-gana*) or in the extremely simplified phonetic syllabary called *kana*. In seventeenth-century Kyoto, the tea ceremony offered the best exposure to the indigenous script tradition. From the mid-sixteenth century, merchant tea enthusiasts had seized upon the writing of courtier Fujiwara no Teika, first for its elegant, aristocratic imagery and subsequently for its visual style. Instead of the thinly brushed, delicately linked manner of *kana* calligraphy called *jōdaiyō*, Teika's work displayed a brusque, expressive manner (fig. 14). By the seventeenth century, the increased popularity of the tea ceremony and accessibility to copybooks and court poetry teachers established the Teika style as a vehicle for anyone with claims to aristocratic and tea genealogies.

Kenzan's ancestors had also made great contributions to

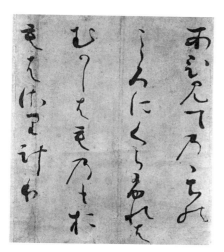

14. Fujiwara no Teika: Page from the *Ogura Shikishi.*

wayō. His great uncle Kōetsu, heralded as one of the greatest calligraphers of the day, paid greater attention to the relationship between written text and underlying paper design. He was a master of contrasts — of painted motif to character, of Chinese *kanji* to Japanese *kana,* and of thickly inked lines to thinly inked ones. Something of that pulse can be seen in Kenzan's script, but without Kōetsu's conscious elegance.

Three documents from the 1680s and 1690s attest to Kenzan's early development in calligraphy. Since the provenance of two of these pieces is well established in the Konishi archive and the other is closely related stylistically, an understanding of their structural and rhythmic tendencies will provide a standard for authenticity. That standard can — and

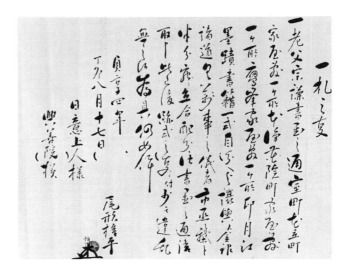

15. Receipt for inheritance of Ogata Gompei (Kenzan).

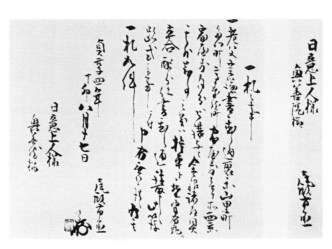

16. Receipt for inheritance of Ogata Ichinojō (Kōrin).

64

17 and 18. (Above, left) "Orthodox" version of character *ji* (self), and (above, right) Kenzan's version of *ji* (see inheritance receipt, line four, eighth character; *Ōtotsuka o Yogiru no Ki*, line one, eighth character).

19 and 20. (Below, left) "Orthodox" version of character *sho* (to write), and (below, right) Kenzan's version of character *sho* (see inheritance receipt, line one, sixth character; *Ōtotsuka o Yogiru no Ki*, line fourteen, ninth character).

will — be compared with the poetic inscriptions and lengthy signatures on Kenzan ceramics, which are always difficult to authenticate. A contrast of writing intended for private and public consumption may also provide character insights: what was the distance between Kenzan the person and the Kenzan persona?

Kenzan acknowledged the legacy from his father in an inheritance receipt, dated 1687 (fig. 15), preserved in the Konishi archive. Since it is difficult to discuss such a work in isolation, let us compare the receipt with one submitted about the same time by Kenzan's brother Kōrin (fig. 16). At a glance it is obvious that Kenzan maintains a lucid, open composition, not only as a whole, but within the individual characters (figs. 17–20). The writing of Kōrin is, in comparison, dense and untidy. Kenzan's writing avoids excessive vertical linkages between each character, endowing each graph with its own space. In contrast, Kōrin allows the line to broaden as it changes direction; the resulting contours are similar to those of a twisted ribbon. Kenzan takes pains to contrast fat opening strokes with the thin and tentatively linked strokes that complete the character. This fat-and-thin contrast lends a conspicuous rhythm to the writing as a whole. In sum, where his brother is content to write in a casual, cursive manner, Kenzan is asserting himself as a conscientious student of script, mindful of problems in composition and brushwork.

Kenzan's most self-conscious calligraphy of these years is *Ōtotsuka o Yogiru no Ki* (A Visit to the Ōtotsuka), a tribute to Ishikawa Jōzan, the most prominent literatus of seventeenth-century in Kyoto. Jōzan had served the Tokugawa as a page until the 1615 siege of Osaka Castle, when he made an abrupt departure from the military. Inspired by earlier lessons with Kyoto Confucianist Fujiwara Seika (1561–1619), Jōzan built a retreat called Shisendō in the hills northeast of the city in 1641. There he cultivated a scholar's life, maintaining a special reverence for thirty-six outstanding Chinese poets from the Han through Song dynasties. Jōzan composed poetry, developed a distinctive manner of calligraphy, and achieved posthumous recognition as the Japanese founder of *sencha,* the style of steeped-tea drinking that originated in Ming-dynasty China. Following in the footsteps of Confucianist Hayashi Razan (1583–1657) and other prominent visitors to Jōzan's compound, Kenzan composed this essay (fig. 21) in 1692.

A Visit to the Ōtotsuka

In this, the summer of Genroku 5 [1692], I went walking from my hermitage at Narabigaoka, soon arriving at the eastern part of the city. Mount Hiei was to the south, the Kamo River to the east. The village of my destination was Ichijōji Yabunosato; comfortably situated near Hachidai Tennō, it was a quiet, inviting place. Near the stone torii, a deep, mysterious forest of pines could be seen. Local people call this place Sagarimatsu (Descending Pine). Some two hundred strides further to the east, I entered the brushwood gate of the hermitage. The mountains seemed deep and forbidding, with luxurious plumes of bamboo overhead; three paths led off. This was Jōzan's place of eternal retirement — although the master had passed on, his living place was unchanged.

Jōzan originally served Shogun Ieyasu but early in life a desire came upon him to escape the world into retirement. After traveling around the country, he settled in Kyoto, where in Kan'ei 18 [1641], in his fifties, he obtained this land as a place of retirement and built a hut on it, calling it Shisendō. Jōzan commissioned portraits of thirty-six great Chinese poets from the Han to Song dynasties; he inscribed representative poems on each portrait, and hung them on the four walls. This was the beginning of the custom of admiring thirty-six great Chinese poets in our country.

Over this Jōzan built a small three-storied tower, with the inscribed plaque Shōgetsu Ro [Moon-Viewing Room]. With an unobstructed view from all four sides, the luxuriant view of the surrounding forest spread out like the universe. At night it was like being inside the moon. Slightly to the east another small room was built. At first Jōzan named it Ryōgei So [Entertainment Pursuit Room], but after discovering the treasury of literature in its library, he changed the name to Shiraku So [Pleasure Attainment Room]. Beyond the fence, I could see a rock formation suggesting a waterfall. This was Sengo Baku [Ignorance-Cleansing Fall]. In front of that was a garden with hundreds of flowers, and beyond that a small hollow. A gate outside the hermitage was called Rōbai Kan [Old Plum Gate]; two or three plum trees were growing there. They reminded me of certain passages of Chinese

今者壬申首夏步自雙岡之艸堂
將遊洛東矣四明之南鴨川之東
到干一林叢號一乘寺藪里而入
大天王穩堂地也石葉表之修松樹
森〻古怪可觀居民鮮曰下松矣行東
二百步許而入柴扃中山深人稀茂
林條竹相接三径是則東溪石先生
之所樓遲也先生既没其跡猶依籍
馬先生初仕
東照大神君少有隱淪志後遊于列國
或居於京師寬永十八年辛巳先生歲
五十餘遂求此地以爲退休之慮抹茅
縛屋経営詩僊堂畫漢晉唐宋之
詩人三十六輩像自書其詩以揭四
壁是我邦撰詩僊之濫觴也堂之上題
架三重小樓額曰嘯月樓四面空洞
森羅萬象唯在一瞬之中堂之東有

21. Detail from *Ōtotsuka o Yogiru no Ki* (A Visit
to the Ōtotsuka).

poetry. Behind the hermitage was a place inhabited by a woodcutter, the son of a former servant. The dwelling was called Yakuen Ken [Jumping-into-Abyss Hut]. But now no one knew much about the site. To the east of the kitchen there was a well, called Kōkō Sen [Spring of the Vital Region]; its waters were said to be good for the spleen.

In spring, the paths were showered with blossoms of cherry and pear; in summer, water cascading over rocks gave cool relief. In autumn, the moon could be seen in Migiri Pond and the valley was red with maple; in winter, snow was high in the surrounding mountains. In the morning, one could gaze out on lazily floating clouds; in the evening, there was smoke rising from homes in the city. The long expanse of the Kamo River could be envisioned winding down to Osaka Castle and town. Beyond the grounds the rustling of pines sounded like ancient court music; the chant from a nearby shrine protected this home. These were the ten places and twelve views of the Ōtotsuka.

The name Ōtotsuka [Concave-Convex Roost] comes from the famous Chinese temple whose walls were painted with flowers which appeared to have real hollows (ō) and protrusions (totsu), but when seen from close up were in fact quite flat. In addition to the features described above, there were many other things too splendid for words.

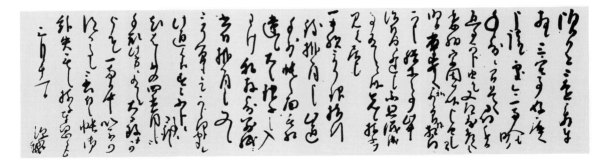

22. Letter to Kōrin.

Jōzan had six possessions which he treasured. These included a scepter, a whisk of horsehair, a chair, a desk, a kettle, and a Chinese zither. Hayashi [Razan's sons Shunsai and Dokkōsai] wrote poems about them, which still remained. The description of the thirty-six poets, the poem on the landscape, and these six articles were still intact. Jōzan's writing was in the Tang style, classic in feeling.

Jōzan's virtue came to the attention of our emperor, and his fame even reached beyond our shores. In the day of the flower or the night of the moon, he enjoyed relations with men of learning, who reaped a rich harvest from the friendship. He disdained sullied riches, but fostered poor men of purity. He lived his life without wife or child.

After Jōzan died, Shisendō was passed on to his adopted son Kazuma, then on to Hiraiwa Senkei, who died soon afterward. Ataka, the present occupant, is a descendant of Jikkyū, the younger brother of Miyoshi Chōkei. Even though he was of a good background, Ataka lived for a long time among the common people in obscurity; now he lives alone at the hermitage. He told me he had no desires save protecting the legacy of Jōzan.

On the walls of the Shisendō there still hung the paintings of the Chinese poets, together with a portrait of the master by Kanō Tan'yū, on which was inscribed a poem by Jōzan himself. This was very true to life and I felt as if I was in his presence.

In the garden there was a small shrine over which hung a plaque inscribed Gasen Shi [Shrine of the Self-Willed Heart]. Anyone who comes here is compelled to reflect about the past; I joined my hands and prayed. After returning to the house for tea and conversation, the sun had begun to set.

Regretfully, I had to depart, but I look forward to returning. I left this poem with Ataka as a gesture of thanks:

The distant flow of the Kamo
Invites a mood of solitude.
The verdure engulfs Ōtotsuka,
Its tower lit by sunset.
Wordlessly enraptured by its beauty:
Captivating,
Like autumn crimson.

[signed] Shūseidō Reikai
[sealed] Narabigaoka Sanjin
[sealed] Reikai

Although this work is not part of the Konishi archive, it shares important kinships with the inheritance receipt: neat rows of evenly spaced characters leaning to the right; a strong, thickly inked opening in many characters with short, frequently unconnected strokes to follow; and an airy structure overall. The similarity of individual characters also helps establish this as a reliable specimen of Kenzan's early style. The tall, open character structure, rounded individual strokes, and pattern of pressure variation is suggestive of Southern Song-dynasty scribe Zhang Jizhih, whose work was popular in temple and tea-ceremony circles in Japan. While a specific model is difficult to establish, it is apparent that Kenzan, informed by the *bokuseki* tradition and a few copybooks, was attempting a script style that would evoke antiquity.

In contrast to this public style, a specimen of Kenzan's private style can be found in a 1696 letter to Kōrin (fig. 22). The highly abbreviated characters suggest that the writing was done with some urgency, and the style lacks distinction. It could be from the hand of any dilettante who could turn out a polished script on demand but reverted to mediocrity in private. This, I believe, is the difference between a skillful calligrapher and a great calligrapher. For the latter, there is no inside or out — even a scribble will be full of interest and energy.

In his years at Nakatachiuri and Shūseidō, Kenzan absorbed worlds of learning, and in calligraphy, he gained a tool through which those worlds might be expressed. That tool would find its real test in ceramics, a supremely difficult medium for the calligrapher. Kenzan's brush would have to fight with clay, which is super-absorbent; fight with metallic pigments, which have the consistency of chalk; and fight with fire, which burns away the fine traces of the brush. Kenzan would have to rethink the internal principles of the art, but this inner struggle would lead to outer expansion: on clay his script would become large and generous. The interaction between calligraphy and ceramics, which was to become one of Kenzan's major contributions to Japanese art, began at Narutaki, his first kiln.

1. Quoted in Kobayashi 1948, 70.
2. Oishi Shinzaburō, *Edo Jidai* [The Edo Period] (Tokyo: Chukō Shinsho, 1977), 150–54.
3. Crawcour 1961, 93.
4. See Ben Befu, *Worldly Mental Calculations: An Annotated Translation of Ihara Saikaku's Seken Munazan'yō* (Berkeley: University of California Press, 1976), 60.
5. Crawcour 1961, 121.
6. From Saikaku's *Kōshoku Nidai Otoko*, quoted in Kobayashi 1948, 89.

Chapter Three
IN THE
NORTHWEST
MOUNTAINS
(Narutaki, 1699–1712)

A host of questions surround Kenzan's decision to open a kiln at Narutaki in 1699. What could have motivated him to abandon the world of the scholar-gentleman? What implications did the decision have for the other kiln in the district, that of Nonomura Ninsei? What convinced Kenzan that as a non-specialist he could succeed in the competitive arena of commercial ceramics? And perhaps the most fundamental problem is the actual production of the Kenzan kiln. How do we sort through the mountain of false essays that bear the Kenzan name? What do the authentic pots tell us about Kenzan's synthesis of ceramics and design? In this chapter, documentary evidence on the Ninsei and Kenzan workshops will demonstrate that the collapse of the former was a catalyst for the creation of the latter. Statements made by Kenzan himself suggest his vision for the new enterprise — and for his role as a designer. Finally, we will propose methods for authenticating Kenzan ware, and identifying the two major types made at Narutaki.

In a series of molded earthenware pots decorated with painting and poetry, Kenzan recalled the high-minded pursuits of the amateur artist. In his stoneware vessels, produced largely on the potter's wheel, he recreated "classic" domestic and foreign pots from the heyday of the tea ceremony a century earlier. Kenzan underlined his intentions with two pseudonyms that he signed and sealed on the pots: "Shōko" (Veneration of the Ancient) and "Tōin" (Hermit Potter). But here we encounter still more questions: Why would a hermit potter build a large climbing kiln, hire a staff of trained artisans, and produce enough pottery to receive mention in contemporary fiction and gazetteers? How can Kenzan's amateurism be reconciled with his mass production?

FROM HERMIT TO HERMIT POTTER

An entry in the diary of Kenzan's friend Naba Yūei shows that Kenzan was using his Narutaki land as a resort as late as 1698. Early in the next year, however, the official diary of the Ninnaji temple (*Onki*) shows a flurry of activity at the site (fig. 23). On the eighth day, third month, 1699, Kenzan asked temple officials for permission to build a kiln on his land at Narutaki — and the request was granted the following day. An entry for the first day, seventh month of 1699 records Kenzan's request for firewood; presumably the kiln was completed and ready to fire. On the thirteenth day, eighth month, 1699, Kenzan received a copy of pottery notes from the Ninsei workshop; its contents are copied into the master's own *Tōkō Hitsuyō*. An entry on the twentieth day, eleventh month, 1699, reveals the first sign of a finished pot: *Onki* shows that Kenzan presented "for the first time" a personally made (*tezukuri*) tea bowl to Kanryū (1662–1707), the Ninnaji prince-abbot. Kiln preparations thus consumed the four seasons of 1699: official permission in spring, construction of the kiln in summer, pottery making in autumn, and the first firing in early winter. Ogata Kenzan had embarked on a career in ceramics that would span the next forty years.

This sudden and serious commitment (after all, Kenzan could have made pots as a hobby) calls for an explanation; three reasons can be proposed. The first and most obvious is that Kenzan enjoyed creative and expressive endeavors, and had some confidence in his abilities. There is no trace in his biography of events that would fuel a negative or pessimistic view of life, or of circumstances that would preclude a more extensive involvement in the arts. The second is that for Kenzan, who was living off an ever-shrinking inheritance, those talents could be put to practical advantage. Here we must be mindful of how the Japanese merchant class had successfully overcome cultural barriers and subsumed alternative lifestyles into its own. In Kenzan's case, his years of seclusion presented less a hindrance to productivity than a source of

23. Reconstruction of Kenzan's Narutaki compound, based on 1732 records preserved in Hōzōji, Kyoto, and on excavations of the Narutaki kiln.

ideas that could be merchandised. Here, too, there were precedents. His older brother Kōrin, who had probably begun painting as a hobby, was beginning to receive commissions for his brushwork. The establishment of Kenzan's cousin Sōn'yū as heir to the Raku family of potters also represents an example of how once-wealthy merchant scions moved into the trades. In the highly competitive and tightly regulated Tokugawa society, however, a successful conversion was nearly impossible without a franchise. Surely the Ogata had positioned young Sōn'yū with the Raku for that very reason; likewise Kōrin sought the honorary court title *hokkyō*, which he received in

1701. The need for enfranchisement brings us to our third
point — how the demise of the Ninsei kiln created both an
incentive and opportunity for Kenzan to assume a career in
ceramics design.

Kenzan was a student of Ninsei — or so it is written in
Japanese ceramics lore. After all, the workshop of the celebrated potter Nonomura Ninsei, located south of the Ninnaji
gate in Omuro, must have been very near Kenzan's own
Shūseidō villa. And since Kenzan acquired his Narutaki
mountain land five years before his actual kiln opening, it has
been speculated that study under the old master had inspired
Kenzan to prepare a workshop site of his own. But other
evidence suggests that the exchange was of a somewhat different nature. As we saw in the last chapter, the Ninsei kiln was
showing signs of difficulty as early as the 1670s; the Ninnaji
diary indicates that the workshop struggled into the last years
of the seventeenth century. The original Ninsei was probably
dead by 1690, but six diary entries in the decade that followed
reveal that his children were granted audiences with the
Ninnaji prince-priest, and received stipends. On the seventh
day, ninth month, 1698, Ninsei's eldest son Nonomura
Seiemon petitioned the temple for firewood. Finally, on the
fourth day, second month, 1699, Seiemon requested permission to fire the kiln. That is the last Ninsei-related mention in
the *Onki* — or for that matter in any contemporary document.
The Ninsei workshop simply disappeared.

Kenzan petitioned the same Ninnaji authorities who governed the Ninsei kiln to open his own workshop within one
month of that final mention. He received the copy of Ninsei's
pottery notes (itself tantamount to a license to practice) within
five months of that petition, and as he would later write,
Seiemon assisted him from the time of the opening. Was this
all coincidence? It is impossible to avoid the assumption that
Kenzan had subsumed the Ninsei tradition under his own
name. Private capital and personal leadership must have been
sought after at every Kyoto kiln. Most city workshops —
including Ninsei's — had been established at imperial temples
during the spate of government-sponsored rebuilding in the
early to mid-seventeenth century; but official subsidies shrank
markedly after the death of Tōfukumon'in in 1678, and more
efficiently organized regional industries were becoming fierce
competitors. The only recourse was privatization under the

urban merchant, who by 1700 possessed nearly all the cash in the realm. I suspect that in the course of conversations with local officials and the Ninsei potters, Kenzan became sympathetic with the plight of the workshop. When the final collapse came, he had a plan to mobilize its techniques and personnel.

Further inquiry into this mobilization demonstrates just how different Kenzan was from Ninsei. In every respect, the two were far apart. While Ninsei was an artisan recruited for his technical skills, Kenzan was steeped in the gentlemanly arts, inspired by the merchant tradition of *sakui*. Like the tea masters and amateurs who preceded him, Kenzan saw himself as an artist and host who created not merely objects but entire environments. So while Ninsei left the dreaming to his patrons, Kenzan envisioned the larger cultural meanings first and then marshaled the human and technical resources to express them. Instead of manipulating clay, he manipulated ideas. This operational concept emerges in Kenzan's two pottery manuals. The earlier of the two, *Tōkō Hitsuyō* (Potter's Essentials), was written in Edo in the third month of 1737; the *Tōji Seihō* (Ceramic Techniques) was written during a visit to Sano some six months later. In the former Kenzan tells us:

> From 1699, I lived at Senkei (Izumi) northwest of the capital; there I began to make ceramics. Since the location was in the northwest quarter of the city, I signed "Kenzan" on the pots that were made there. At that time I employed a craftsman named Magobei who was a relative and apprentice of the Oshikōji family workshop. He was a skilled workman and proficient at firing the kiln. Seiemon, the oldest son of Ninsei, also came to my kiln and assisted me. From these two men I received the secret traditions of Oshikōji earthenware as well as [the stoneware traditions of] Ninsei ware of Omuro.

Evidence for the design of the wares emerges in the *Tōji Seihō:* "The shapes of the vessels and the patterns were created by me, and in consultation with my brother Kōrin; all of the early painting was by Kōrin."

These passages reveal Kenzan not as a lone potter toiling in the hills, but as the owner-operator of a ceramics workshop not only modeled after the Kyoto urban prototype but absorbing two of its most important traditions. Kenzan took responsibility for design but left the manual chores to artisans.

Trained assistants such as Seiemon and Magobei would fabricate the pots, paint some of the simple designs, and glaze and fire the wares. Those with expertise in the brush — including Kōrin and Watanabe Soshin, whom we will meet later — would execute more sophisticated designs. Kenzan would then personalize the ceramic designs with calligraphic inscriptions and signatures. In addition to Kenzan's own signature there are generic Kenzan marks painted, stenciled, and impressed by the workshop staff.

Without validation in actual work, however, such pronouncements are little more than speculative. Here is the most formidable challenge in Kenzan studies: how to wade through all the fakes. All told there must remain, in Japanese and foreign collections, about five thousand wares with the Kenzan mark; I have seen and handled over half of them. Needless to say, most of these have little to do with Kenzan himself, but with every Kenzan publication the jumble of sincere homages and patent forgeries grows, contributing to confusion and distrust. To restore some clarity to Kenzan's career, it is absolutely necessary to attempt a systematic organization — not only of Kenzan's own work but of all the others as well. I began by dividing the pieces that I had surveyed into eight categories:

> shapes (including function)
> techniques (low- or high-fired, type of pigment or enamel)
> decor (painting subject and style)
> border patterns (the secondary patterns usually used as
>   framing devices)
> inscriptions (the type and style of poems inscribed)
> signatures (the content and style of the personal or
>   workshop mark)
> monograms (Kenzan occasionally used a personal
>   monogram, or *kaō*)
> seals (content and style of seals)

After much grouping and regrouping, I managed to isolate clusters of pots that shared similar materials, decoration, signature, etc.; how, then, to locate these clusters in the two-and-a-half centuries of Kenzan-style production? Clues could be found in four places: in works with inscribed dates; in well-documented collections (especially nineteenth-century Western collections) where certain clusters appeared en masse; in the general stylistic development of Kyoto ceramics from the mid-eighteenth through the twentieth centuries; and in the relationship between certain designs and illustrated (and dated) publications. From these clues, one could begin to see a Kenzan "period" style: the way Kenzan was envisioned by copyists in the late eighteenth century, the early nineteenth century, and so on. Examples of these groups, and the criteria used to divide them, are delineated in Appendix 3.

But how about the *real* Kenzans? Some of the clusters included works dated to Kenzan's time, among them pots with decisive painting, skillful calligraphy similar to that in his authentic letters, and consistency in signature style. Most important, in each pot the components functioned together to produce allusive designs. These I believe to be authentic products of the Kenzan workshop — that is, produced under Ogata Kenzan's supervision, with a varying degree of personal participation by the master himself. Let us now examine two such authentic clusters associated with the first kiln at Narutaki, which operated from 1699 to 1712: *kakuzara*, earthenware plates conceived as a facsimile painting; and *utsushi*, stonewares based on classic tea-ceremony wares. Still more authentic clusters will be introduced in following chapters and in Appendix 3.

THE POT AS PAINTING: *KAKUZARA*

shapes: molded square and polygonal forms
techniques: earthenware with underglaze enamels
decor: academic-style painting
border patterns: Japanese textile patterns or patterns from Chinese ceramics
inscriptions: extensive use of Chinese and Japanese poetry
signatures: long, heraldic signatures
seals: "Tōin" and "Shōko" relief-style seals, painted
monogram: bag-shaped (*kinchaku*) monogram on some pieces
(for affiliated pieces see Appendix 3, Groups 1–2)

In photographs, certain Kenzan wares look more like paintings than pots. These flat, "cornered" plates (*kakuzara*) are typical of Kenzan's early work in earthenware. Bearing a date of 1702 is a set of twelve flat plates decorated with the theme of Fujiwara

24. Square plate with design of plum and mandarin duck.

no Teika's waka poems of birds and flowers for the twelve months (fig. 24). Each piece is painted with a bird-and-flower composition relating to a specific month on the front, with the matching Teika poem copied out on the back.

From a potter's viewpoint, the *kakuzara* is an unusual concept indeed. The external referents are not in ceramics, but in wood or lacquerware shapes. The front of the finished work resembles a painting and the back looks like a poem card. Even the forming technique is something of a violation — clay resists molding into flat, rectilinear shapes, and such vessels will frequently warp and crack in the course of manufacture. The degree of difficulty is evoked in the name Kyoto potters give to this genre — *sashimono*, or cabinet work. The exact method has been debated, but in a pottery manual attributed to Kenzan's adopted son Ihachi the following technique is recorded:

> For square, six-sided, and eight-sided vessels . . . roll out a slab with a rolling pin, and drape that over a mold. Over that lay a fine silk cloth that has been rinsed and wrung out; turn it [the mold and the clay draping it] over, transfer it to a dry plank, and take out the mold. Gently press in the [upright] edges [of the plate, which will have bulged out in the process of transfer]; experience will tell you how much. For finishing the

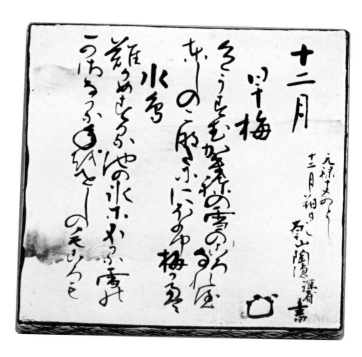

25. Inscription and dated signature on verso.

square [and polygonal] pieces, sharpen a blade and trim the edges. The greater the number of sides, the more careful you must be in trimming. After trimming, cover the form with a coarser, damp cotton cloth and finish. You can smooth out the warps at this stage. Then dry in a shaded place for at least three days.

Kenzan was exploiting the Kyoto potter's skill in making shapes derived from crafts other than ceramics. Around the same time that Kenzan opened the Narutaki workshop, other potters in the city were making such facsimile items as ceremonial offering stands (*sambō*), fans (*uchiwa*), vases in the shape of a quiver (*ebira*), and stacked boxes (*jūbako*). But Kenzan was the first to attempt facsimile paintings, not only in terms of shape but in the application of the pigments — his so-called underglaze enamels. After a preliminary low-temperature (bisque) firing, green, yellow, purple, blue, red, white, and black were applied directly to the unglazed surface. When the painting was complete, the entire surface was coated with a low-fire transparent glaze made of lead oxide and powdered silicate rock, and fired again. The transparent glaze coating caused the contours of the painting underneath to blur slightly — an effect akin to painting on absorbent paper. This technique effectively circumvented the raised, beaded effect common to the overglaze enamel decoration seen on Ninsei or Arita wares. Since Kenzan's pottery manuals attribute these recipes to the Oshikōji potter Magobei, it can be assumed that Kenzan learned of the underglaze enamel technique from him.

For the painting itself, Kenzan chose a subject with an esteemed pedigree. The Teika birds and flowers had been paired in painted compositions from the seventeenth century by such masters as Karasumaru Mitsuhiro (1579–1638), Kanō Tan'yū (1602–74), Tosa Mitsuoki (1617–91), and Kōrin's presumed teacher Yamamoto Soken (active 1683–1706). Kenzan's father and brother painted them, too. Kenzan's plates could have been inspired by these versions or by a set of illustrated poems in a popular book, *Shigi No Hanegaki* (Fluttering of Snipe's Wings), published in 1691. In the Kenzan set the working of the trunk and branches, and especially the dotted outlining of the birds, fall squarely within the style of the Kanō school, which under the leadership of Tan'yū was the official academy in Edo. Given that Yamamoto Soken had trained in the Edo Kanō style, was in frequent attendance at the Nijō salon, and is known to have decorated folding screens with the theme, he seems a logical contributor. Soken also had an adopted son, Kazuma (1679–1760), whose name emerges in the Nijō diaries as well.

As a designer, Kenzan paid attention to detail. The outside walls of the plates have painted patterns suggesting the fabric borders of a mounted painting. Some versions of this set (there are about six sets in all) have stenciled patterns of wisteria and peonies on the outside walls, but this early version is the so-called Narihira lozenge associated with the *Tale of Ise* hero Ariwara no Narihira. Surely this pattern was deliberately conceived to complement the classical subject — further evidence of the degree of unity in the features of design. Indeed, we shall see that in Kenzan's monochrome plates with Chinese-derived landscape patterns, the edge patterns are usually the cloud and palmette scrolls found on Chinese ceramics.

The quality of the painting on the front of these pieces is matched by Kenzan's calligraphy on the verso (fig. 25). The plates' size, the underlying decoration of colored swatches to simulate the traditional cloud-patterned paper (*kumogami*), and the composition of the poetry is inspired by the poem card, or *shikishi*. The earliest *shikishi* of the Heian period varied widely in

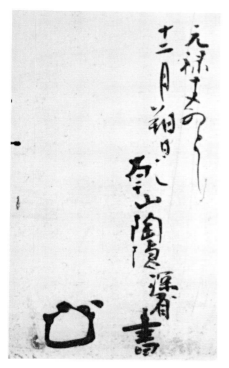

26. Detail of verso. (Fig. 25)

size but averaged approximately 13 cm. square; today's *shikishi* is conventionally fixed at 21 × 18 cm. or 24 × 21 cm. Kenzan's plates, at 16.8 cm. square, thus fall in the middle of this evolution.

The poems were composed by Fujiwara no Teika in 1214 for Prince Dōjo (?–1249), then abbot of the Ninnaji. The example illustrated here reads:

Twelfth month:

Plum blossom (*ume*)
It is that time
When snow buries the colors of the hedge;
Yet a branch of plum is blooming
On this "side"
Of the New Year

Mandarin Duck (*oshi*)
The snow falls on the ice of the pond
On which I gaze;
Piling up, as does this passing year on all those passed
And on the feathered coat of the mandarin duck,
The "bird of regret."[1]

Writing appears elsewhere in world ceramics — examples can be seen in short verses on certain Chinese blue-and-white porcelains, in religious exhortations on wares from Persia, or in patriotic slogans on Staffordshire wares from England.[2] In Kenzan ware, however, calligraphy as an art form is a central focus. Kenzan was skillful enough to evoke the style of past masters; the model observed for these poems is, appropriately, Fujiwara no Teika, whose style of writing was very popular in the seventeenth century. Since it is Kenzan's personal handiwork, calligraphy also provides the most reliable standard for authenticity. The neat columnar composition, airy and somewhat tall character structures, and thick-thin linear contrasts apparent in Kenzan's early calligraphy are in evidence here — especially in the titles of the poems.

Kenzan was the first Japanese potter to brush his signature consistently onto the wares. The twelfth-month plate of this set bears the mark "Kenzan Tōin Shinsei Sho" (Written by the Hermit Potter Kenzan Shinsei; fig. 26). Since the "Kenzan"

27. Rectangular plate with design of landscape. Painting by Soshin.

mark is used throughout the potter's career and undergoes distinctive changes, it is worthwhile to note its initial style: a strong axial orientation to the upper right is in evidence. The first two (upper) strokes of the *ken* radical are emphatically brushed, with the second stroke proportionally longer than the first. The stem (right part) of the *ken* has been simplified into a hook-like shape, executed in two pulses: the engagement, a lifting of the brush, and then re-engagement with sustained but moderate pressure. The addition of *sho* was conventional when copying an external source. A personal monogram (*kaō*) known as the moneybag, or *kinchaku*-shape monogram, follows the signature. Some claim that the shape is an extreme simplification of the *sei* in Kenzan's personal name, Shinsei. All evidence suggests that this monogram was used only on works from Kenzan's Narutaki period; after Narutaki and especially in Edo he seems to have used a cipher resembling the character *ji* (meaning "thou" or "in that way").

If these pots were really facsimile paintings, were they ever intended for use? Various theories have been offered. The softness of the low-fired body, the difficulty of handling a flat shape with low sides, and the fact that there is painting where food would be placed would all seem to preclude anything but display. Yet in the Nijō family diaries, a Kenzan ware *suzuributa* (literally "inkstone cover") is mentioned. Despite the name, the *suzuributa* was a flat wood or lacquer tray used from the Heian period to display flowers and candy; in Kenzan's day it was used to hold light snacks. That Kenzan conceived of some of these plates for such use is suggested in his box inscription for an eight-sided flat plate in a private collection in Japan: *hakkaku kabon*, or eight-sided candy dish.[3] The separation of the Teika pictures from the poems also suggests a contest wherein participants might be called upon to recite the unseen poems for the particular month pictured. Pairing a refined discipline like poetry guessing (*uta awase*) with simpler culinary amusement is seen elsewhere in late seventeenth-century culture. For example, the need to associate the tea ceremony with the diversions of the pleasure quarters is reflected in a contemporary tea procedure called *shichiji shiki* in which players receive roles by drawing cards.[4]

In contrast to the native preferences in the Teika plates, a Chinese world is represented in a number of rectangular plates with monochrome landscape decoration bearing Hōei-era

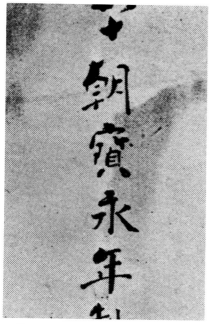

28. Era mark on verso.

(1704–11) marks (figs. 27, 28). Here the underglaze-enamel technique is used to reproduce monochrome ink painting. The pigment, called *kuro e* (black painting) by Kenzan, is an iron oxide blackened by the addition of impure cobalt. The covering glaze is the Oshikōji formula of lead and silica oxides. The edge patterns, hand-painted around the pictures, variously include cloud arabesques or waves, sometimes interspersed with ogival panels containing floral motifs. The schemes are derived from Chinese ceramics, particularly stonewares from the Cizhou and Jizhou kilns, and porcelains from Jingdezhen, all of which were prized in Japan.

The subjects here are landscapes. In contrast to the intimate Teika motifs and poems, these paintings are intended to transmit the remote and high-minded hermit's world as celebrated in Chinese poetry and painting. Paintings combining poetic inscriptions and landscape painting were also executed in Japanese Zen temple ateliers from the fourteenth century. At the highest level of aspiration, the picture served as an imaginary and idealized retreat from the mundane business of the temple.[5] Two particular styles are in evidence: one in which linear contours are prominent, and a more diffuse style known as "splashed ink" (*haboku*). Over the course of the fifteenth century, these paintings evolved from the personal expression of monk-painters into refined products from the hand of professionals like Sesshū (1420–1506). Kanō-school masters further codified those styles from the seventeenth century on.

The sophistication of the brushwork on these plates suggests that they, like the Teika set, were executed by professional painters. Yamamoto Soken could well have painted such compositions for Kenzan. Another name that emerges in connection with these plates is Soshin. In fact, a faint "Soshin" intaglio seal is found on the plate illustrated here. In Chapter 6, we will meet a "Watanabe Soshin," an apparent collaborator with Kenzan's adopted son Ihachi. Tellingly, the *so* ideogram in Soshin matches that of the Nijō salon painters Yamamoto Soshin and his son Kazuma (Sosen), suggesting that they all belonged to the same atelier. The name of Rimpa-style painter Watanabe Shikō (1683–1755) has been presented as an alias for Watanabe Soshin, but Shikō was still quite young in the opening decade of the eighteenth century; his later activities center around official service with the Konoe family of court aristocrats.

As in the Teika plates, the unity of design elements in the landscape plates is remarkable. In poetic inscriptions on the front or extended signatures on the back, Kenzan's calligraphy is now intended to evoke a Chinese mood. At the beginning of each inscription is an ovoid "head" seal, or *kambōin,* reading "Kenzan." Like other seals used on Kenzan ceramics, it is made with yellow ochre to resemble the real cinnabar seals used by painters. As mentioned at the beginning of this chapter, it was Kenzan's preference in these early works to finish the inscriptions with painted (not impressed) square relief-style seals reading "Shōko" and "Tōin." In a later stage, from about 1712, the seals became stenciled rather than painted, and in the third decade of the century Kenzan workshop products exhibited seals reading "Kenzan" and "Shinsei." These changes are helpful in dating and authentication.

The calligraphy style in these plates (especially evident in the signatures) exhibits the open and somewhat vertically elongated character structure of the early Konishi specimens. Calligraphy is sometimes described as an art of dots and lines, and in these authentic early pieces the sense of "dot" is still stronger than the sense of "line."

That the "pot-as-painting" theme continued through the Narutaki years is seen in a piece dated 1711, a rectangular plate decorated with poems and imaginary portraits of six classical poets (fig. 29). Edges turned outward and decorated with floral arabesques frame the subject: six figures painted in thin outlines and translucent washes of blue, green, yellow, and brown, accompanied by their titles and representative poems:

Gokyōgoku Sesshō Saki no Dajō Daijin
[Fujiwara no Yoshitsune, 1169–1206]:

Awaking in my hut
To think how lonelier
Must they be who,
Living in the mountains
See the moonlight seeping between the trees.
[*Shin Kokinshū,* no. 395]

Jū Ni Ietaka
[Fujiwara no Ietaka, 1158–1237]:

I look up at the moon

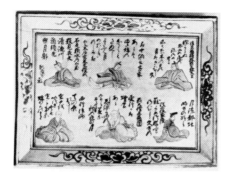

29. Rectangular plate with design of six classical poets.

30. Inscription and signature on verso.

And think,
Lonely is the dawning sky
Seen from the palace
In the moon.
[*Shin Kokinshū*, no. 392]

Zen Chūnagon Teika
[Fujiwara no Teika, 1162–1241]:

With each day's passing
Already mid-autumn is behind us.
Isn't it a pity to see
The waning moon?
[*Shin Chokusen Wakashū*, no. 261]

Saki no Daisōjō Jien
[Jien Daisōjō, 1155–1225]:

As night deepens,
The smoke from the boiling brine
Will cease to rise.
Pray, wait with patience for the autumn moon
That will shine over Shiogama.
[*Shin Kokinshū*, no. 390]

Kotaigū Daifu Shunzei
[Fujiwara no Shunzei, 1114–1204]:

In each myriad droplet
Dancing through the rocks
The light of the moon
Clarifies the river
Of Kiyotaki.
[*Zoku Shi Kashū*, no. 185]

Saigyō Hōshi
[Priest Saigyō, 1118–90]:

Be it the rays from the
Rock door at Amanohara
Or that from the
Nocturnal autumn moon —
Brilliant is the light.
[*Zokugo Chokusen Wakashū*, no. 323]

This is a contest. A theme is selected — in this case the moon — and the participants must assemble verses on the subject by the great poets. This competition of poems from different periods (*jidai fudō uta awase*) can be traced back to about 1200, when it was devised by a retired emperor, Gotoba (1180–1239); he pitted fifty "ancient" (8–10th c.) poets against fifty "contemporary" (11th–12th c.) poets.[6] Portraits of the master poets matched with their verses had been painted as early as the twelfth century, and some three centuries later village associations or local aristocrats had the bards painted on votive plaques (*ema*).[7] Astoundingly, this facet of the tradition was also seized upon by Kenzan: on the back of his plate, there are two lugs for hanging it, plaque-fashion. Just why Kenzan selected this particular group of poets is unclear, but the same six poets are the subject of a sketch left by Kōrin in the Konishi archive.

The signature on the verso (fig. 30), executed in a script more heavily and confidently inked than that on the pieces from Kenzan's first decade of work, reads: "Made and written in the spring of 1711 by hermit potter Shōkosai Kenzan of Kyoto at the request of a patron in Sesshū [Hyōgo Prefecture]." Painted seals beneath the signature read "Shōko" and "Tōin." A plate of identical size and with the same inscription on the verso was recorded in the Tomkinson collection in 1898, though its present whereabouts are unknown.

The appeal of these glazed *kakuzara* made at Narutaki stems from at least three factors. First, the extent to which every element of the pot contributes to the design is remarkable; nothing seems to be left to chance. This harmony and integration of design elements is characteristic of authentic Kenzan ware as a whole. A second is the sheer novelty of the design. Kenzan was not merely trying to emulate painting; had he wanted to take ceramic decor to the limits of pictorial expression — to the extent seen, for example, in the *famille rose* wares of eighteenth-century China — he would have compromised the medium. One senses instead a deliberate conceptual dissonance — between painting and ceramics, between function and non-function. A third point is the high-culture flavor of the decoration, which evoked both literary classicism and amateurism, or art-as-play. In the case of the former, there were ample precedents; evocation of some bygone era, whether it was the age of Ariwara no Narihira or Ashikaga Yoshimasa, dominated much of the artistic discourse of the seventeenth century.

As mentioned in Chapter 1, this was not mere nostalgia but a renegotiation of identity after a long period of civil disruption. In the Teika plates, Kenzan was playing not only on class associations but personal ones. The Teika poems, it will be remembered, were originally conceived for the Ninnaji temple prince-abbot, and five hundred years later Kenzan was working under the Ninnaji jurisdiction. The Nijō family of courtiers were the traditional guarantors of the Teika tradition, and Kenzan was a frequent guest of Nijō scion Tsunahira. Kenzan created such works not merely to please courtly customers; diary references suggest that the plates were given to the aristocrats. The strengthening of the association between Kenzan ware and the court added inestimable allure to the pots for a more general audience. This strategy had already been used to great advantage by tea masters like Kobori Enshū, who boosted the value of newly made tea caddies by giving them names from classical poetry, and Kanamori Sōwa, who seems to have been successful in promoting Ninsei ware as representing the taste of the Kyoto court. In using symbols that were suggestive of privilege, Kenzan and his merchant patrons were buying into a genealogy denied them by birth or politics.

As for the signs of amateurism, the inclusion of words like "hermit potter" and "veneration of the past" appear as value enhancements as well. Indeed, if Kenzan was a true hermit, why would he have to declare it — or why would he have to make ceramics at all? In this sense it is worthwhile to distinguish between real amateurism and its professionalization. The former disregards technique, finish, and marketability; the latter seeks marketability through a conscious rejection of technique and by changing the boundaries between maker, object, and consumer. On the other hand, saintly expectations of Kenzan are our own, not his or his patrons'. A cultivated merchant would naturally fuse personal interests with business, and it is as the first cultivated merchant who ever operated a ceramics workshop that Kenzan made his mark. Kenzan seems to have understood that Kyoto potters could no longer just sell technique. He took the sensibilities cultivated at his Shūseido villa — a love of nature, an affinity for tea and the classics, and the pursuit of inner calm — and infused them into ceramics.

The thickly textured surfaces of Ninsei wares were replaced by quick, painterly impressions. Such decoration was sufficiently allusive to attract a diversity of patrons: royalty such as the Nijō and Takatsukasa families and the Ninnaji prince-priests; the pleasure-loving townsmen typified by the notorious spendthrift Nakamura Kuranosuke; and Kenzan's own circle of literati. Had Kenzan concluded his career after making only these vessels, his mark on Japanese ceramics would be great.

THE POT AS ANTIQUE: *UTSUSHI*

shapes: mostly wheel-thrown forms such as tea bowls and food containers

techniques: stoneware, with underglaze and overglaze pigments

decor: simple patterns from earlier ceramics traditions

signatures: mostly simple "Kenzan" marks, painted or impressed

(for affiliated pieces see Appendix 3, Group 3)

Little has been written on the early stonewares — the "main" kiln (*hongama*), as the technique was called by Kenzan. In fact, before the 1940s it was commonly thought that Kenzan didn't manufacture stonewares at all. Since the early earthenwares have been preserved in greater number, and many of them are inscribed with dates, those pieces have formed the basis for pronouncements about Kenzan's work. Here, evidence is presented for a much larger high-temperature operation, principally in copies of classical wares for the tea ceremony. These copies, which are really creative interpretations, are known as *utsushi*. The practice has a long history in Kyoto ceramics.

Kenzan's Narutaki kiln site lies on the grounds of the Hōzōji temple in Ukyō Ward, Kyoto. A record from 1930 mentions a site about two meters wide and twelve meters long containing large numbers of shards, kiln fragments, and setting tools.[8] In the summer of 1986, when the back yard of the temple was being dug up for the installation of a drainage system, I made an interesting discovery. A sloping layer of blackened soil about ten meters long was exposed at a depth of about one meter; the size of the area matched the earlier report. A climbing kiln twelve meters long would have had about three chambers; Kenzan could have fired around one thousand small-to-medium-size pieces per firing. It is well known that wood-firing climbing kilns fire imperfectly, generating flawed pots at the rate of about thirty to fifty percent. Assuming that the kiln was fired a few times a year for twelve years, the midden (waste piles) should have been conspicuous. What was the Narutaki stoneware production like, and what happened to those remains? As in all matters dealing with Kenzan, the answer was not easily found.

Kasuga Junsei, who first reported the site, dug fragments four times in 1928 and 1929. Some of the shards now kept at Hōzōji match Kasuga's description, but a very large number was reported to be in his possession when he entertained a visitor in 1942.[9] Kyoto antiquarian Ninagawa Teiichi (son of Ninagawa Noritane, the dealer who supplied nineteenth-century Boston collector Edward S. Morse with his ceramics) plundered the site twice in the 1930s, carrying away, in Kasuga's words, "wheelbarrow loads" of shards. A small but important sampling of that group is now housed in the Kyoto National Museum. In the summer of 1986 I was introduced to Ninagawa Chikamasa, who still occupies the old family residence now in the shadow of the Kyoto bullet-train station. It was exciting to see Noritane's nineteenth-century ledgers with descriptions and sale prices of wares now in Boston and Salem, but Chikamasa had failed to locate any fragments in his storehouse.

The next Hōzōji dig was conducted in 1942 by the banker and amateur potter Kawakita Handeishi (1878–1963). It appears from Handeishi's report that he too dug up a lot (he was assisted by five people, including potters Arakawa Toyozō and Miyanaga Tomoo), but only a few pieces made their way back to the Hōzōji. In the summer of 1987 I obtained an audience with Kawakita Sadahisa, Handeishi's grandson, at the family's vast estate at Tsu, Mie Prefecture. The Kawakita storehouse had crates of shards from all over Japan, along with a box tantalizingly labeled "Kenzan" — but it was empty! There may be one other cache of Kenzan shards on the grounds of the Hōzōji itself. Some Kenzan experts maintain that an old well just below the kiln site was backfilled with shards during a cleaning, but a building now occupies that spot. In this study it can only be assumed that the shards kept at Hōzōji and the Kyoto National Museum are representative, and the following comments on Kenzan's early stoneware are based on that corpus. Since the pieces excavated are from the site worked by

31. Fragment of tea bowl in the style of late Ming Dynasty enamelled ware (*gosu aka e*).

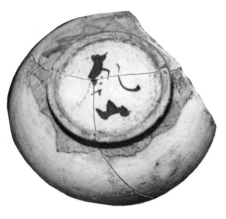

32. Signature inside foot ring.

Kenzan between 1699 and 1712, they do constitute solid evidence for dating and an authentic standard.

Kenzan's interest in *utsushi* was grounded in nearly a century of such production in Kyoto workshops. The interest of Kyoto tea practitioners in reproductions of Korean tea bowls and Chinese tea caddies is amply documented in *Kakumei Ki,* the diary of Kyoto priest Hōrin Shōshō. The shards excavated from the suspected kiln site of Nonomura Ninsei also reveal an intense interest in *utsushi,* especially tea caddies. In the notes that Kenzan received from the Ninsei workshop there are numerous recipes for these facsimiles. Kenzan's own early interest in tea and fine furnishings for the ceremony is documented in the 1690 *Shūseidō Ki,* and his recorded inheritance of "utensils" — which is close to synonymous with tea ware — hints that he studied tea in his youth.

The tea ceremony was one vehicle for the popularization of high culture at the end of the seventeenth century. As the number of tea practitioners increased, so did the demand for commodities that would confer upon their owners some association with the "golden age" of a century earlier. These items might include texts, like the 1691 *Nambōroku,* a manual of secret teachings attributed to the great master Sen no Rikyū, or vessels in that period style. A guide to these classic pots, the 1694 *Wakan Sho Dōgu* (Compendium of Domestic and Foreign Utensils), illustrates some forty-seven varieties of ceramics, all of them intended for use in the tea ceremony. The booklet's woodblock printing with phonetic glosses indicates that it was intended for widespread consumption. Kenzan's interest in evoking these earlier styles is confirmed in his much-used pseudonym "Shōko." In his low-fired plates he evoked Chinese and Japanese classicism through painting and calligraphy, and in his high-fired wares he would reach for classicism in ceramics. Tradition and not fashion, "ancient" China and Japan rather than Ninsei or Rimpa style, seemed to govern Kenzan's stylistic preferences in the early years of the Narutaki enterprise. Incidentally, the same seemed to be true of Kenzan's cousin Sōn'yū, who was attempting to evoke the Raku ware founder Chōjirō in his own work.

Aside from the antiquarian spirit in design, the technical basis for these early stonewares came from the Ninsei workshop; as we have noted, part of Kenzan's pottery manual is in fact a copy of the notes granted by the Ninsei potters in 1699.

33. *Gosu aka e*-style ware: Bowl with diadem and disc pattern.

In the prologue of his manual Kenzan writes, "The techniques of pottery fabrication, glaze manufacture, clays and pigments were transmitted to me, Ogata Kenzan Shinsei, from Nonomura Ninsei who lived in front of the Ninnaji temple in northwest Kyoto." But times had changed. Ninsei was interested in reproducing the iron-glazed tea caddies, Chinese *temmoku,* and Korean-style tea bowls that were popular in the first half of the seventeenth century; Kenzan had little interest in these somber monochromes. He wanted to make copies of painted wares — late Ming Chinese and Vietnamese porcelains, Chinese Cizhou stonewares, and Oribe and Karatsu stonewares from Japan. For this, Kenzan made use of Ninsei's underglaze iron and cobalt pigments, the transparent stoneware glaze to cover them, and of course, his stable of overglaze enamels.

Among the more complete excavated specimens in the Ninagawa group in the Kyoto National Museum is a tea bowl in the style of a late-Ming enameled ware commonly referred to as *gosu aka e* (fig. 31). Potted in a buff clay of fine texture, the piece has been covered with white slip in an attempt to approximate porcelain. A large "Kenzan" signature is painted inside the foot ring (fig 32). A cobalt pigment is used for horizontal bands around the mouth rim, disc motifs on the interior wall, and a wave pattern around the outside of the foot ring. Overglaze-enamel decoration would have completed a resemblance to the Chinese prototype (fig. 33). *Gosu aka e* (sometimes called Swatow ware by Western collectors) was first manufactured in the Jiajing era (1522–66) in Jima, Fujian Province. The style was especially admired by Japanese tea enthusiasts, who imported it from the early seventeenth century. In the ceramics primer *Wakan Sho Dōgu* it is ranked next to *Shonzui* (a blue-and-white decorated porcelain made in the late Ming dynasty for export to Japan) and *nishikide* (overglaze enameled ware); plates, bowls, and ewers are listed as the principal shapes. Arita porcelain bowls decorated with discs and diaper patterns, recently discovered in a waste pit below the remains of the Edo villa of the Kaga Daishōji domain, suggest that the style was being reproduced in Japan no later than 1650–80.

Another prominent classic in the *Wakan Sho Dōgu* is Vietnamese (Annam) ware. The book mentions that contemporary products were uninspiring, but that pieces from an earlier day were admired among teamen. In the collection of the Kenzan shards at Hōzōji, there is a well-preserved specimen of an Annam-style tea bowl (fig. 34). Annam ware was probably fired from the fourteenth to fifteenth century in the Champa kingdom south of present-day Hanoi. While it may have been influenced by underglaze-blue decorated porcelain of the Yuan and Ming dynasties, its softer firing and blurred underglaze motifs of flowers, grasses, clouds, and insects are distinctive (fig. 35).

These wares were imported into Japan in the seventeenth century, where the underglaze-blue decorated variant was called *shiboride* and an overglaze-enamel type *beni* Annam. Early attempts at imitating the style in Japan are associated with Chin Gempin (1587–1671), a potter employed at Ofuke, the official workshop for the Owari Tokugawa clan. The Kenzan version replicates the distinctive Annam high foot and slightly everted mouth rim. Over the thickly potted body of fine white-buff clay, bird-and-flower motifs are executed in a thick cobalt pigment. Those motifs are framed with bands that encircle the vessel; brusque vertical lines around the outside of the foot ring probably stand for lappets. The piece is unsigned and was never glazed. The old abbot at Hōzōji told me he used to lend the piece to local grammar-school teachers for their history lectures, only to find that less and less of the piece came back each time.

The only dated work testifying to the early high-temperature production is a large bowl in the style of Chinese Cizhou ware (fig. 36). The thickly potted body was totally covered with white slip, which served as a ground for painting in iron pigment. The glaze is transparent. Motifs include bands of cloud and palmette-chrysanthemum scrolls alternating with ogival panels which contain stylized peonies. The self-fulfilling inscription on the base (fig. 37) reads: "Made in Great Japan by Kenzan hermit-potter Shōkosai Ogata Shinsei

34. Annam-style tea bowl with patterns of birds and flowers.

35. Annam ware: Bowl with design of floral scroll.

36. Bowl with Cizhou-style designs of peonies and chrysanthemum scrolls.

37. Signature and inscription on base.

of Kyoto, in imitation of a rare vessel from Korea; 1706." A painted relief-style seal following the inscription reads "Shōko." Of special interest is Kenzan's use of the inscription to provide a built-in historical context for the vessel.

Kenzan was of course mistaken about the source of the piece — he was copying a Chinese, not a Korean model. As the traditional Japanese name for Cizhou ware, *Egōrai* (painted Kōrai, or painted Korean), implies, the Chinese product was long confused with a Korean one. Cizhou ware, a folk ceramic manufactured in north China from about the tenth century, was originally produced in the form of plain white-slipped storage bottles and jars; the slip was used to cover an impure stoneware body and sometimes to approximate a more elegant neighbor product, Ding ware. From the eleventh century, sgraffito techniques in iron became common, and a century later underglaze iron painting on the white slip began to replace the sgraffito. Ogival panels surrounded by scroll patterns and containing landscape, bird-and-flower, figural compositions, and occasionally calligraphy were common in twelfth-century decor. These motifs became more dynamic and abbreviated in the Yuan and Ming dynasties, and there was progressively less use of sgraffito. That Kenzan based his work on a Ming-dynasty prototype, quite possibly of the Jiajing era (1522–66), is suggested by a likeness of the scrolled motifs in his work to a 1541-dated *guan* jar in the Herbert F. Johnson Museum, Cornell University (fig. 38). Cizhou ware appears never to have been intended as an export ware, and it was probably introduced into Japan as a container for export goods.

38. Cizhou ware: Tall jar with design of crane in landscape.

39. Fragments of Oribe-style tea bowl.

40. Fragments of Oribe-style square dish.

Kenzan extended his classicism to Japanese models, particularly Oribe ware, the eccentric style produced in Mino (Gifu Prefecture) from the early years of the seventeenth century. In the section of his *Tōkō Hitsuyō* pottery manual called "Seto with crackle clay," Kenzan mentions "Wares in the taste of Furuta Oribe such as incense containers, plates, and cups made in red clay and painted in black and white." In his *Tōji Seihō* pottery manual, in a section entitled "Recipe for green glaze applied to Seto-style vessels," there is a sketch of a plate with a partial application of a contrasting glaze and the note: "Black [iron pigment] is painted on top of the white [slip areas], and green glaze is applied to the red clay [areas left undecorated]." Among the Narutaki shards, there are two pieces testifying to this Oribe interest: a fragmented tea bowl with design of young pine in snow (fig. 39), and a flat tray shard decorated with white stripes surrounded by black (fig. 40). Both of these patterns have strong connections to Oribe wares, particularly to a variety called Narumi Oribe (figs. 41, 42). The absence of extant Kenzan wares in an overt Oribe style may signify a limited interest in copying them, but a set of broader lessons is nevertheless apparent in many Kenzan wares: creative use of white slip, irregular shapes, and sensitivity to vessel shape in the painted design. Kenzan ware might even be seen as an extension of Oribe ware — polished by the master's personal cultivation.

Kenzan experimented with another style closely allied to Oribe: Karatsu ware, a Korean-influenced stoneware from Kyushu. A Narutaki fragment (fig. 43) and extant specimens of a food dish in the shape of a lily blossom (fig. 44) display the texture and coloration common to a variety of painted Karatsu called *Egaratsu*. The shape may be inspired by the split-pepper (*wari zansho*) type of lobed food dish popular at Karatsu kilns (fig. 45). Another Karatsu-style Kenzan piece, a small food container with a lattice motif in underglaze iron, features not the usual painted signature but a "Kenzan" seal impressed into the clay (figs. 46, 47). Similar pieces can be found in the Karatsu repertoire (fig. 48). I know of only two other extant works with this seal, but I have seen it on a number of fragments from the Narutaki site.

My explorations of the Narutaki kiln site at Hōzōji also turned up a fragment of underglaze cobalt-decorated porcelain (fig. 49). Kenzan noted in *Tōkō Hitsuyō* that Kyoto potters

41. Oribe ware: Tea bowl with stripe design.

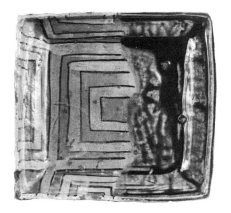

42. Oribe ware: Square dish with linear designs.

43. Fragment of Karatsu-style food dish in lily shape.

were experimenting with a porcelain-like clay from Hira village in Kōshū (present-day Shiga Prefecture), and that he had purchased some. Kenzan complained that the material didn't fire out to a pure white when used alone, so he added to it an equal amount of white clay from Akaiwa village in Bungo (Oita Prefecture). The Narutaki site has yielded several porcelain fragments; the one that I found has a quatrefoil panel containing a stylized peony with an interlocking cash (*shippō*) pattern in the spandrels. The original piece, probably a large bowl, was heavily potted, painted in a rather impure cobalt, covered with the standard transparent glaze, and then fired. Kenzan's manual tells us that these porcelain pieces were put into saggars and set in the hottest place in the kiln.

Despite his obvious reliance upon Ninsei stoneware recipes, Kenzan displayed an independent attitude toward reproduction. For example, Ninsei crafted all of his *utsushi* from three local clays: Yūgyō, Yamashina, and Kurodani. Kenzan, on the other hand, stated in *Tōkō Hitsuyō* that for ceramics any clay would do, but that if one was really interested in a true copy it was necessary to secure materials from the country in question. Ninsei, a production potter, was satisfied with topographical resemblance; Kenzan seems to have attached more importance to an intrinsic foreign quality. As F. W. Mote writes of Chinese painting, recovery of the past might be little more than slavish copying in some minds, but for others it could be a revolutionary archaism, one that could compete with the present.[10] The extent of Kenzan's transformations suggest the latter.

Did Kenzan's first venture meet with financial success? We must remember that Kenzan wares were not produced as "art" — the word does not appear in period literature — but as things subject to the market forces as well as private enjoyment. That Kenzan had some business acumen, and was mindful of how a certain image might resonate for the consumer, we have discussed in these pages. The exact financial picture, however, suffers from an absolute dearth of records. Let us attempt, however, a highly speculative scenario — a year's income for the Narutaki stoneware kiln. A three-chamber climbing kiln would have fired around a thousand small-to-medium pots. Assuming that Kenzan fired three times a year, and that he suffered a 50% loss in the kiln, he would have produced fifteen hundred stoneware pots. There

44. Karatsu-style food dish in lily shape.

45. Karatsu ware: Food dish in shape of split pepper.

46. Karatsu-style cylindrical food dish with design of lattices.

are no records on the prices that Kenzan wares fetched, but a quick survey of period literature, including popular novels, tea masters' diaries, the Konishi archive, and pawn shop notes, gives a general idea of price structure (prices are in *kamme* — 8.3 pounds of silver, which equaled 1000 *momme*):

Misoya takatsuki (a famous tea caddy)	58 *kamme*
Painting by Sesshū	12.9 *kamme*
Kōrin lacquer box	500 *momme*
Sōtatsu painted screen	180 *momme*
Ninsei tea-leaf jar	87 *momme*
Shigaraki-ware flower vase	11.6 *momme*
Seto food containers (set of 5)	27 *momme*
50 small Arita porcelain bowls	10 *momme*
10 Arita porcelain plates	75.4 *momme*

It is of course impossible to calculate seventeenth-century silver into contemporary currency, but to put these prices into some perspective, in the 1690s a cook could be hired for 80 *momme* a year; highly skilled potters at provincial kilns were making 300 to 500 *momme*; Kōrin's top salary as an official painter for the Sakai daimyo was the equivalent of 3 *kamme*. The probable price range for a Kenzan ware must have been between the 87 *momme* for the Ninsei tea-leaf jar — probably the top price that a contemporary ceramic could fetch — and the 7.5 *momme* for an Arita plate. I would thus venture an estimate of 10 *momme* for a fine Kenzan piece or for a whole set of lesser-quality vessels. If Kenzan produced and sold 1500 of these in a year, his gross income would be 15 *kamme* per year. Deducting two-thirds for shipping and commissions leaves 5 *kamme*. Then Kenzan had to pay salaries and costs — perhaps 1 *kamme* for the skilled potters Seiemon and Magobei, and perhaps 750 *momme* for clay, glaze, and firewood. This leaves 3.25 *kamme* yearly income for Kenzan — not a fortune, but enough to maintain a very comfortable level of living. Generally speaking, production costs seemed to have been low; it was at the other end, sales, that the problems occurred. The price of rice — the index for all commodities in Kenzan's heyday — fluctuated radically (price per share).

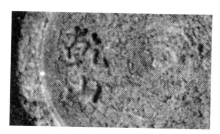

47. Impressed seal on base.

1700: 100 *momme*

1710: 90 *momme*

1712: 200 *momme*

1720: 50 *momme*[11]

Sales of Kenzan ware were surely affected by these price cycles. The rise in 1712 is especially conspicuous. Kenzan may have felt the pressure to increase production and sales, for in that very year he came down from the mountain and opened shop in the center of the city.

1. Translation in Edward Kamens, "The Past in the Present: Fujiwara Teika and the Traditions of Japanese Poetry," *Word and Flower* (New Haven: Yale University Art Gallery, 1989), 30.
2. Phillip Rawson, *Ceramics* (London: Oxford University Press, 1942), 166–67.
3. This box inscription is illustrated in Mitsuoka Chūsei, ed., *Rimpa Kōgei Zenshū* [Collection of Rimpa Crafts], Kenzan sequel no. 3 (Kyoto: Kōrinsha, n.d.), cat. no. 21.
4. Robert Kramer, *The Tea Cult in History* (doctoral diss., University of Chicago, 1985), 55–59.
5. See Shimizu and Wheelright, eds., *Japanese Ink Paintings* (Princeton: Princeton University Press, 1976), 26–27.
6. See John M. Rosenfield, et al., *The Courtly Tradition in Japanese Art and Literature: Selections from the Hofer and Hyde Collections* (Cambridge: Fogg Art Museum, 1973), 160–61.
7. Maribeth Graybill, "The Immortal Poets," in Shimizu and Rosenfield, eds., *Masters of Japanese Calligraphy: 8th–19th Century* (New York: Asia Society Galleries/Japan House Galleries, 1984), 96–97.
8. Kasuga 1930.
9. Kawakita 1942.
10. F.W. Mote, "The Arts and the 'Theorizing Mode' of the Civilization," in Murck, ed., *Artists and Traditions* (Princeton: Princeton University Press, 1976), 8.
11. Based on estimates provided in G.B. Sansom, *Japan: A Short Cultural History* (Rutland, Vermont and Tokyo: Charles E. Tuttle, 1977), 472.

48. Karatsu ware: Cylindrical food dish with design of lattices.

49. Fragment of porcelain from the Narutaki kiln site.

Chapter Four
RETURN TO THE PRESENT
(Chōjiyamachi, 1712–31)

In his "classicizing" ceramics at Narutaki, Kenzan expressed admiration for achievements of the past. His best works spoke of the pleasures that he and his cultivated comrades found in pursuits such as poetry, painting, and the tea ceremony. During this first decade of work, Kenzan had the funds and patrons to support the manufacture of such precious items; but a much larger market was beckoning. In urban Kyoto, his brother Kōrin was producing designs of compelling freshness and simplicity for an audience of newly risen townspeople. In moving back to the city in 1712, Kenzan gained access to Kōrin design and the full resources of the urban craft world. His works began to address fashion. He had Kōrin decorate the flat plates with images popular with the merchant class. He took ordinary stoneware vessels — even disposable vessels — and decorated them with elegant designs that belied their otherwise common nature. He made pots that were not simply clever grounds for the painter, but acted as three-dimensional paintings themselves. This contradictory play of signs, seen also in costume and vernacular literature, followed the aesthetic ideal of the urban commoner. Kenzan's foray into the world of fashionable ceramics is commonly said to represent an artistic decline, but the work from this new Chōjiyamachi kiln brought Kenzan ware into the mainstream of Japanese ceramics design, a place it still occupies today. At Chōjiyamachi, Kenzan returned to the present.

THE WORLD OF KYOTO FASHION

Verdure and seclusion may succor the heart of the poet, but not the potter. After a dozen years of work at the Narutaki kiln, Kenzan decided to move back to the city. A municipal record called *Kyoto Oyakusho Muki Taigai Oboegaki* states that in 1712 Kenzan dismantled the kiln, granted the land to someone else, and moved to a place called Nijō Chōjiyamachi in downtown Kyoto. There, according to the document, he maintained a ceramics business, firing his pots in rented space at Awataguchi and Gojōzaka, kiln centers located on the eastern slopes of the city. What was the reason for the move? For the record, Kenzan simply claimed that the old location was "inconvenient."

There were more than a few conditions that may have made Narutaki a difficult place to work. It lacked supplies (good clays have yet to be found in this part of Kyoto) and it was far from centers of distribution. Such an enterprise could survive through custom orders by wealthy patrons, but the collapse of the wealthiest merchant houses from unpaid daimyo loans, coupled with the spectacular rise in prices, may have precluded sufficient patronage from that quarter. Downtown Kyoto, on the other hand, was a thriving center of craft production. The notes of Engelbert Kaempfer (1651–1716), a member of a Dutch delegation passing through Kyoto in 1691, depict a city in which nearly every house seemed to be engaged in a productive trade, making goods of the highest quality. Kyoto products were so famous that even bad imitations, if bearing some kind of Kyoto trademark, would sell.[1]

The supporters of that economy were the so-called new townspeople, or *shinkō chōnin*, who had established themselves in the city over the course of the seventeenth century. Their sheer number and purchasing power greatly influenced the course of Japanese crafts. Instead of filling custom orders generated though personal contacts, urban workshops were beginning to mass-produce and mass-market all kinds of items — even high-quality pieces. Patterns of consumption were shaped by popular media. In textiles, for example, woodblock-printed pattern books — *hiinagata* — informed the consumer of designs that were au courant. And while those designs were promoted as exclusive, many of them could now be bought right off the shelf. In 1683, Mitsui Hachirōbei opened a draper's shop in Edo, making cash sales from an inventory of ready-made goods. The Mitsui printed their shop logo on umbrellas, provided free clothing to popular actors for display on stage, and even distributed handbills to potential customers. Fashion was thus mediated by easily identifiable symbols. As Kaempfer astutely observed, the Kyoto trademark in itself was enough to guarantee sales — even of spurious items. The stage was set for the emergence of celebrity designers who would become involved not only with custom orders, but with large wholesale markets. One of them would be Kenzan.

Nijō Street, the location of Kenzan's new Chōjiyamachi workshop, was the major business thoroughfare in the city, linking the military administrative center at Nijō Castle with the wharves of the Takase Canal. The street was lined with the ateliers of armorers, printers, and lacquerers, as well as offices of moneylenders and foreign trade agents. The Takase Canal was the principal artery to the entrepot city of Osaka where, from the second half of the seventeenth century, specialized wholesale brokers had been distributing ceramics to the entire realm. Kenzan's workshop, probably sandwiched into a narrow urban lot (fig. 50), must have bustled as well, for its penetration of these markets is first noted in 1713, when his ware was listed among prominent Kyoto products in the popular encyclopedia *Wakan Sansai Zue*. The celebrated dramatist Chikamatsu Monzaemon (1653–1724) wrote Kenzan wares into his 1715 play *Ikutama Shinjū* (Love Suicide at Ikutama). The hero of the drama, an Osaka ceramics dealer named Koheiji, talks of selling "fifteen or sixteen *ryō* worth of *nishikide* Kenzan Otowaware tea bowls, bowls, and plates" from his father's stock. Although the reference is garbled, the suggestion is that the ware was being stocked by the Osaka merchants. Kenzan ware thus enjoyed broad esteem in the second decade of the eighteenth century, but the achievement was hardly Kenzan's alone. Backing him was his brother Kōrin, who reigned as the city's most celebrated designer.

By the time Kenzan moved to Chōjiyamachi in 1712, Ogata Kōrin had been active in painting and design for at least fifteen years. The first hints of Kōrin's artistic career are recorded in the diary of Nijō Tsunahira: a request in 1695 for Kōrin to paint five fans for presentation to the Empress Dowager, and in 1700, a reference to Kōrin painting on a box for sweets. A related mention can be found in the 1699 popular book *Kōshokumon Denjū* (Instructions in Love), in which Kōrin is said

50. Kyoto urban ceramics workshop, after an 1882 painting by Kōno Bairei.

to have painted "black pines on white satin [kimono]." In the absence of further evidence, it would appear that Kōrin first indulged in decorative painting as a diversion rather than an occupation. From 1701, however, Kōrin was awarded the honorary *hokkyō* title and began to show rapid development as a painter of screens and scrolls. His early painting exhibits two preferences that would endure throughout his career: one for the ink monochrome tradition imported from China and naturalized by generations of painters in Japan; and the other for the colorful decorative style developed by Tawaraya Sōtatsu and his followers. We shall see that both types would have an impact on Kenzan ware.

Kōrin's rise as a painter coincides with the appearance of a new friend and important supporter, Nakamura Kuroemon Nobumitsu (1669–1730) — better known by a later name, Kuranosuke. From 1601, when Tokugawa Ieyasu opened a silver mint in Fushimi (moved to Kyoto proper in 1608), men of the Nakamura, together with other upper-class merchants, were appointed to supervise the coinage. Kuranosuke was promoted to the position of Custodian of Bullion in 1700, and within a year he was using his mint connections to help Kōrin. A document in the Sumitomo family collection entitled *Dōza Tomechō* (Ledger for the Copper Mint) mentions Korin as a member of a delegation sent from Kyoto to inspect a newly opened copper mint.

The prosperity of mint officials like Kuranosuke had its origins at the highest levels of authority. In 1695, the government yielded to the advice of finance minister Ogiwara Shigehide (1658–1713) and debased the currency to stem huge deficits in the treasury. Every time the currency was recoined — and that happened five times between 1695 and 1707 — the mint took a four to six percent commission. These manipulations also encouraged embezzlement, counterfeiting, and speculation on the part of the mint workers, and every indication is that Kuranosuke himself exercised few scruples. His home on Muromachi, near Ryōgaechō (Money-changing Quarter), was palatial. Under seventeen thousand square feet of roof were thirty-three rooms, four storerooms, tea houses, a stage for Noh drama, and enclosed gardens. This kind of extravagance gave rise to the Ryōgaechō style (*Ryōgaechō fū*), a term synonymous with fashion and foppery.

Kōrin's contribution to Ryōgaechō style emerges in

Okinagusa, a mid-eighteenth century gazetteer. An anecdote in this record depicts him agreeing to help Kuranosuke's wife in a suburban fashion show, apparently the rage of the day. At the appointed hour, various contestants arrived in gilt and embroidered finery, each as "resplendent as rays from heaven." Kuranosuke's wife, however, demurely stepped from her palanquin dressed in a simple white robe with a black overgarment. This disappointed everyone until it was realized that she was accompanied by a maid dressed more sumptuously than anyone in the crowd. This witty inversion of high and low culture and of half-obscured lavishness — ironically encouraged by governmental sumptuary laws — was held by the new townspeople to be the epitome of chic. It would also become an element of Kenzan-ware design.

Kuranosuke, who spent half of his official service in Edo, may also have provided introductions for Kōrin in the military capital; the painter is known to have lived there from about 1705 to 1709. No doubt he was lured by the prospect of steady employment painting for provincial warlords, all of whom were compelled by the shogunate to maintain villas in the city. In a 1708 entry in *Tekikō Sayō,* the official record of the Sakai clan, Kōrin is listed as an employee, receiving twenty rice shares for his services. But in letters to a friend, Kamishima Gen'in, Kōrin describes in ambivalent terms the chore of having to reproduce work in the style of Muromachi-period ink painters Sesshū and Sesson for his conservative warrior patrons.

Despite the security of his Edo position, Kōrin returned to Kyoto in 1709. Plans for a house built at Shimmachi, Nijō Kudaru, in 1711 demonstrate a new resolve; a spacious edifice with storehouses, a tea house, and large painting studio attest to affluence and productivity (an impressive building based on those blueprints was recently erected behind the MOA Museum in Atami, Shizuoka Prefecture). The following year Kenzan came down from Narutaki to take up residence at Chōjiyamachi a few blocks down the street.

In terms of character, Kōrin and Kenzan were light years apart. Kōrin had spent his youth in seeming pursuit of urban pleasures, while Kenzan was quietly working away in the suburban hills. What they both shared was artistic energy — and it was reaching its prime at the beginning of the Chōjiyamachi period. Kōrin's work as a painter had begun with crafts decoration, and that sensibility continued to inform his brushwork. In painting scrolls and screens, Kōrin achieved exquisite decorative compositions that combined naturalism with bold, abstract design. By the time Kōrin returned from Edo, Kenzan had been working in ceramics at Narutaki for ten years — ample time to grasp both the technical and formal possibilities of the craft. These were just the right tools needed to harmonize with Kōrin's superb brushwork and compositional sense. From our overall survey of Kenzan wares, at least three clusters can be associated with the Chōjiyamachi years, which spanned from 1712 to 1731: Kōrin-Kenzan *kakuzara*, which feature quickly brushed popular designs by Kōrin himself; *futajawan* and *kawarake*, which are ordinary "blanks" decorated with Rimpa (Kōrin)-style designs; and *katamukōzuke* and *sukashibachi*, pots whose shapes were altered in accordance with their painted designs.

KŌRIN-KENZAN
KAKUZARA

shapes: molded square and polygonal forms
techniques: earthenware with underglaze iron painting
decor: simplified figural and floral subjects
border patterns: lattices, floral rosettes, and other simple
　　linear patterns
inscriptions: Chinese poetry, in five- or seven-character
　　lines
signatures: short, typically "Written by Kenzan Shinsei"
　　after the poems
seals: "Tōin" and "Shōko," stenciled
monograms: Kōrin uses a monogram resembling the
　　character *kotobuki*
(for affiliated pieces, see Appendix 3, Group 6)

Two *kakuzara* from the very end of the Narutaki period, both dated 1711, hint at a changing emphasis in Kenzan-ware design. They are a square plate with a painting of a pine branch (figs. 51, 52), and a square plate with a painting of a plum branch (figs. 53, 54). The same techniques and shapes that Kenzan employed in the early part of his career are in evidence, but the decoration speaks of greater abbreviation and immediacy. Instead of a carefully wrought landscape or bird-and-flower composition, there is an isolated subject without the slightest hint of a spatial setting. Absent are the lengthy poetic inscrip-

51 and 52. Square plate with design of pine branch (above) and signature on verso (right).

53 and 54. Square plate with design of plum branches (above) and signature on verso (right).

tions that accompanied the subjects on the earlier earthenware plates; the plum branch is paired with a mere four-character inscription. Using a Chinese poetic designation for plum, composed of the characters for "crossing" and "slanting," Kenzan writes:

The plum: pure but fleeting.

The spirit of brevity is continued in simple border patterns that feature the auspicious *ru yi* and castanet motifs on the inside, and lattice patterns with floral panels on the outside. Kenzan has reserved his calligraphy for a signature on the back of the pine plate, which reads: "Made in the spring of 1711 by the hermit potter of Kyoto, Japan, Kenzan Shōkosai Shinsei." While the painting in these two plates seems a little too deliberate to be from Kōrin's hand, the overall style relates

55. Square plate with design of willow. Painting by Kōrin.

56. Square plate with design of monk Hotei. Painting by Kōrin.

57. Signature on verso.

stongly to a group of works bearing his signature, to which we now turn.

Central to the Kōrin-Kenzan collaboration are a small number of *kakuzara* with decorating in iron under a transparent lead glaze. The subjects are the "lucky gods" Jurōjin, Hotei, and Daikoku, popular with the newly risen urban townspeople, as well as birds, flowers, and trees. Each motif is accompanied by a signature, variously containing Kōrin's name, his *hokkyō* title, or a favorite pseudonym, Jakumyō. A majority of the plates bear poetic inscriptions by Kenzan, and all bear his signature. Although there are several dozen of these plates extant, only thirteen of them seem to be beyond suspicion: ten in the Fujita Museum, Osaka (originally part of a set of twenty), and three other pieces. Illustrated here are square plates with respective designs of willow, the legendary monk Hotei, and the Chinese poet-calligrapher Huang Shangu watching gulls (figs. 55–59). The lightness and sharpness of Kōrin's brushwork, together with Kenzan's poetry, have endeared these plates to generations of connoisseurs. Even in prewar Japan, when standards of authenticity for Kenzan wares were at their strictest, these collaborative works were held up as exemplary. The problem lies in dating them.

Since Kōrin and Kenzan are probably Japan's most famous art collaborators, the nature and timing of their dialogue have attracted much debate. The controversy stems from the absence of even a single dated work from the accepted corpus of collaborative pieces. In his *Tōji Seihō* pottery manual, Kenzan writes, "The shapes and designs for the vessels I worked out together with my older brother Kōrin, and all the early painting was by him. Later I used a Kōrin style, and gradually added my own ideas." At face value, this statement suggests that Kōrin was on hand from the very opening of the Narutaki kiln in 1699, and most scholars have followed that line. Since Kōrin was flourishing as a painter in the years just prior to his death in 1716, it is assumed that he would have had little interest in "minor" arts like ceramics. Also, the idea of a stalwart and filial Kenzan giving his rogue brother an early boost made a heartwarming story. Be that as it may, our research places the collaborative works in the second decade of the eighteenth century, when Kenzan was established at Chōjiyamachi. Five reasons can be advanced.

First, the shape, size (22 × 22 × 3 cm. throughout), and

58. Square plate with design of Chinese calligrapher-poet Huang Shangu watching gulls. Painting by Kōrin.

59. Signature on verso.

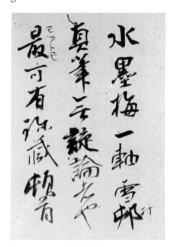

60. Detail from five sheets in a book of Kōrin memoranda.

general composition of the painting match the 1711 pieces just introduced. Second, as far as the medium permits, Kōrin's brushwork displays the wet, sharp marks characteristic of his late work in painting proper. This sharp touch in Kōrin's late ink painting, usually referred to as his quick-stroke (*sokuhitsu*) style, is thought to stem from those years in Edo, where he was required to work in the Muromachi-era monochrome style. Third, the border patterns are nearly identical to the two 1711 pieces: a single line drawn around the perimeter of the painting; the auspicious *ru yi* and castanets on the inside walls; and lattices and floral rosettes on the outside walls.

A fourth point concerns the calligraphy. Kenzan's inscriptions and signatures here display more boldness and fluidity, and individual characters feature an expansiveness and thickness of line — propensities that were encouraged by more than a decade of work in ceramics. When writing with coarse mineral pigment on rough, absorbent surfaces, the brush must be loaded and each movement must be decisive and inclusive. Any attempt to execute delicate gestures will cause the brush to stick. Even if they could be brushed, these subtle nuances would likely vanish in the heat of the kiln. Kenzan had to embolden his script, and that change can be located in a document from the Konishi archive, datable to about 1711: five sheets in a book of Kōrin memoranda (fig. 60). Kenzan wrote these sheets for Kōrin to use in inscribing, signing, and authenticating paintings. The style of the individual characters, and even the language used, compares favorably with the inscriptions on the collaborative plates.

A fifth and final indicator of a later date concerns the "Tōin" and "Shōko" seals, now stenciled rather than painted, as was the case in the early Narutaki pieces. Oddly, these stenciled seals are placed upside down on all of the thirteen finest works that bear seals.

The evidence for a comparatively late date for the joint works — from 1709, when Kōrin returned from Edo, until 1716, the year of his death — now seems quite compelling. The question remains as to why Kenzan claimed in his 1737 pottery notes that Kōrin helped him from the very start. Did Kenzan, writing from a late-life perspective, simply equate Kōrin's contribution with the time that the kiln gained broad popularity? Or does there exist a body of early Kenzan ware decorated by Kōrin's hand? I prefer the former explanation, but the issue has become one of those East-West feuds endemic to Japanese scholarship. Defending the early dating is a Kyoto-Osaka axis of ceramics specialists, apparently galvanized by a remark at a 1982 symposium that Kenzan specialists (most of whom then resided in western Japan) were lazy. In Tokyo, specialists in painting stood behind their assessment that the brushwork on the collaborative pots represents Kōrin's later style. For now, it seems that Kōrin did seriously begin to help Kenzan from the very late Narutaki or early Chōjiyamachi years. Furthermore, his assistance extended beyond painting *kakuzara* to providing designs for a new line of stonewares, which make up our second Chōjiyamachi cluster.

PAINTING ON BLANKS: *FUTAJAWAN* AND *KAWARAKE*

shapes: round forms, including bowls and dishes
techniques: stoneware, with designs in white slip,
   underglaze iron, and cobalt
decor: Rimpa (Kōrin)-style painting
signatures: simple "Kenzan" signatures, painted
(for affiliated pieces, see Appendix 3, Group 7)

Although there are a few traces of Kōrin design in the stoneware shards from the Narutaki kiln, his sensibility emerges fully at Chōjiyamachi. It can be dated in a set of five covered bowls (*futajawan*) with designs of cranes and reeds (figs. 61, 62). The wooden box for the set appears to be original, and it is inscribed with a date of 1713 — a year after Kenzan moved from the Narutaki hills to Chōjiyamachi. A few more pieces with the same design exist in separate collections.

The dynamic decor scheme — cranes fly and rest, appear and disappear — obscures very plain bowls and covers. They were probably thrown in rapid succession as "blanks" — without any prior knowledge of, or interest in, how they would be decorated. When I lived in Gojōzaka, the old potters' quarter in Kyoto, greenware and bisqueware makers called *kijiya* customarily turned out large quantities of these blanks. Even in the early 1980s, their labor was cheap — undecorated bowls like this could be had for less than a dollar. Porters could always be seen carrying the blanks to the decorators — *ekakiya* — who also worked independently. At the final stage, the bowls were brought to kiln operators, or *yakiya,* for stoneware

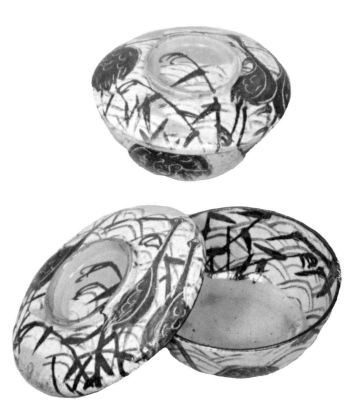

61. Lidded bowls with design of crane and reeds.

62. Signature inside foot ring.

or enamel firing. The *ekakiya* in my neighborhood answered to wholesalers (*ton'ya*), although the decorators' ideas — especially those found to be marketable — were heeded.

Had Kenzan relinquished his command of the manufacturing process to a specialized metropolitan system? In a sense, yes. The Kyoto magistrate's record *Kyoto Oyakusho Muki Taigai Oboegaki* states that Kenzan borrowed space in the kiln centers of Awataguchi and Gojōzaka after the move to Chōjiyamachi. In his *Tōkō Hitsuyō* pottery manual he rather proudly confesses to using blanks from such places as Arita and even Holland. But Kenzan was no mere decorator. From the years of work at Narutaki, he realized that his forte was in surface design; it was not necessary to maintain a large workshop staff and a climbing kiln. In downtown Kyoto, one could order shapes and secure kiln space at any time. So in exchange for overall control, his commitment to surface treatment was intensified. The innovation would have a lasting impact — from this time on, urban workshops in Kyoto would be organized around master designer-decorators rather than potters proper. Kenzan's synthesis of ceramics and design would become an institution.

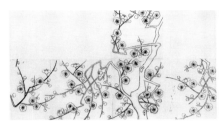

63. Ogata Kōrin: Sketch for a stacked food box.

The use of white slip, cobalt, and iron constitutes an important new technical ensemble. In the first stage of the decorating, irregular patches of white slip were applied to the bowls. Kenzan was particularly proud of his slip technique, and divulges the formula piecemeal in his pottery manuals: to fine white clay from Akaiwa village in Bungo (Oita Prefecture) he added about twenty percent silica — probably to prevent excess shrinkage. To render the slip suitable for application to bisqueware, Kenzan first calcined the clay (biscuited the clay in dry powder form). This would also reduce shrinkage by eliminating organic matter and chemically combined water. A seaweed syrup called *funori* was added to promote suspension, adhesion, and to slow drying. The result was a fine, dense material suitable for both painting and broad application. In the Narutaki underglaze-enamel pieces, slip had been used as one of the colors in the painting; in the 1706 Cizhou-style bowl, it was used as a total covering. There is, however, no evidence of these slip patches at Narutaki; nor was the composition carried inside the forms as it is here.

After the slip application, patterns of waves, reeds, and cranes were brushed in an impure cobalt and iron. The outlines of the cranes were etched through the iron in a technique hitherto unseen in Kenzan products: needle incising, or sgraffito (*kugibori*). After the decorating, the pieces were dipped in a transparent stoneware glaze; Kenzan always used Ninsei's formula of Namase (Hyōgo Prefecture) feldspar and ash (Kenzan recommends hardwoods called *kashi* and *enoki*). My experiments with these materials and recipes leads me to believe that Kenzan's stoneware, like most Kyoto stonewares today, was fired to a temperature of about 1230 degrees C. — a little lower than we usually fire ours in the West.

While Kōrin's signature is nowhere to be found on these Chōjiyamachi stonewares, his influence is unmistakable. A large group of sketches in the Konishi archive, many of them intended for the decoration of round fans, lacquerware objects, and incense wrappers, show Kōrin's efforts to adapt elements of his Rimpa-school forebears to a variety of three-dimensional objects. For example, Kōrin would "wrap" his figures around forms (fig. 63), thus creating dramatic cropping effects from an otherwise naturalistic tableau. The principle is vividly illustrated in wrappers designed by Kōrin for incense and quite possibly for food (fig. 64); although most of them are

64. Food wrapper with Kōrin-style design of cranes.

65. Att. Hon'ami Kōetsu and Tawaraya Sōta-tsu: Elongated poem card *(tanzaku)* with design of cranes over water.

now mounted as hanging scrolls, in their original configuration as folded wrappers the motifs alternately appear and disappear in rhythmic tension. This particular set of bowls also may have been inspired by a work from the era of Kōetsu and Sōtatsu, an elongated poem card with a design of cranes over water (fig. 65), which was wrapped around and into the pots. The placement of motifs on far (inside) and near (outside) surfaces, coupled with the cropping effects, make for a kinetic vision.

Kenzan's revolutionary use of white slip provided the perfect device for harmonizing these two-dimensional schemes with round forms. For centuries, the composition of painting on ceramics had been conditioned by the shape of the vessel. For example, the standard scheme in underglaze blue porcelain of the Yuan- and early Ming-dynasty China consisted of bands of stylized decor, such as cloud scrolls, at the base and mouth rim of the vessel; these would in turn frame a band or circular area of pictorial motifs like flowers or dragons. Usually the picture was symmetrically placed and, if possible, repeated at fixed intervals. In the late sixteenth and seventeenth centuries, Japanese potters in Mino and to some extent Arita experimented with other concepts, but hardly with the assimilative power of Kenzan. By using these oddly divided slip patches (analogous to the pattern fields seen in Kōrin's painting) as a compositional ground, the painting was released from the confines of square or circle. The paintings could, in a sense, exist independent of the vessel form. This was an all-important breakthrough in the history of Kenzan ware. The most pedestrian vessels — like these lidded-bowl "blanks" — might now possess a rich and variegated surface.

At the level of allusion, these surfaces embody an interesting contradiction. By reserving bare patches of clay and by

66. Lidded bowls with design of spring grasses.

using impure cobalt and iron pigments, Kenzan was invoking the rustic taste of the sixteenth-century tea master. On the other hand, the painted motifs suggest the elegant world of court poetry. That Kenzan consciously exploited this tension is seen in certain lidded bowls with designs of spring grasses (fig. 66), where the painted area may disappear completely when revolved away from the viewer. As we hinted at the beginning of this chapter, the new townspeople appreciated this play between unadorned and decorated surfaces; we are reminded of Kōrin's plainly clad fashion contestant with sumptuously dressed maid in tow. Other stonewares from the Chōjiyamachi Kenzan kiln show similar strategies. Kenzan had found a language appropriate not only for urban taste and Kōrin design, but also for the mass-produced blanks that were readily available in the new downtown location. Essential to the new style was white slip, an ideal material for dividing vessel surfaces into dramatic design fields.

We presume that work on these prefired blanks was a major part of the early Chōjiyamachi production. Unfortunately, the 1713 lidded bowls are the only Chōjiyamachi stonewares that can be firmly dated. But if the key features of the 1713 bowls — simple shapes, painting fields established by asymmetrically placed patches of white slip, Rimpa-style subjects, use of subdued iron and impure cobalt pigments, and use of the *kugibori* incising technique — are taken as a baseline, other pieces can be provisionally dated as well. An important example, one that also adds some stunning new features, is a set of round food dishes with individual designs (figs. 67, 68).

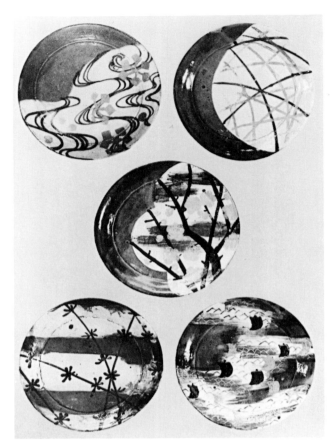

67. *Kawarake* with individual designs.

68. Verso with signature.

This variety of handmade dish, made of a coarse, iron-rich clay and conventionally used in undecorated biscuit form, is called *kawarake*. The Kenzan-style decorated *kawarake* is another unusual mixture of humility and sophistication. Semi-disposable earthenware plates were made in Japan since ancient times; archaeologists have excavated them by the carload from hundreds of sites. In Kyoto, *kawarake* were made from the ninth century as offertory as well as ordinary eating wares; the potters were attached to temples, shrines, and sometimes imperial villas. Known workshops include the Fukakusa potters, affiliated with the Daigoji temple, and the Saga potters, who worked with the Nonomiya shrine. In the fifteenth century, one group of potters from the Saga community moved to Hataeda in north Kyoto, inaugurating a production that has lasted down to the present. According to a seventeenth-century record on the Hataeda workshop, pots were made by flattening a ball of clay into a pancake shape and molding that around the flexed elbow. There were a variety of

69. Ogata Kōrin: Sketch of blossoming plum.

70. Ogata Kōrin: Sketch of flowing water.

standard sizes, the more common being about twelve, fifteen, eighteen, and twenty centimeters in diameter. These were packed in a simple cylindrical kiln and fired all morning; the following day, vendors would cart off the bulk of the merchandise, which would be sold to the common folk.[2]

Here the *kawarake* has been appropriated as a ground for Kōrin-style patterns. Sketches in the Konishi archive show just how masterful Kōrin was in reducing detail and engaging in selective distortion. His single elements are characterized by simple, full forms and supple contours (figs. 69, 70). It is in the total design of the set, however, that Kenzan makes his own allusive statement. First, each of these plates has a completely different motif — a concept known as *egawari*. The notion of irregular sets has a long heritage — as early as the fourteenth century it was praised by Yoshida Kenkō in his essay collection *Tsurezuregusa* (Essays in Idleness), and some two centuries later it was cultivated by practitioners of the tea ceremony. But few producers were capable of assembling diverse poetic images into a single, unified set. To facilitate these individual designs, Kenzan used his white slip in a new manner: instead of merely using it as a field, he endowed it with a pictorial value that would interact with the painting on top of it. In the plate with a plum design, the white forms the contour of a single blossom against the dark, unslipped portion of the surface; in the plate with snowflakes on water, the slip becomes the water. In the other three plates, it works variously as waves, bands of mist, and the autumn moon.

For the painting itself, Kenzan added overglaze gold to the already established palette of cobalt and iron. The absence of gold or silver enamel in early dated pieces or in the Narutaki shards suggests that Kenzan did not use the technique extensively in his first decade of production. Gold enamel is troublesome — it requires a very low-temperature firing to fuse the material to the glazed surface. There were many gold- and silver-leaf specialists in the city, however — indeed, Kenzan was surrounded by them at Chōjiyamachi. Gold designs on a crude brown "disposable" pot carried the suggestion of frivolous consumption that the towspeople adored. There is even a Kōrin episode to match: on an outing with his fellow dandies, the painter carried his lunch in plain bamboo-sheath wrappers instead of the usual sumptuous lacquer box. These earthy sheets, however, were decorated on the inside with patterns in gold and silver — and when he was finished eating, Kōrin nonchalantly tossed them into a stream. Disposable income and its manifestation in commodities had become art.

As in other works, Kenzan's exacting sense of design continues into places unseen. In this case, the white slip has been carried over onto the bottom edges of each plate. On one of those white edges the front design is continued, and on the other, iron lines form a frame that includes a "Kenzan" signature. These framed signatures, like others at Chōjiyamachi, lack the calligraphic flourish of the Narutaki version. Painted with deliberation and seemingly following a set model, they seem more like a trademark than a personal signature. Obviously, it was neither possible nor necessary for every one of these works to bear the master's personal touch. Continuity of materials, manufacture, and pictorial style, coupled with minor variations in brushwork, imply that these works were decorated and signed by several artisans closely following diagrams — for design *and* signature — provided by Kōrin and Kenzan. The basic similarity of the design elements here to the 1713 lidded bowls suggests that the *kawarake* too were made in the early Chōjiyamachi years.

The collaboration of the Ogata brothers in earthenware painting and stoneware design was as short-lived as it was felicitous. Kōrin seemed to have premonitions of his demise: in 1713, the same year that his son Saijirō was born, he addressed wills to wife Tayo and to his only legitimate son Juichirō (born 1700), who had now joined the Konishi family. To Tayo, he expressed concern over Juichirō's future, and over the continuation of the Ogata blood line. Juichirō was encouraged not to forget his obligation to Kuranosuke and the Konishi. In 1714, Kōrin's ally Nakamura Kuranosuke and four other cronies at the mint were charged with corruption. Kuranosuke was found guilty of excessive luxury and collusion with government treasurer Ogiwara Shigehide, and was exiled to the remote Miyake Island south of Edo. The scandal deprived Kōrin, and probably Kenzan, of a circle of friends and patrons.

On the second day, sixth month, 1716, Kōrin died. His final decline must have occurred after visiting the Nijō with New Year's greetings in the first month of that year. In the meantime, the large number of pattern books with Kōrin designs published in the second and third decades of the eighteenth century suggests that Kōrin's work — or at least his name —

was booming in popularity. The celebrity status may in part account for the appearance of Kenzan ware in popular contexts, as well. As mentioned earlier in this chapter, scholars have long maintained that employment with Kenzan in the early years of the Narutaki kiln gave Kōrin the impetus he needed to become a great artist. Now it appears quite the opposite — that it was Kōrin's painting and design that helped Kenzan ware become a truly popular product. Kenzan's own additions to this legacy appear in our third and final Chōjiyamachi cluster.

PAINTING AS POT: *KATAMUKŌZUKE* AND *SUKASHIBACHI*

shapes: wheel-thrown and drape-molded forms, some carved
techniques: stoneware, with underglaze pigments and overglaze enameling
decor: Rimpa (Kōrin)-style motifs
signatures: simple "Kenzan" signatures, framed
(for affiliated pieces, see Appendix 3, Group 7)

According to the Nijō family diaries, in 1723 Kenzan accompanied his patron Tsunahira on a visit to the famous Kasuga shrine in Nara. This is Kenzan's last recorded appearance in Kyoto, but his work seems to have continued. An entry in the Nijō record the following year mentions the presentation of a "Kenzan-ware square tray" (*suzuributa*) to the noble Takatsukasa family. In 1725, Kenzan ware appears in another noble context: the *Kaiki,* diary of courtier and aesthete Konoe Iehiro (1667–1736), records the use of Kenzan-ware plates at a tea ceremony. Even after Kōrin's death, then, the production at Chōjiyamachi was sustained at a level of quality suitable for such elevated patrons. We shall now examine a variety of stoneware designs that probably originated during the second decade at Chōjiyamachi, ca. 1720, and continued until Kenzan's departure for Edo in about 1731.

At this stage of his career Kenzan developed a concept almost the reverse of his earliest square plates. Instead of subordinating traditional ceramic technique and form to facsimile painting, he began to see how he could make the painting harmonize with the space of the traditional vessel. Pot as painting became painting as pot. The experiment is manifested in sets of food dishes with the shape of the vessel

71. Food dishes with design of maple leaves on the Tatsuta River.

72. Verso with signature.

contoured with the painted design — the so-called *katamu-kōzuke*. There are at least three themes extant: maple leaves on the Tatsuta River, chrysanthemums, and peonies. Here we shall examine a set of six plates with designs of autumn foliage on the Tatsuta River (figs. 71, 72).

These pots were formed by a technique called drape-molding, whereby a slab of clay is laid over a convex mold. When the form was rigid, a foot ring was turned on the wheel. After a biscuit firing, the pieces were decorated in white slip and underglaze painting. Patches of slip all functioned as pictorial elements — in this case, water patterns that vary compositionally with each piece. Linear accents were added in an impure cobalt pigment. Each piece was coated with a transparent glaze and fired to stoneware temperature. For the final step, maple leaves were painted in red, yellow, and green overglaze enamels and fused in an additional low-temperature firing.

The contours of the maple leaves are carried out to the very edges of the plate. Coordinating the shape and painting on three-dimensional objects had some history prior to Kenzan. In such Rimpa designs as the fans made by the Sōtatsu atelier or the Kōetsu-style domed lacquer boxes, there is a sensitivity between painted composition and the shape of the object. It was seldom if ever the case, however, that the painted subject actually became the shape of the vessel; that idea seems to have been adopted most enthusiastically by potters. An early example is the so-called *kosometsuke* type of blue-and-white porcelain made in late Ming China for export to Japan; sets of *kosometsuke* food dishes in such shapes as oxen, fans, and melons were popular in the tea-ceremony meal from the early seventeenth century. Similar experiments were undertaken in Oribe ware at the same time. From about 1660, the porcelain potters in Kyushu began to slab-mold dishes to match their intended painted decoration; Nabeshima porcelains in particular achieved a high degree of sophistication around the turn of the century. Mindful of these precedents, Kenzan must have tried a few experiments at Narutaki; a shard of one such shaped plate is still preserved at Hōzōji. But Kenzan did not simply make a pot in the shape of a single pictorial element; he formed the vessel out of a complex composition. In this endeavor, he made use of patterns left by his older brother, one of which — the opulent maple-leaf shape (fig. 73) — is seen in these Kenzan-ware plates.

The bottoms of these plates also display some new features; in underglaze cobalt or iron, Kenzan added a small, complementary motif, such as pine needles or abbreviated water patterns. In the center of the foot ring, a patch of white slip surrounded by an iron pigment frame is inscribed "Kenzan." The shape of the stem of the *ken* character, which is now executed in a single downward pulse with a sudden lift of the brush at the very end of the stroke, is very close to the personally signed works from the master's late-life residence in Edo. Another similarity between these pieces and all of the Edo pieces is that the entire vessel is covered with glaze. Accordingly, they were probably made shortly before the Edo trip, circa 1720–30.

The pot-as-painting concept is most fully realized in a number of deep openwork bowls, or *sukashibachi* (figs. 74, 75). Aside from the perforated stands made for prehistoric wares, openwork became fashionable in the seventeenth century; it is seen in Bizen and Oribe stonewares, Arita and Kutani porce-

73. Ogata Kōrin: Sketch of maple leaf.

74. Bowl with openwork design of pine in snow.

75. Verso with signature.

lains, and in a few wares from Kyoto. Kenzan, however, was the first to conceive of the holes as part of the painted decoration. These bowls were thrown and trimmed on the potter's wheel; while the piece was still a bit soft, the rim was irregularly carved and holes cut out. White slip was used in diverse ways: as a solid field, as a brushed accent (*hakeme*), or as part of the painted composition. The subjects, typically seasonal flowers and foliage, were rendered in a combination of underglaze and overglaze colors; in the example illustrated here, the pine bark, branches, and needle details are in underglaze iron, and the green foliage is in overglaze enamel. The voids suggest space between branches, stems, and flowers, and the carved rims suggest the upper contours of foliage. Although nearly impossible to convey in a photograph, these pieces display a remarkable sensitivity to the user's visual perspective. When examined from a thirty- to forty-five-degree elevation, the pieces impart the experience of peering through trees or clumps of flowers. Phillip Rawson, writing about analogous effects in Ming- and Qing-dynasty porcelains and Cretan jars, maintains that when the pot itself provides a third dimension for its painted surfaces, the viewer is transported to a "world whose scale is determined by the images on the pot," rather than the disassociative effect of seeing painted decoration with an arbitrarily established frame of reference.[3] In the Kenzan *sukashibachi*, the effect can be attributed to clever juxtaposition of painted pattern and openwork as well as careful adjustment of interior and exterior painting. The interest in pictorial effects anticipates Kenzan's Edo work in painting proper, in the last decade of his life. The signatures, enclosed in frames on the fully glazed bottom of the bowls, constitute further evidence for manufacture in the decade just prior to that move, the 1720s.

Pundits have long maintained that after the first ten years at Narutaki, the master suffered an artistic downturn. He had forfeited his own kiln and then lost his older brother; he had to depend on borrowed facilities in the city, and there eked out a living by mass-producing sets of functional wares instead of those painterly square plates. It is true that Kenzan relinquished a secluded site and private kiln ownership for a conspicuous place in the metropolitan production system. Instead of a mountain retreat, his shop at Chōjiyamachi probably resembled those still found on Gojō Street in present-day Kyoto: a wide storefront, behind which is a raised area for business negotiations, packing and display of stock, and limited production. Decorators work in adjacent rooms, and fire low-temperature underglazes and enamels in a small kiln in the enclosed yard. Greenware production and high-temperature glazing is parceled out to neighboring groups of specialists.

The old Chōjiyamachi interpretation needs reassessment, however. First, the idea that having one's own kiln is essential for making good pots is a twentieth-century conceit; since the Kenzan style was based on surface decoration and not special glaze effects, maintenance of a kiln provided no special salvation. Kenzan could hire metropolitan greenware makers and kiln masters just as Kōetsu and Kōrin hired lacquer specialists. Kōrin's death was an undeniable setback, but before he died the older Ogata brother had transmitted to Kenzan not only paintings and patterns, but a way of design firmly rooted in Japanese paper, lacquerware, and textile traditions, and richly articulated in the work of the earlier Rimpa masters. Kenzan brought that legacy into ceramics.

Finally, do pots that are functional and made in sets constitute an artistic decline? Although the fact is rarely mentioned, Kenzan also made sets at Narutaki — he had always made sets. Are overtly functional wares inherently inferior to non-functional ones? In a recent essay, potter Warren Frederick defends physical function in light of the more pluralistic spirit in contemporary art criticism:

Art functions through sensory impacts that affect us physi-
cally, emotionally, and conceptually. Artists choose the particular means most suitable to convey their intended meaning.
. . . Physical function is one more vehicle for expressing
artistic content. Physical use is merely a more complicated
level of art's ever-present sensory impact, albeit far more
influenced by personal, social, and cultural factors. African
and Eastern cultures provide the best examples of physical
engagement and provoke infinite aesthetic responses.[4]

Function is thus just as deserving of privilege as other
factors in ceramics, but just because certain Kenzan wares seem
to be more immediately functional does not make them better
pots. Rather we must consider the type and quality of
mediation in any given work. The highly skilled painting and
personal calligraphy on the flat plates evoked the ethos of
literati art, generally accorded the highest rank in East Asian
material culture. The enthusiastic critical evaluation that they
receive is understandable in that light. Of signal importance,
however, is that Kenzan's conceptual growth did not cease with
that genre. Armed with designs from his older brother, he
began to treat ceramics less as a novelty than as a medium with
its own peculiar potential. He embraced the concept of set
making and produced *egawari* sets as a poetic response. He
worked with blanks, but exploited their seemingly pedestrian
shapes and materials in distinctive designs. He modified
shapes for design purposes without mitigating their utility. His
physical participation in many of these stonewares is difficult
if not impossible to prove; here the "site" of mediation is at
the design stage. But the designs were his. In returning to the
tradition of the vessel, Kenzan found the extraordinary in the
ordinary.

Gojōzaka is a working neighborhood in east Kyoto. Tour-
ists will know it as the gateway to the Kiyomizu temple or as
the location of potter Kawai Kanjirō's house; for motorists, it is
where the national highway rises out of the city basin into the
hills. Exhaust fouls the air, so much that in the 1960s the city
was forced to close the numerous climbing kilns that had
dotted the landscape from Kenzan's time. But Gojōzaka is still
potter's territory; shells of the old kilns lie behind newer
buildings, and greenware and enamel specialists continue to
ply their trades in impossibly narrow workshops. Saggars

planted with flowers line the streets. I lived in Gojōzaka for over two years before discovering the nearby Saifukuji, a small temple lost among the flower shops, cafes, and its considerably more famous ecclesiastical neighbor, the Rokuhara Mitsuji. According to a legend passed down in Saifukuji, Kenzan's patron Nijō Tsunahira restored the temple in 1726, and Kenzan and Nijō's nephew, Prince Kōkan, had their first meeting here. We will now turn to evidence suggesting that in 1731, Kenzan accompanied this prince to Edo, never to return to his native city.

1. Engelbert Kaempfer, *The History of Japan,* III (trans. J.G. Scheuchzer; Glasgow: James MacLehose and Sons, 1906), 21.

2. Nakanodō Kazunobu, *Kyoto Yōgei Shi* [Kyoto Ceramics History] (Kyoto: Tankōsha, 1984), 30–31.

3. Rawson 1971, 187–88.

4. Warren Frederick, "An Aesthetic of Function," *New Art Examiner* 13:1 (September 1985), 42–43.

Chapter Five
A POTTER'S PILGRIMAGE
(Edo, 1731–43)

From a Kyoto perspective, Edo in the early eighteenth century was still a cultural hinterland, and certainly not a mecca for ceramics production. Kenzan's years there have traditionally been seen as the most obscure part of his career — and as something tantamount to exile. These accounts ignore the fact that the city had begun its own distinctive florescence in the mid-seventeenth century, when the shogun decreed that all daimyo and their retinues spend alternate years in his attendance. This created not only an instant class of consumers but an extensive service infrastructure. The military aristocracy supported their own artists-in-residence, but those who served the military — either in ritual or logistical capacities — now had the wherewithal to support alternative activities. Therein we find Kenzan. There is now enough evidence to connect him to salons in the city, where he was admired not as a craft designer but as a person of cultivation and heir to his older brother Kōrin, who had himself lived in Edo some years before. Kenzan's work in ceramics and painting now emerges in the context of collegial gatherings, or *ozashiki* — at Rinnōji, part of the Tokugawa ecclesiastical center; in Sano, a town outside Edo where Kenzan was hosted by local amateurs; and in Fukagawa, the Edo center for haiku poetry.

It is also in Edo where Kenzan at last showed his hand — and indirectly, his heart. Undaunted by the lack of facilities, the old man now decorated all of his pots and took up the brush to paint on paper as well. The work from this late period may lack the technical finesse and crisp finish of the Kyoto years, but the sense of intimacy is unmatched — a final, personal journey, mapped by his surviving pots and paintings.

THREE EDO SALONS

Hints of Kenzan's new circumstances emerge in a letter addressed to Kōrin's son, who had taken the name Hikoemon upon adoption into the Konishi family. The letter, still preserved in the Konishi archive, is dated twenty-eighth day, first month, 1737. Kenzan offered New Year greetings to Hikoemon and thanked his nephew for providing care during a serious illness in the year just past. Kenzan mentioned an audience that Hikoemon's colleague Hasegawa Chōbei had with a certain Junkō, saying that it went just as well as one that had been granted to Hikoemon. In return for Kenzan's arranging the audience, Chōbei had ordered Kenzan ceramics.

Junkō was another name for Prince Kōkan (1697–1738), the third son of Emperor Higashiyama and the nephew of Kenzan's longtime patron Nijō Tsunahira. Kōkan was sixth in a line of imperial princes serving at the Tendai-sect temple Rinnōji (within the larger temple complex of Kan'eiji), located in what is now Ueno Park, Tokyo. From the time of the first Rinnōji prince-priest, Morizumi (a son of Gomizunoo), the duty of the Rinnōji ecclesiastics was to make three yearly pilgrimages to the Tokugawa mausoleum at Nikkō, and less frequent sojourns to Kyoto. It was the function of Rinnōji, together with temples on Mount Hiei in Kyoto and Mount Nikkō in Tochigi, to protect Japan's rulers from the inauspicious northwest quarter.

Kōkan had been a priest since the age of twelve. In 1714, at the age of eighteen, he set out for Edo, where he took up residence at Rinnōji; his predecessor, prince-priest Kōben, bestowed the Kōkan title at that time. In the fifth month of the following year, Kōkan became head of the temple. For tonsured princes, it was the highest post attainable, with revenue totaling ten thousand shares of rice, about five times that of top-ranked courtiers in Kyoto. Kōkan made his first return to Kyoto in 1718, and thirteen years later, in 1731, he once again returned to his native city. There he took part in investiture ceremonies for his nephew, Prince Yasuyoshi (1722–88), who would eventually become his successor under the name Kōjun. Although the date of Kenzan's move is not recorded, it is plausible that after having become acquainted with the prince in Kyoto, Kenzan accompanied him back to Edo in that same year.

More about Kenzan's career in Edo emerges in secondary sources. According to *Sumidagawa Hanayashiki,* a pamphlet

Key to Map
1. *Rinnōji*
2. *Iriya (Uguisudani)*
3. *Imado*
4. *Asakusa (Sensōji)*
5. *Nagasakichō*
6. *Rokkembori*
7. *Bashō's house*
8. *ex-Nagasakichō*
9. *Fuyuki*
10. *Naraya*

KENZAN IN EDO

UENO

MUKŌJIMA

SUMIDA RIVER

N

EDO CASTLE

HONJŌ

FUKAGAWA

KIBA

76. Kenzan's commemorative stone in Iriya.

published in 1820 by Kenzan revivalist Sahara Kikuu, and *Koga Bikō*, the mid-nineteenth-century painting history, Kenzan settled in Iriya, located at the foot of the slope behind the Rinnōji temple (see map). The area is also known as Uguisudani, or Warbler Valley. According to one legend, Kenzan made a present of Kyoto warblers to Kōkan, and they multiplied, hence the name.[1] A concrete stele marking Kenzan's presence in the neighborhood has been erected on a smog-infested traffic island across from the Iriya subway station (fig. 76).

Why had Kenzan left Kyoto? There is little evidence to support the traditional belief that he was dispirited or in financial distress. As we shall describe in the next chapter, he was prominent enough to set up an adopted son, Ihachi, as his Kyoto successor, and at an imperial temple, at that. Kenzan was probably tempted by the opportunity to see this bustling new city, especially since it had been home to his two older brothers. And then there was Kōkan, to whom Kenzan probably transferred his loyalties and affections upon the death in 1732 of his longtime friend and patron Tsunahira. Kenzan's

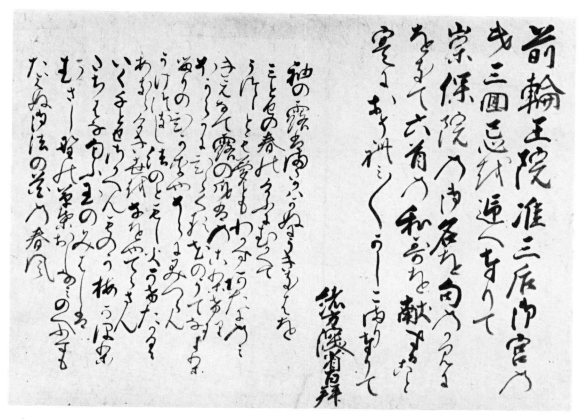

77. Lamentation poems for Prince Kōkan.

intimacy with Kōkan is evident by his ability to arrange audiences for his nephew and colleagues. It appears that Kenzan acted both as a companion and as a kind of cultural attaché for the prince. Furiku, a pseudonym that Kenzan adopted in Edo and used on his letters and paintings, even has ancient connotations in Chinese as "princely tutor." An anecdote in the *Koga Bikō* relates one occasion, on which Kenzan was presented with some new garments for an audience with the prince; two days later a visitor to his workshop found him wearing the same clothes, encrusted with clay. Kenzan seems to have made some pottery under temple auspices; his *Tōkō Hitsuyō*, written in the third month of 1737, portrays a still-active potter. He may have also taught the prince something about painting. One report maintains that in the Shōoin subtemple, Nikko, there is a painting by Kōkan signed with the art-name Keishū.[2] Such pleasures were short lived, however. On the ninth day, third month, 1738, Kōkan officially retired; six days later, he was dead at the age of forty-two. He was buried in a special grave at Rinnōji under the posthumous name Sōhōin. Kenzan embedded that name in a moving set of lamentation poems composed on the third anniversary of the prince's death (fig. 77):

Six poems dedicted to the third anniversary of the death of Prince Kōkan, former abbot of the Rinnōji, with the first syllable of each verse [in the Japanese] arranged to read Sōhōin [the prince's posthumous] name:

In sleeves still drenched
With undried tears,
Forlornly
I greet a third spring.

Is it a dream
Or this world?
Fruitlessly,
I linger on,
Like dew still moist.

Brightly,
The flower opens
From its pedestal.
Blue rays of light
Fill the sky.

By your transmitting
The light of the dharma,
Even brighter
Is the light
Of this world.

Long may you bloom
In fragrances of
Plum and orange
On the steps
To the heavenly palace.

Though the reed plains
Of Musashi may be
Flattened,
Eternal as the spring winds,
The flower of your Buddhahood.

A second site for Kenzan's late-life activities was Sano, a village just north of Edo, in present Tochigi Prefecture. A visit to the village by Kenzan had long been part of local lore, but area schoolmaster Shinozaki Genzō found solid evidence after a decade of investigation in the 1930s and early 1940s. The trail began with his discovery of a booklet of verses entitled *Sanjūrokkasen* (Thirty-six Poets); an inscription on the last page stated that Kenzan had copied out the poems at the request of a person named Sudō Tosen early in the winter of 1737. Investigations of old local families established that Tosen was indeed from Sano. Then Shinozaki found hints of ceramics production in Sano — oddly enough, in an American source. The 1901 *Catalogue of the Morse Collection of Japanese Pottery* showed an illustration of a hand warmer by Kenzan-style potter Ida Kichiroku (1791–1861) marked, "Made in Sano for Matsumura Kosei Eitei by Kenzan Tōin Shinsei and copied by Kichiroku." The Matsumura were the hereditary bailiffs of the region; Shinozaki visited a family matriarch and heard recollections of Kenzan wares passed down in her family.

Finally, on November 28, 1940, Shinozaki was invited to view what appeared to be an original Kenzan pottery manual — the *Tōji Seihō* — in the collection of the wealthy Takizawa family in nearby Ujiie village. The manual bore a date: "Ninth month, eleventh and twelfth day, Kenzan [at] seventy-five [1737]." The Takizawa also possessed several Kenzan wares, and one of them, a shell-shaped dish decorated with pine and cherry blossoms, bore the inscription, "This vessel formed and fired by the gentleman Ōkawa at Sano; *Gembun hinoto mi,* two days after *chōyō* [ninth day, ninth month, 1737]." On the opposite side was written, "Painted by Kenzan." That confirmed Kenzan's presence in Sano at the time the *Tōji Seihō* was written. As we shall see below, Takizawa also owned two other Kenzan pots which bore inscriptions naming "Ōkawa Kendō" and "Sudō Tosen" as benefactors.

From the accumulated evidence, Shinozaki concluded that Kenzan was active in Sano in the ninth month of 1737, and was hosted by Sudō Tosen, Matsumura Kosei Eitei, and Ōkawa Kendō, all of whom were found to have headed prosperous and interrelated local families. Ōkawa Kendō's link with Kenzan was strengthened further in 1954, when researcher Suzuki Hancha published sections of a Kendō diary also owned by Takizawa; it transcribed parts of a letter posted by Kenzan in Edo, and detailed Kendō's preparations for the 1737 visit. Taken as a whole, the extant materials suggest that while in Sano, Kenzan produced a small number of ceramics and wrote out the *Tōji Seihō* manual. We shall see in Chapter 7 that Shinozaki's research also provided fodder for the spectacular New Sano Kenzan scandal that broke in 1962.

In addition to the Rinnōji and Sano salons, Kenzan can now be connected to a cultural circle in Fukagawa, a district on the far side of the Sumida River. This section of Edo had been home to Matsuo Bashō (1644–94), the celebrated master of haiku, the allusive seventeen-syllable verse form. Born into a low-ranking samurai family in Ueno, a city in present Mie Prefecture, Bashō received local instruction in poetry, and went on to achieve some renown in his home province. In 1672 he moved to Edo, where after some years he, and the hut he lived in, received the name Bashō after a banana tree presented by a student. The Bashō Hut in Fukagawa served as home base for the master's wanderings, journeys of personal discovery that fueled his poetry. Drawing upon the experience of travel (*tabi*) for its evocations of detachment, union with nature, spiritual liberation, and even impending death, Bashō's pilgrimages through the Japanese countryside form the backdrop for some of the most moving poetry in the Japanese tradition. One of those walking tours, a 1691 sojourn to Kyoto, took him to Saga, within hailing distance of Kenzan's Shūseidō. There is no hard evidence to support it, but given Kenzan's interests in those days, it is not inconceivable that the two men could have met.

While in Edo, Bashō supported himself by teaching haiku and calligraphy. His large circle included not only literati but professional artists such as painter Hanabusa Itchō (1652–1724) and lacquerer Ogawa Haritsu (Ritsuō; 1663–1747); Haritsu is even alleged to have been a student of Kenzan. Just east of Bashō's Fukagawa home was Kiba, a maze of canals built by the government to hold timber harvested in the mountains and rafted downriver. Since city-wide conflagrations occurred with astonishing regularity, the demand for lumber was enormous. The merchants of Kiba were among the city's most wealthy, and contributed to local culture. Timber and fish magnate Sugiyama Sampu sponsored Bashō's stay in Fukagawa, and after the master's death the merchants continued to support the arts. There is now enough evidence to suggest that Kenzan was one such beneficiary.

The first hints of Kenzan's reception in Edo poetry circles occurred in 1733, when haiku poet Kikuoka Senryō published an Edo gazetteer entitled *Kindai Seji Dan* (Present-day Talk):

> Ogata Shinsei of Kenzan ware:
> He began firing with clay from Narutaki in Saga. Since Narutaki mountain (*zan*) is located to the northwest (*ken*) of the palace, the kiln took the name Kenzan. Shinsei is the younger brother of Ogata Kōrin and he is still alive. He can compose both Chinese and Japanese poetry.

Senryō's description suggests that Kenzan's reputation in Edo was built not only on his ceramics but on his cultivation. Other poets singled him out for admiration. Kenzan is mentioned in a haiku left by Senryō's friend and Bashō follower Naitō Rosen. The verse was based on a popular seasonal sweet called *ikuyō* (many-a-generation) *mochi*, made by a merchant named Kihei, located at Ryōgokubashi Nishizume in Edo:

> A fragrance of plum:
> And *ikuyō mochi*
> Served on Kenzan ware.[3]

Another contemporary, Shōji Katsutomi of Yoshiwara, described a pair of Kenzan-ware plates in his 1738 poetry collection, *Dōbōgoenshū* (Cave-Lair Verse Garden). These plates had Chinese poetry on the front and Japanese poems on the back, and were signed "Copied out by Kenzan, age seventy-eight." Other gentleman-scholars in Kenzan's circle may have included the two men whose names appear as recipients of his pottery manual, *Tōkō Hitsuyō*: Isshian Rankei, whose use of the syllable *ran* suggests either an interest in literati or Dutch studies, and Minakami Rosen, whose "Tōenkyō" (Living Amid Kiln Smoke) seal affixed to the manual hints at the playful approach of an amateur who dabbled in ceramics.

Kenzan has been connected with at least two art-loving timber merchants from Fukagawa. The mid-nineteenth century painting history *Koga Bikō* states that while in Edo, Kenzan resided both in Iriya and at the house of Sakamoto Beishū (1704–77) in Rokkembori, a section of Fukagawa. Fond of haiku and painting, Beishū was a possible benefactor. The 1820 *Sumidagawa Hanayashiki*, on the other hand, agrees with the Rokkembori address, but relates that Kenzan's host was "timber merchant Naramo" — another name for Naraya

Mozaemon (?–1714), whose serendipitous possession of lumber stock suitable for work on the Tokugawa mausoleum at Nikkō in 1683 led to a vast fortune. Kenzan's contemporary would have been third-generation Naraya scion, Yasuzaemon, whose circle of friends included painters, doctors, and haiku poets. Through the building of the Nikkō complex, the Naraya may have formed a relationship with its companion temple, Rinnōji, which in turn could explain the link with Kenzan. Since the Naraya and Beishū were both culture-loving merchants with villas in Fukagawa, the confusion is understandable.

The precise sequence of events in Kenzan's last years is unclear. Iriya was ravaged by fire in 1737, perhaps prompting the travel to Sano and residence in Fukagawa. Kōkan died in 1738. A flood in Fukagawa in 1742 may have forced Kenzan from that site. He never disclosed his whereabouts in a letter to Konishi Hikoemon on the nineteenth day, first month, 1742. In it, Kenzan congratulated his nephew upon his promotion to a new position in Osaka, and expressed relief that Hikoemon was looking after Tomi and Ichisuke. According to Konishi papers, Tomi was one of Kōrin's illegitimate daughters. Since Hikoemon and Tomi were Kōrin's children, perhaps Ichisuke was another Kōrin descendant; indeed, the *ichi* of his name is written with the same character as that in Kōrin's boyhood name, Ichinojō. On the reverse side of this letter, Kenzan expressed shock and grief over the death of Kōrin's widow Tayo in the winter of 1741, at the age of seventy-seven. The tone of the letter intimates a long friendship with and respect for this woman.

What were those last years like for the old man — unmarried, childless, and now deprived of Kōkan, his greatest patron? Surely the sentimentalists are correct in asserting that he had moments of loneliness and nostalgia. Yet the writing style and content of his letter to Hikoemon conveys a strong spirit, and his late work also prompts the assumption that he was a positive, forward-looking human being. Despite his apparent contentment and activity, however, Kenzan's health may have given out. A passage from a bailiff's diary called *Ueno Oku Goyōnin Chū Kampō Watari On Nikki* (Diary of Official Attendants to the Ueno Prince for the Kampō Era) relates that a doctor brought news to the local bailiff that Kenzan, ill for some time, had finally expired. Kenzan's landlord Jirōbei met with the local officials, and it was decided that since Kenzan had no local temple affiliation he would be buried at a place called Zen'yōji.

Zen'yōji was a branch temple of the Rinnōji, and the official cemetery for retainers of the prince-abbots. Parts of the bailiff's record, especially statements that "Kenzan had no temple affiliation" and that the Rinnōji office "donated one *ryō* [a unit of coinage] to cover expenses" have often been taken to mean that Kenzan was penniless and was given what amounted to a pauper's burial. Of course Kenzan had no temple of his own in Edo; he was of Kyoto stock, from a family so wealthy that they had maintained their own chapel, Kōzen'in, at Myōkenji. Thus a temple had to be chosen, but for an official — not a pauper's — interment; with wealthy patrons and admirers, Kenzan was not in the dire straits heretofore described. That final resting place can still be found at Zen'yōji, now located in the Nishi Sugamo area of Tokyo. The gravestone (fig. 78) is inscribed with two death poems and a brief epitath:

78. Kenzan's gravestone (front), Zen'yōji.

[Front]
> Pleasure and pain once passed
> Leave naught but dreams
>
> All my life through
> These eighty-one years
> I have done what I wished
> In my own way;
> The whole world
> In a mouthful.
>
> Reikai Shinsei Koji.

[Back]:
The deceased was from Kyoto. In days past he worked at Narutaki [in the northwest mountains]; therefore he was called Kenzan. He achieved fame as a potter. His family name was Ogata. He died in the third year of Kampō, sixth month, second day.

That "world in a mouthful" emerges in a cluster of ceramics attributed to the Edo years; these pots mark a final journey, both over geography of the present and cultural spaces of the past.

EDO CERAMICS

shapes: molded, wheel-thrown, and handbuilt
techniques: earthenware, with underglaze and overglaze
    colors
decor: Rimpa (Kōrin)-style subjects, now more painterly
inscriptions: short Japanese poems
signatures: typically include Kyoto referents
seals: occasional Shōko, painted
(for affiliated pieces, see Appendix 3, Group 10)

In 1635, at the behest of third-generation Tokugawa shogun Iemitsu, the Takahara kiln was transplanted from Osaka to Asakusa, Edo. Its production of Korean-style tea bowls for use in shogunal ceremonies represented the earliest efforts at glazed ceramics in the new capital. A half-century later, one Shirai Hanshichi started the Imado kiln just up the Sumida River. Some thirty years after that, Hanshichi II expanded production beyond the earthenware braziers, or *dōburo*, to glazed pieces. The most activity, however, was at the tile kilns, which probably existed from the very start of the city's construction, and must have flourished after 1720, when commoners were given the right to have tiled roofs. Suitable deposits of iron-rich clay lined the banks of the Sumida; quantities of tile were made at Imado, and just downriver there was another kiln at Honjō. There was also a kiln at Kenzan's Iriya.

Shimpen Musashi Fudoki Kō (New Musashi Topography), published in 1828, mentions Iriya as an alternate name for the Sakamoto district; its principal trades were farming and making earthenware (*dōki*) for the shogunate and the "Nikkō Gomonshū" (Rinnōji). The potters included Matsui Shinzaemon and Jin'emon. Five years before this publication, painter and Rimpa revivalist Sakai Hōitsu wrote to a friend about the potter Tazaburō from "among Kenzan's followers in Iriya." Apparently the Kenzan tradition had been handed down in a continuously functioning group of potters. That community, sustained by patronage from the shogunal and imperial establishment at Rinnōji, may have extended into recent times: Aimi Kou wrote that early in this century there existed a ceramics quarter (*yakimono yashiki*) in a section of Iriya.[4] In Edo, Kenzan was not surrounded by experts of Kyoto caliber, but he was still among people who could make and fire pots.

The kind of facilities available in Edo, along with state-

ments in Kenzan's pottery manual, provide some hints as to
what kind of ceramics he would produce in his new environs.
In the last section of *Tōkō Hitsuyō*, the master recorded the
alteration of a glaze to make it melt faster, which "is desirable
for gatherings (*ozashiki*) or for amateurs." In the last decade of
his life, Kenzan was hardly interested in extensive stoneware
production. Low-fired ceramics had a technical simplicity and
immediacy compatible with the poets and amateur artists with
whom Kenzan fraternized in Edo. One could paint, glaze, and
fire these pots in the course of an afternoon. In the same
section of his manual, he also included a group of pigment
recipes called "Kenzan exclusive" (*Kenzan ichiryū*), indicating
his efforts to devise a broader palette for earthenware. In
Kenzan's Kyoto designs, color was created in two different
ways. There was the Oshikōji-inspired manner of decorating
with colored lead glazes under a transparent lead glaze; as we
saw at Narutaki, this made for a slightly blurred effect similar
to the way painters' pigments were absorbed on paper or silk.
The other method featured Ninsei's overglaze enamels; since
the addition of glassy frit made them bead up on the surface,
the effect was explicitly ceramic in nature. In this late-life
experiment, however, Kenzan combined underglaze and overglaze formulas and used them both under and over the
glaze — for the sake of vibrant color. Obviously these effects
made an impact on Kenzan's Edo patrons, who had never seen
ceramic colors used in such a free, painterly manner.

Kenzan's new technical centerpiece was a white enamel. It is
extremely difficult to paint in white on ceramics. One can
paint in white slip under the glaze or bring out a white clay
body in reserve, but without the aid of the traditional Western
opacifier, tin oxide, or modern materials such as zinc or
zirconium, it is difficult to produce a white color of density
and stable contour. Nonetheless, Kenzan found a formula for
white — a mixture of prefired, finely ground white clay mixed
with white frit (a prefired glass) and a little lead carbonate.
Kenzan used this white alone as a pigment, and also used it as a
base for subtle blends of color. For example, a touch of red
pigment (Kenzan advocated *rokuban*, which is a calcined iron
sulphate) added to the white produced a pink; green added to
the white gave a light spring green. Kenzan had devised a paint
box for amateur potters.

The interest in chromatics clearly emerges in a series of

141

79. Square plate with design of white lily.

80. Signature on verso.

ceramics from those last years. The earliest known piece, inscribed to the effect that it was made in Edo in 1736, is a square plate painted with a design of white lily, formerly in the Masaki Chiharu collection, Tokyo, and now accessible only through photographs (figs. 79, 80). The entire vessel is coated with a pea green earthenware glaze. The central motif is a single lily; stem and leaves are painted in iron pigment and the blossom in the new white enamel. The outlines of those elements are incised in Kenzan's characteristic *kugibori* technique. To the right of the flower is a field of white in the shape of the stylized clouds seen in classical narrative painting (*suyari*). The poem, painted in black pigment on the cloud patch, reads:

> Is it the flickering flame,
> Still lingering from night?
> Or the morning dew,
> Glistening —
> On a solitary lily?

A rectangular white patch on the verso is inscribed in black pigment, "This was made by Kenzan of the Heian capital ["Heian Jō Kenzan"] in the opening year of Gembun [1736],

81. Dish in the shape of an abalone with design of pine and cherry trees.

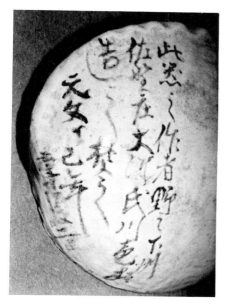

82. Inscription on base.

83. Signature on side.

while staying in Bukō [Edo]." The design is full of suggestion: the square painting ground is divided in a manner reminiscent of ancient calligraphy sheets or the broken field textile designs called *katamigawari*. At the same time, it uses the potter's technique of *kugibori* and displays Kenzan's newfound interest in color, highlighted by the white enamel.

A series of pieces made in Sano — these are *authentic* Sano pieces, made in 1737 — bear the new palette as well. An abalone-shaped plate with a design of pine and cherry blossoms (figs. 81–83) is coated with a very pale green glaze; the cherry blossoms are a delicate pink. An inscription on the back reads "This vessel was formed and fired by the gentleman Ōkawa at Ya no Shū, Sano, ninth month, eleventh day, 1737." On the opposite side a small panel reads, "Painted by Kenzan." This is the first work in which Kenzan explicitly acknowledges his role in painting. A charcoal container (*hiire*) with monochrome motifs of orchid, plum, and narcissus in separate ogival panels features cloud patterns in the spandrels colored blue, yellow, light green, purple, red and pink (figs. 84, 85). An inscription inside the foot ring reads, "Made by Kenzan by request during a brief stay at Sano, in Temmei, at the house of the gentleman Ōkawa." While these two vessels are executed in a buff-colored clay, the Sano series also includes a set of round plates, potted in the red clay more characteristic of eastern Japan; one of them is a plate with a summer landscape design (figs. 86–88). On an irregular white enamel patch that breaks down the roundness of the form is a grove of pines and deciduous trees, painted in iron and green. A problem with the kiln apparently caused the entire surface to darken and the copper in the green pigment to reduce to a dull red. On the unaffected verso, a few broad strokes of white serve as a ground for a haiku poem written by patron Sudō Tosen in response to Kenzan's painting:

> Not here [in this landscape]
> But the dweller of this space —
> The cuckoo.

Tosen   [Signed Tosen]

A small white slip patch on the side opposite is inscribed, "Made by Kyoto Kenzan at Ya no Kashū, Sano." The three other plates in the set are unfinished, lacking the final transpar-

84. Charcoal container (*hiire*) with motifs of orchid, plum, and narcissus.

85. Signature inside foot ring.

86. Dish with design of summer landscape.

ent glaze coat. One of them, a plate with a design of a hollyhock, depicts the flower in rich color over a white enamel ground (figs. 89, 90). Each color represents one of those late-life Kenzan recipes: the light green comes from a mixture of rock copper and white; the red flowers from ochre and iron sulphate; the pink flowers from the red and white; and the pale blue from black (iron and impure cobalt) and white. The two other plates bear designs of chrysanthemums and bush clover, respectively. All three have a white signature panel like that on the summer landscape plate, but the signature in the unfinished pieces merely reads "Kenzan." In place of the haiku there are latticed squares in a matrix of undulating lines.

Still another pot announces Kenzan's peregrinations, in this instance not to Sano but to Nagasaki. An incense case shaped and decorated after a toy top is inscribed, "Made by Kyoto Kenzan ["Keichō Kenzan"] Shinsei during a brief stay in Nagasaki" (figs. 91, 92). Ceramics historian Mitsuoka Chūsei has suggested that Kenzan may have accompanied finance minister Ogiwara Shigehide on an official trip to that city in 1697.[5] Yet Kenzan never mentioned a trip to Nagasaki in his otherwise detailed pottery notes. There is, of course, more than one Nagasaki in Japan, including a Nagasakichō several blocks northeast of the Rokkembori section of Fukagawa, a short distance from the villas of the wealthy timbermen linked with Kenzan. In this incense box, the use of "Keichō," common during Kenzan's Edo years, and the proximity of the strong but unaffected handwriting to the inscriptions on the lily plate and the Sano pieces further attest to manufacture late in Kenzan's career. The piece has a thickly formed body potted in a dark clay. On the domed lid, bands have been painted in red, yellow, blue, purple, and iron underglaze colors; the inside of the top and bottom are coated with a frothy green enamel.

That same green surface can be seen in another probable Edo manufacture, the well-known tea bowl with a design of moonflowers (figs. 93, 94). With its black ground, white flower with yellow pistil and large green leaves, and calligraphy in white, the moonflower bowl is one of the most striking designs from the Kenzan oeuvre. The large spheroidal shape vaguely resembles a Raku-ware tea bowl, but the piece is thrown on the potter's wheel rather than being carved out in the Raku fashion. The expansive size may have been selected to accommodate the poem and floral motif executed in Kenzan's new

87 and 88. Poem on back of rim, composed by Sudō Tosen (above) and signature on back of opposite rim (right).

89 and 90. Dish with design of hollyhock (above) and signature on back of rim (right).

colors. The painting and poem are derived from the "Yūgao" (Moonflower, or literally, "Evening Faces") chapter of the eleventh-century classic *Tale of Genji*, where a vine of these night-blooming flowers leads the shining prince to a new paramour — the "lady of the evening faces." Kenzan combined two of the original Genji poems in his inscription:

> Upon approaching
> In the glistening dew;
> How unexpected,
> The blossoming
> Of the evening face.

Here ceramics technique, painting, and calligraphy combine to produce a very special lyrical effect. On top of a plain red earthenware vessel, possibly the best that could be obtained from the rustic Edo greenware makers, Kenzan applied a wash of his "exclusive" black enamel to create the appropriate

91 and 92. Incense container with design of toy top (above) and signature on base (right).

93. Tea bowl with design of moonflowers.

94. Signature outside foot ring.

nocturnal atmosphere. The flower, calligraphic inscription, and leaves — painted in Kenzan's dense white and green enamels — loom out of the night. The extensive and skillful use of the new recipes, the stock character of the vessel, and the style of the "Kenzan" signature in white on the outside of the foot ring all commend this piece to the master's stay in Edo.

Kenzan had not totally abandoned himself to coloristic effects; a small tea bowl with horse designs, inscribed "Made by old man Kenzan at seventy-nine," testifies to a continued interest in monochrome (fig. 95). This bowl was hand formed and carved — perhaps by Kenzan himself — and its red clay body coated with white slip. The horses are inspired from Kōrin's sketches (fig. 96), although Kenzan's heavy hand and anatomical liberties contrast tellingly with the Kōrin touch.

What may be Kenzan's latest work in ceramics is a set of ten rectangular plates in the shape of elongated poem cards (five are illustrated in figs. 97–99). The verso of one plate is marked "Copied out by Kenzan at eighty-one," which would date the piece to Kenzan's last year, 1743. The elongated poem card, or *tanzaku*, has a long history; the oldest extant example is from the hand of monk-poet Yoshida Kenkō. The early cards were smaller than today's and were intended primarily for spontaneous jottings rather than formal compositions. It was customary to introduce a blue cloud pattern at the top of the card and a purple one at the bottom in the process of making these papers, and Kenzan duplicated the effect with diffuse washes of cobalt and manganese. On that ground Kenzan copied out ten poems, one per plate.

Inscriptions on the matching box handed down with this set announce the design concept: ten "styles" of *waka* poems —

146

95. Tea bowl with design of horses.

96. Att. Ogata Kōrin: Sketches for Kenzan ware (detail).

waka jūtai. This idea was first articulated in *Wakatai Jisshu* (Compendium of Ten Waka Styles), a small book thought to have been written in 945 by Mibu no Tadamine, one of the editors of the imperially authorized waka anthology, the *Kokinshū*. Several centuries later the great poet and critic Fujiwara no Teika listed what he called *waka jūtai* in a letter to a student:

> Those styles which I have called "fundamental" are the following four of the ten styles about which I have written to you previously: the "style of mystery and depth," the "style of universally acceptable statement," the "style of elegant beauty," and the "style of intense feeling." It is true that we occasionally find, even among these, poems which have archaic elements, but their overall effect is such that their archaic style is not displeasing. After you have developed the ability to compose freely in these gentle and amiable styles, such others as the "lofty style," the "style of describing things as one sees them," the "style of interesting treatment," the "style of novel treatment," and the "style of exquisite detail" are quite easy to master. The "style of demon quelling force" is difficult to learn, but after you have attained the necessary proficiency I see no reason why you cannot master that also.[6]

For these plates, Kenzan did not compose his own verses but instead chose classical works that he felt matched the ten styles. The poems are inscribed on the front and the respective style names, followed by a Kenzan signature, are written on the verso. The style names and poems (I have added the poets and sources in brackets) are as follows:

Mysterious:
The hours before dawn
Seem saddest of all to me
Since that leave-taking
When I saw in the heavens
The pale moon's indifferent face.[7]
[Mibu no Tadamine, *Kokinshū* 625]

Lofty:
In the shifting clouds
One can sense

97. Rectangular plates in the shape of elongated poem cards (*tanzaku*).

The coming storm —
In the mountains of Katsuragi
Leaves of the spindle tree flutter.
[Fujiwara no Masatsune, *Shin Kokinshū* 561]

Intense Feeling:
The pines along the cove
Of the Oi river
Have attained old age —
Should we inquire of royal visits
Of ages past?
[Sakanoue no Korenori, *Zoku Kokinshū* 1662]

Elegant Beauty:
I had hoped
To have long life
Under your reign —
Only to find myself
Growing old.

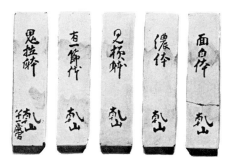

98. Signatures and style names on verso.

99. Inscribed box.

[Nijōin Sanuki, *Shin Kokinshū* 1634]

Universally Acceptable Statement:
When I often awake
In the long autumn night
From my heart
I pray
For the emperor's long reign.
[Fujiwara no Ietaka, *Shin Kokinshū* 1758]

Interesting Treatment:
What can I do?
I have made a retreat
Deep within a bamboo glade
Only there to find
The ways of the world.
[Fujiwara no Shunzei, *Shin Kokinshū* 1671]

Exquisite Detail:
In days past
Where we gathered brushwood
At Kataoka,
Nothing remains
But a mountain path, overgrown.
[Jakuren Hōshi, *Shin Kokinshū* 1632]

Describing Things as One Sees Them:
After a day hunting
Upon Katano field,
And spreading brushwood under me,
I see the moon reflected clear
In the rapids of the Yodo.
[Fujiwara no Kinhira, *Shin Kokinshū* 688]

Novel Treatment:
Having been to Matsushima,
I only long to go again —
May the hut
At Ōjima
Not be swallowed by the waves.
[Fujiwara no Shunzei, *Shin Kokinshū* 933]

Demon Quelling:
Like the clouds
Of yesterday,

100. Tea bowl with design of rose.

101. Inscription and signature on opposite side.

> Vanished on the mountain wind
> Is the vow —
> That you made to me.
> [Fujiwara no Ietaka, *Shin Kokinshū* 1294]

The separation of the style names from the poems recalls Kenzan's early Teika twelve-month plates, where users would have to guess the poems from the painted motifs. On these plates, one would have to speculate as to which one of Teika's styles was evoked by that certain poem. As in Kenzan's earliest work, literary classicism, gaming, food presentation, and calligraphy are richly intermingled.

The inscriptions on the plates and matching box show full-bodied characters with thickly inked lines; Kenzan's hand was still steady at eighty-one. Contours are soft and rounded, with even less exposure of the brush tip than his mid-career writing. The composition is skillfully coordinated with the vessel shape and the characters exhibit sensitive mutual relationships. It is in this area that imitators of Kenzan's calligraphy usually failed. Common sense would suggest that calligraphy and ceramics are ill-matched — the freshness and immediacy of the mark are compromised by the fire. Kenzan nevertheless achieved a superb harmony of these arts throughout his career. This synthesis may appear to be the triumph of a good designer, but had Kenzan not been a skilled calligrapher to begin with, it could never have been achieved.

Kenzan's late ceramics also include high-temperature work, although it was probably limited to enamel decoration on prefired and glazed blanks. A representative work is a tea bowl with a rose design formerly in the collection of the Tendai-sect Bishamondō temple in Yamashina, Kyoto (figs. 100, 101). The rose is painted in overglaze red and green enamels with underglaze black lines under the leaves; the petals are outlined in gold. An inscription in overglaze black enamel reads:

> Continuing from spring
> And into summer;
> Emitting its fragrance duly.

Was Kenzan looking back to Kyoto as spring, and Edo as summer? The signature reads, "Inscribed and painted by Kyoto refugee Kenzan Shinsei at Tōei Shaji," and is followed by a written "Shōko" seal. Tōei Shaji signifies Rinnōji, the

Tendai-sect temple presided over by Kenzan's patron Kōkan; the bowl thus constitutes further evidence for the relationship between potter and prince. The ordinary shape, abrupt trimming of the foot, and premature glaze termination are typical of the Takahara kiln in nearby Asakusa. The Bishamondō provenance suggests that the piece was handed down in ecclesiastical circles.

Among all Kenzan ceramics, the Edo pieces possess the most succinct set of diagnostic features. This is ironic, since an assessment of Kenzan's Edo style has never been attempted. The content and style of the signature are especially helpful. In contrast to his earlier, long Chinese-inspired signatures identifying him as a potter of "Great Japan," on the Edo pieces, Kenzan frequently prefaced his name with "Karaku," "Heian Jō," and "Keichō" — poetic equivalents for Kyoto. The stronger focus on Kyoto reflects the fascination that his Edo patrons and indeed, most Japanese living outside the city, had for the ancient capital. The "Kenzan" signature itself is strong and consistent (refer to the set of *tanzaku* plates just discussed for a good example), and structurally represents a continuation of the mark seen in the *katamukōzuke* and *sukashibachi* from the last years in Kyoto. The radical and stem of the *ken* now occupy an equal amount of space. The *zan* is tightly integrated with the *ken,* and the first stroke of the *zan* — the vertical member in the middle of the character — is brushed off center to the right. This is a subtle but reliable feature of late production. Other diagnostic features include use of a simplified character *sho* (written by) and the character *ga* (painted by). Kenzan frequently painted a "Shōko" seal on these late works as well.

Besides identifying his origins on these late pots, Kenzan was also eager to claim his current whereabouts: the pieces are variously inscribed "at Edo," "at Tōei Shaji," "at Nagasaki," and "at Sano." Here is a hint that Kenzan, inspired by a long tradition of Japanese religious and literary pilgrimage, had embarked on one of his own. Like Bashō and other great poets, Kenzan used his creations to mark physical place and cultural spaces of the past simultaneously. As he moved across the landscape of eastern Japan, he also traveled though moments in Japanese tradition, ranging from Teika poetry to Raku-ware ceramics. There was also a personal poignancy in the journey eastward: Edo had been a home for his now-departed brothers, and Sano was his mother's birthplace. The late ceramics, then, testify to a final visit to places both poetic and personal — more of that "world in a mouthful."

PAINTING

In Kyoto, in the shadow of his talented brother, Kenzan lacked the conviction to paint. In Edo, however, he was seen as heir to the Kōrin tradition — and there is even evidence that he endeavored to pass the mantle on. *Ogata Ryū Ryaku Impu* (Brief Compendium of Ogata-School Masters), published in 1815 by Edo painter Sakai Hōitsu, mentions Tatebayashi Kagei, originally a doctor from Kaga (Ishikawa Prefecture), who first came to Edo under the name of Shirai Sōken; he was a student of Kenzan and the "third-generation Kōrin." Hōitsu's sequel edition of *Kōrin Hyakuzu* (A Hundred Kōrin Pictures), published in 1826, states that in the ninth month of 1738 Kenzan gave Kagei an album of fans that Kōrin painted after the style of an even earlier Rimpa predecessor, Sōtatsu. As a physician, Kagei may have been a person of some cultivation, a likely participant in the circle of haiku poets and amateur painters frequented by the master. Those art-loving companions probably encouraged Kenzan to manifest his cultivation in painting and calligraphy, and though he may not have had dazzling manual skills to show his admiring hosts, a combination of personal cultivation and certain technical propensities would enable him to produce images of freshness and power.

Kenzan's painting calls to mind the Japanese axiom *Daikō wa setsu naru gotoshi* — great skill, at a glance, appears unskillful. Despite its unstudied appearance, Kenzan's brushwork has garnered countless admirers, its appeal stemming from the fact that there is no obvious leavening of skill or finish. One might imagine that he disregarded technique altogether and just took simple pleasure in making the work. Such an approach to painting naturally invites comparison with that of his older brother Kōrin. Where Kōrin's brush is sharp, quick, and light, Kenzan's is rather ponderous. Such a difference may well be attributed to differences in character as well as degree of professional training, but there are other factors. Whereas Kōrin was a painter who occasionally worked in the crafts, Kenzan came from a thirty-year sojourn in crafts to the world of painting proper.

As we discussed in the opening chapter, the incremental nature of production, task specialization, and the intractability of the materials used in ceramics, textiles, and lacquerware are impediments to spontaneous personal expression. As a potter Kenzan had succeeded in overcoming many of those limitations, but the need to harmonize all the design elements demanded, as a rule, painted decoration that was simple and impersonal. Paradoxically, when translated back into painting proper, such a style appears very personal indeed. Kenzan further personalized his painting with poetic inscriptions; what is unusual about these inscriptions, however, is that they were appended to a mode of representation that had for centuries progressively shed itself of obvious reference to literature. When mated with simplified motifs, Kenzan's calligraphy is intrusive if not overwhelming. This reworking of the relationship between painted picture and written word is one of the peculiar achievements of Kenzan the painter.

Kenzan's method of composing a painting was also informed by his work in ceramics. Almost all the decoration in Kenzan ware was done in small formats, such as flat plates and cylindrical tea bowls. The painting on such objects had to spread horizontally. Since Kenzan made very few tall forms like flower vases and water jars, he never developed vertically oriented compositions. When translated into painting proper, we see a predilection for small square and horizontally oriented rectangular formats. Kenzan avoided the tall hanging scroll, and when he worked with it, there is a sense of discomfort.

A rigorous analysis of some three hundred extant "Kenzan" paintings — taking into account formats, materials, subjects, composition, brushwork, and content and style of inscriptions, signatures, and seals — suggests two authentic clusters: a polychrome Japanese style inspired in some measure by Kōrin, and a monochrome Chinese style with roots in Zen painting and salon amateurism. We begin with characteristics of the former:

> format: small hanging scrolls; possibly some tall scrolls and
>   folding screens
> materials: thick mineral pigments on paper
> subjects: poetic themes and Rimpa-style flowers and grasses
> inscriptions: Japanese poetry
> signatures: typically "Shisui (violet verdure) Shinsei"
> seals: typically "Tōzen" (oblong relief), "Shūseidō" (oblong
>   intaglio), "Shinsei" (square relief), "Reikai" (square relief)
>   (for other Kenzan paintings see Appendix 3, Group 17)

A theme familiar to Kenzan is seen in a set of album leaves illustrating Fujiwara no Teika's *waka* poems of birds and flowers of the twelve months (fig. 102). The twelfth-month leaf is signed, "Copied by Shisui Shinsei [Kenzan], age eighty-one," which would date the work to 1743, the last year of the artist's life. Teika's calligraphy and poetry have already been seen to occupy a prominent place in the art of Kenzan as well as his Ogata forebears. Teika was also popular with Bashō's followers, who may well have been sponsoring these paintings. In this set, an interest in contour and color juxtaposition over naturalism, use of highly stylized motifs, such as Kōrin's sinuous water pattern, and the occasional use of the *tarashikomi* blotting technique all suggest the decorative Rimpa painting tradition inaugurated by Sōtatsu and brought to new heights by Kōrin. Kenzan's composition is even inspired by Kōrin sketches: designs for medicine cases (*inrō*) for the first, sixth, and seventh months, preserved in the Konishi papers, are close to these versions (fig. 103).

102. Wild pinks and cormorant, originally from a set of twelve album leaves depicting Fujiwara no Teika's poems of birds and flowers of the twelve months.

103. Ogata Kōrin: Wild pinks and cormorant.

For all its precedents, this set represents one extreme of the Rimpa painting tradition. The pictorial elements are flattened and simplified like ceramics decoration, and have the same plane and contour arrangements seen in the Chōjiyamachi bowls and plates. Just as the white slip patches create a compositional anchor in the ceramics, here the ink wash, which variously suggests mist, hillocks and water, performs a similar function. Set among these planes are barely believable trees, birds, flowers, and architecture depicted in arbitrary scale and languid brushwork. The sense of flatness and fatness conveys the peculiar spatial (on three-dimensional objects illusionistic painting is redundant) and material world of the ceramics decorator. One could easily envision these paintings wrapped around tea bowls.

Crowding the painting is Kenzan's inscription:

Sixth month

Chinese pink (*tokonatsu*)

I even miss the weather of this parched month,
Usually spurned for its hot sun,
Because it is the month when the Chinese pink,
"Of everlasting summer,"
Comes into bloom.

Cormorant (*u*)

As swiftly as the flares disappear
Upstream in the river where the cormorants fish
On this short summer night
This month of parched weather, too,
Will soon be gone.[8]

Painting and calligraphy have been combined in various ways in the history of Japanese art. In Chinese-influenced religious and literati painting, the inscription is typically placed in a carefully chosen block of space in the upper part of the picture. In the indigenous tradition, calligraphy permeates painting: in the *uta e* tradition the script may be scattered asymmetrically, and in the *ashide e* style it may be hidden among pictorial elements. While Kenzan was probably cognizant of those traditions, his writing is exuberant, even intrusive — it dances in and around the painting. Never in the *uta e* tradition had delicacy been so summarily abandoned.

The perennial theme of Japanese poetry and painting, "iris bridges" (*Yatsuhashi*, figs. 104, 105), also provided a vehicle for Kenzan's calligraphic appetite. The picture is simple: Eight horizontal strokes in a silvery ink form the plank bridges and a few malachite stalks and azurite blossoms depict the irises. Even the subtle sense of movement provided by Kōrin in his famous versions of the theme is absent here — this is a ground for calligraphy. The inscription, from the ninth chapter of the classic *Tale of Ise*, begins from bottom right:

104 and 105. Iris Bridges (*Yatsuhashi*, above) and detail of signature and seals (right).

Someone glanced at the clumps of irises that were blooming luxuriantly in the swamp. "Compose a poem on the subject, 'A Traveler's Sentiments,' beginning each line with a syllable from the word 'iris' [*kakitsubata*]," he said. The man recited:

Karagoromo	I have a beloved wife
Kitsusu nareneshi	Familiar as the skirt
Tsuma shi areba	Of a well-worn robe
Harubaru kinuru	And so this distant
	journeying
Tabi o shi zo omou	Fills my heart with grief.[9]

The casual touch and scattering technique recalls the writing on the Teika pages. In the lower left corner, the signature "Shisui Shinsei" obscures oblong and rectangular intaglio seals reading "Shūseidō" and "Shinsei," respectively, the former suggesting that Kenzan was recalling his scholar-gentleman days at the Shūseidō hermitage. If Kōrin's famous *Iris* screens in the Nezu Institute for Fine Arts, which show nothing but the flowers against an empty ground, do the most to deliteralize the *Ise* episode, Kenzan here effects something of a restoration.

Another side of Kenzan's Rimpa-style production is seen in a pair of panels decorated with hollyhocks in the Cernuschi Museum, Paris (figs. 106, 107). Though surely inspired by

106 and 107. Hollyhocks (above) and detail of signature and seal (right).

Kōrin's supple renditions of these flowers, Kenzan's composition is a stark collage. On a gold-leaf ground, two isolated clumps of flowers sink below the frame while the third is positioned in the upper right-hand corner. The sense of artifice is acute: contours are hard and geometric, the stems straight, flowers round. Here the painter has transformed Kōrin's original to the point that it is no longer a copy. Kenzan's inclination toward bulk, lucidity, and artifice, a legacy of his work in thick pigments on space-denying vessel surfaces, emerges fully here.

Other large paintings attributed to Kenzan are problematic. These are, typically, tall hanging scrolls with flowers and grasses as a subject. Most have rather anemic *waka* inscriptions in the open space at the top of the picture. Outlines are heavy, and colors are thick and decorative. Many of them show Chinese-style "host-and-guest" compositions, where a tall element, usually a tree, looms over a smaller animal or flower. This type of composition does not appear in the work of Kenzan's Rimpa forebears, but it occur frequently in work by "Edo Rimpa" painters of a century later, especially Sakai Hōitsu and his circle. Was Kenzan the founder of this later

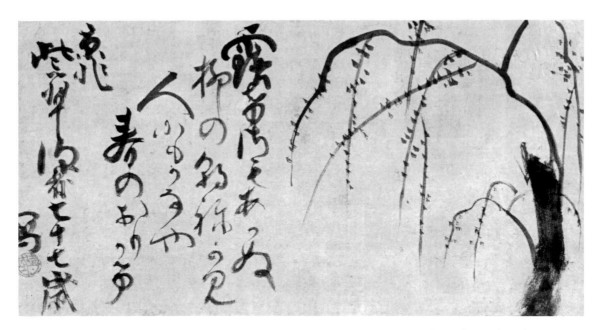

108. Willow in Spring.

109. Signature and seal.

Edo Rimpa style, or were the tall scrolls attributed to Kenzan really late Edo and Meiji productions?

Hōitsu's *Kenzan Iboku* (Extant Painting of Kenzan), published in 1823, reproduced some thirty-three works attributed to the master — many of the tall scroll type — and provided the first survey of Kenzan's brushwork. In contrast to this public Kenzan discourse by Hōitsu is a private one — all of his other documentation on Kenzan paintings, which encompasses box writing and authentication certificates, is for smaller monochrome paintings.[10] Hōitsu sparked a general interest in Kenzan and, by extension, an interest in fabricating Kenzan works. The Kenzan manner imparted the impression that "anybody could paint like that," and it seems that a good number of people picked up the brush to see if that was true. A number of the aspirants were surely painters and enthusiasts in the Edo Rimpa circle of Hōitsu — and it is not inconceivable that Hōitsu himself was involved. I suspect that many of the tall scrolls, including the famous *Flower Baskets,* come out of this mileu.

Kenzan's vision embraced not only the Rimpa manner but the monochrome style favored by the aristocrats, monks, and tea masters of the early seventeenth-century Kyoto salons:

format: small hanging scrolls
materials: ink on paper

subjects: legendary Zen figures and Chinese "gentleman"
    subjects
inscriptions: Japanese poetry
signatures: include "Sanjin" (Dissipated person) and
    "Itsumin" (Refugee)
seals: "Tōzen" (oblong relief), "Furiku" (round relief)
(for other Kenzan paintings, see Appendix 3, Group 17)

Willow in Spring, like most of Kenzan's monochrome ink subjects, is a small, horizontally formatted hanging scroll (figs. 108, 109) whose subject is a single willow tree occupying the right half of the painting. The willow trunk, branches, and leaves are painted with a worn brush in the *tsuketate* manner, which uses single lines for each element rather than building the elements out of bounding lines, washes, or texture strokes. The ink is dark and dry.

The inscription, covering an inordinately large section of the painting, reads:

> Gazing upon the tangled willow strands,
> Lustrous with morning dew,
> I am reminded
> Of her hair —
> And of that spring.

110. Rectangular plate with design of willow.

The key to this unusual balance of picture and word lies in Kenzan's ceramics, particularly a simple type of *kakuzara* made by his workshop late in the Chōjiyamachi period (fig. 110). The gradual enlargement of his script for decorative purposes has obviously spilled over into his painting.

Willow in Spring also constitutes a good example of Kenzan's late calligraphy style. The individual character construction and internal rhythms can be compared with the 1738 lamentation for Prince Kōkan (fig. 77). In the script of both documents, line contours are softer, with little internal modulation and less exposure of the brush tip. Kenzan was still a strong writer, but now without excess embellishment.

Also bearing short, brusque inscriptions are a number of small monochromes; we illustrate *Raizan* (Chinese: Laican) *Roasting Yams* (figs. 111, 112). Raizan, a legendary monk of the Tang dynasty, was famous for his refusal of all official enoluments. Like other Zen heroes, his nobility is rooted in

111. Monk Raizan Roasting Yams.

nothingness; he is typically pictured cooking yams over a fire of dung chips. The inscription reads:

If you are hungry,
And in need of sustenance,
Just roast a yam
And eat it!
That's all there is to it.

These compositions are rooted in the amateur tradition of the Kyoto salons of the first half of the seventeenth century. Similar subjects can be seen in work by Kanō Tan'yū, Shōkadō Shōjō, Sen Sōtan (1578–1658), Karasumaro Mitsuhiro, Konoe Nobutada, and Takuan Sōhō (1573–1645). Paintings become more abbreviated, more amateurish, and more humorous with each generation of Zen painters. Kenzan's ink paintings seem to fall within that tradition; they are hardly as elegant as Shōkadō nor quite as reductive as the nineteenth-century monk Sengai.

There is nothing in the Kenzan calligraphy tradition that prepares us for such haphazard composition and character execution. The arbitrary enlargement of certain *kana* is without

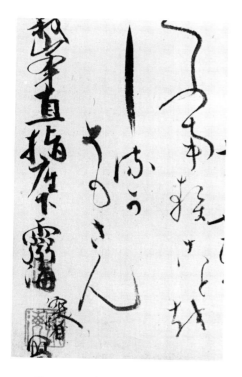

112. Signature and seal.

precedent. The brush tip is exposed with greater frequency, and a very willful pull of the brush in the last strokes of certain characters is unusual. As for the painting style itself, we have little with which to compare it. The figure style is in general rooted in the Zen salon tradition; the occasional addition of *tarashikomi* is a Rimpa feature, and the small facial features in the figures are reminiscent of stylizations by Kōrin. In the absence of any other comparative material, an attribution to Kenzan can be made only with caution. The paintings certainly represent one extreme of Kenzan's art.

In his pottery manual Kenzan had referred to gatherings of patron-cum-amateur artists (*ozashiki*). Surely in the Fukagawa haiku circles there were all types of *ozashiki,* including functions dedicated to painting. Although Kenzan would not be summoned as a specialist painter, to see him as a participant, making a few quick sketches covered with exuberant calligraphy, requires no stretch of the imagination. Despite inevitable bouts with the infirmities of old age, even at eighty-one he was painting and inscribing ceramics. Those works appear fresh, youthful. Even if Kenzan was not skillful, a bright spirit seeps out between each line of his calligraphy, between each flower and rock in his painting.

1. Leach 1966, 91. City gazetteers variously attribute the birds' origin to Mount Hiei in Kyoto or the Tokugawa mausoleum at Nikkō. See Paul Waley, *Tokyo Now and Then* (Tokyo: Weatherhill, 1984), 156.

2. Hirotani 1943, 94.

3. Suzuki Hancha, "Kenzan no Fūkai" [Musings of Kenzan], *Nihon Bijutsu Kōgei* 198 (1955), 14.

4. Aimi Kōu, "Kenzan no Edo Gekkō ni tsuite" [Concerning Kenzan's Trip to Edo], *Tōsetsu* 55 (1957), 16.

5. Mitsuoka 1973, 102.

6. Robert H. Brower and Earl Miner, *Japanese Court Poetry* (Stanford: Stanford University Press, 1961), 246–47. With the permission of the publishers, © 1961 by the Board of Trustees of the Leland Stanford Junior University.

7. Translated in Helen C. McCullough, *Brocade by Night: 'Kokin Wakashū' and the Court Style in Japanese Poetry* (Stanford: Stanford University Press, 1985), 395–96. With the permission of the publishers, © 1985 by the Board of Trustees of the Leland Stanford Junior University.

8. Translated in Kamens, 30.

9. Translated in Helen C. McCullough, *Tales of Ise: Lyrical Episodes from Tenth-Century Japan* (Stanford: Stanford University Press, 1968), 75. With the permission of the publishers, © 1986 by the Board of Trustees of the Leland Stanford Junior University. The *ba* syllable in kakitsubata is the same as the *ha* in the poem: its position in the word causes it to be aspirated.

10. The *Iboku* is reproduced in Gotoh 1982, 59–63. For Hōitsu's authentication certificates and box inscriptions, see Gotoh 1982, 161–65.

Chapter Six
THE TRADITION

113. Ogata Ihachi: Water jar *(mizusashi)* with design of birds, butterflies, and imperial chrysanthemum.

114. Signature on base.

Ogata Kenzan's personal cultivation and uncanny assimilative vision were not assets that could be willed to followers. Yet there is ample evidence for not one, but two lines of successors — one in Kyoto and one in Edo. This seeming anomaly leads to the question of what constituted a tradition in Kenzan's day. Here too one encounters a bifurcation — between an orthodox transmission of skills and knowledge passed down within kinship lines, and the purchase of these rights by amateurs. The latter trend, which began in the seventeenth century, is demonstrated in Kenzan's acquisition of the Ninsei manual. And just as Kenzan helped to fracture the notion of a legitimate succession in Japanese ceramics, his own legacy would be subject to multiple interpretations.

There are at least three reasons to consider the later "Kenzans" in detail. First, their ceramics, painting, and antiquarian activities all shed light on the original master. Second, they assist in authentication: their pots provide a chronology of style, showing how Kenzan was perceived in a given period. These period styles help us in locating and dating forgeries. Third, the followers constitute a remarkable group in their own right. The art name "Kenzan" was passed between dilettantes and artisans and was even inherited by a non-Japanese. While an admiration for Ogata Shinsei is the common thread, the diversity of interpretation makes the Kenzan tradition one of the most fascinating in Japanese ceramics. The later Kenzans — and the scholarly mediators of the tradition — provide more than a two-and-a-half century requiem for a single master.

OGATA IHACHI AND THE KYOTO KENZAN SCHOOL

115. Ogata Ihachi: Tea bowl with design of pine, bamboo, plum, and imperial chrysanthemum.

116. Signature inside foot ring.

Kenzan did not work alone during his years at Chōjiyamachi in downtown Kyoto. His pottery manual *Tōji Seihō* mentions a son, Ihachi: "I have passed [my techniques and style] on to my son Ihachi, who is making both high- and low-temperature ceramics in front of the Shōgoin temple in Kyoto, east of the Kamo River." Another eighteenth-century reference to Ihachi appears in a 1750 genealogy in the Konishi archive, in which Kōrin's son, now using the name Konishi Hikoemon, lists one "Ogata Ihachirō" as a cousin. *Sumidagawa Hanayashiki*, a pamphlet produced in 1820 by Kenzan revivalist Sahara Kikuu, states that late in life, Kenzan adopted Ninsei's son Ihachi, who was referred to as second-generation Kenzan. Kikuu adds that Ihachi's son moved to Edo to serve a samurai, bringing the ceramics line to an end. Since Ninsei's first son was already listed as a kiln owner in the 1670s, it is more likely that Ihachi was a grandson of the famous master.

The key to identifying Ihachi's work lies in the *Tōji Seihō* statement that Ihachi was working in front of the Shōgoin temple in east Kyoto. Shōgoin, a Buddhist temple of the Tendai sect and headquarters for the mountain-climbing Shūgendō cult, was founded in Iwakura north of the city in the ninth century and moved to its present location in 1090. Not long after, it became a temple headed by a tonsured imperial prince (*gomonzeki*). Destroyed in the mid-fifteenth century Ōnin Wars, the temple was rebuilt at Karasumaru Shimotachiuri a century later, and in 1690 was moved back to the present site. A list dated 1863 shows that it had the fifth-largest revenue among twenty-four imperial temples.[1] Kenzan would have had an entrée to Shōgoin either through Nijō Tsunahira, his longtime supporter in Kyoto, or his late-life patron, Prince Kōkan. Thirty-ninth Shōgoin Prince-abbot Chūyo (1722–88) was Kōkan's nephew.

A collection of pots passed down in the Shōgoin can be linked to Ihachi. Three styles are represented: *Kōchi* (sometimes called cloisonné or *fahua ware*), a glazed earthenware with design zones bounded by raised threads of clay (figs. 113, 114); *ai e* (literally indigo picture), a transparent glazed earthenware with underglaze designs in a rich fritted cobalt inspired by Delft ware from Holland (figs. 115, 116); and Raku ware with painted designs on a white reserve ground (figs. 117, 118). Significantly, the original Kenzan pursued none of these styles. In comparison with a signature of his adoptive father's (fig. 119),

117. Ogata Ihachi: Black Raku tea bowl with design of flaming jewel.

118. Signature on opposite side.

119. "Kenzan" signature from *Tōkō Hitsuyō*.

Ihachi's "Kenzan" signature shows some divergent traits: it is smaller in scale; it is less tightly composed; the fourth stroke of his *ken* is exaggeratedly pulled to the right; and the first stroke of his *zan* shows a pronounced horizontal orientation before turning downward.

These facts alone, however, are not enough to identify the Shōgoin potter as Ihachi. Indeed, all of the pieces are signed "Kenzan," not "Ihachi." The missing link is found in an *ai e*-style tea bowl with a design of pine, bamboo, and plum in the collection of the Enshōji nunnery at Obitake, Nara (figs. 120–122). The matching box for this piece, inscribed by the third-generation heir Gosuke, reads, "Made by second-generation Ihachi." The white-buff clay body, the painted decoration, lead glaze, and the signature of the Enshōji piece match the specimens in the Shōgoin. A similar signature is found on another *ai-e* piece, a cylindrical food dish, dated to the Enkyō era (1744–48), which began a year after Kenzan died (figs. 123, 124). The evidence points to Ihachi as the producer of the Shōgoin group, and since the sixteen-petal imperial chrysanthemum appears on some of those pieces, he was probably patronized by prince-abbot Chūyo.

Having identified Ihachi's signature style, we consider evidence for a father-to-son transmission, beginning with numerous square and rectangular plates painted in underglaze iron; a set of such pieces identical to one illustrated here (fig. 125) has a box dated 1724. As we have seen, the *kakuzara* decorated with underglaze iron painting, calligraphy, and border patterns were among the mainstays of the Kenzan workshop. These Ihachi plates continue the concept, but with conspicuous changes in detail. First, in place of the elaborate edge patterns such as arabesques and lattices are highly simplified floral rosettes on the outside and mere dots or short wavy lines on the inside. Second, the painting and inscriptions occupy an equal amount of space; in earlier Kenzan pieces, the relationship was about seventy percent painting to thirty percent calligraphy. Third, the brushwork is deliberate, even clumsy. Fourth, the poems are reduced to a minimum of characters, and the same verses appear repeatedly. Fifth, because of the repetition and the attempt to reproduce what must have been an original Kenzan model, the calligraphy lacks an original flourish. Sixth, instead of the typical "Shinsei" in the signature only *Sei* is written, followed by a simplified character *sho* (written by). Seventh, the

120. Ogata Ihachi: Tea bowl with design of pine, bamboo and plum.

121. Signature inside foot ring.

122. Box inscription (signed and sealed "third-generation Kenzan, Gosuke").

seals read "Kenzan" (relief) and "Shinsei" (intaglio) rather than the original "Tōin" and "Shōko." The overall impression is a compression — or even caricature — of those earlier Kenzan classics.

These monochrome pieces also have a connection to a person working alongside Kenzan and Ihachi: Watanabe Soshin, whom we first encountered at the Narutaki kiln as a decorator for Kenzan's classical flat plates. A square plate with orchid design (figs. 126, 127) features a Kenzan inscription on its verso: "This group was painted by Watanabe Soshin, who works for me when I am tired. He is very skillful. Written by Kenzan Sei." This plate has the same simple flowers and short wavy lines on the raised edges as do the Ihachi versions, but the seals here, although barely visible in photographs, are a small "Shōko" and a large "Tōin" relief seal. A good number of square and rectangular plates bear these particular seals, and quite possibly they reflect the painting (and writing?) of Soshin working along with Ihachi in the second quarter of the eighteenth century. A pottery manual attributed to Ihachi, *Tōki Mippōsho* (Secret Pottery Manual), makes explicit reference to "Watanabe" as a source of painted designs for the ware.

Other Kenzan-inspired designs by Ihachi include four-sided plates with planed surfaces (*kanname zara*), cylindrical tea bowls with paintings and short inscriptions, and *kawarake*. In certain sets of *katamukōzuke* some of the signatures appear to be by Kenzan and some by Ihachi. Where was this collaboration taking place? It is widely assumed that Ihachi joined Kenzan at the Chōjiyamachi workshop, but father and son may have moved out to the Shōgoin together. Only a person with Kenzan's connections could have established a pottery workshop under imperial aegis. It may be that the new facilities at Shōgoin inspired Kenzan to go beyond decorating blanks to designing the *katamukōzuke* and *sukashibachi* that seem to date to the third decade of the eighteenth century. A decade or so of Kenzan-Ihachi collaboration at the Shōgoin now seems a distinct possibility.

The direction of Ihachi's work after Kenzan's departure is found in the abovementioned *Tōki Mippōsho*, now in the collection of the National Diet Library, Tokyo. Although the manual is a late eighteenth-century copy and finishes only with the signature "Kenzan," the general opinion is that the original author, who alludes to "my predecessor [that is, the original

123. Ogata Ihachi: Cylindrical food dish with floral designs.

124. Signature inside foot ring.

Kenzan]" in the text, was Ihachi. An epilogue mentions that Nunami Rozan (1718–77), the founder of the Banko kiln in Kuwana, Mie Prefecture, had gone to Kyoto for study under Omotesenke-school tea master Sen Joshinsai (active 1730–51); during that stay Rōzan received the pottery manual from one Seigo, a disciple of "Kenzan." Rōzan's period in Kyoto would seem to coincide with Ihachi's heyday.

The contents of the *Tōki Mippōsho* portray Ihachi as more of an artisan than a designer. There are instructions on how to calculate for shrinkage; how to make square and rectangular plates; how to mold small containers; how to formulate glazes for Raku ware, with special emphasis on making black Raku ware with reserved white sections for painting; and how to use the bellows in firing black Raku ware. The same emphases are found in works attributed to Ihachi. Flat square and rectangular plates, small incense containers, and Raku tea bowls form the bulk of his work. There is little interest expressed in high-temperature ceramics (the author advises that pieces be brought to the Awataguchi climbing kiln for glazing and firing) and no mention at all of the stoneware glazes learned from the Ninsei workshop.

Formulas and procedures can be passed from master to apprentice, but inspiration cannot be transmitted, even from father to son. To a certain extent Ihachi had been able to absorb and continue a manner of design by working alongside his adoptive father, and that probably accounts for his modest success (suggested by the large number of surviving pieces

125. Ogata Ihachi: Square plate with design of pine.

from his hand). The distance between the abilities of the first generation and later followers becomes especially obvious in the generations following Ihachi's death, which probably occurred early in the second half of the eighteenth century. For a larger Ihachi group, see Appendix 3, Group 12.

Almost nothing is known about Kenzan-ware production in Kyoto in the mid- to late-eighteenth century. One possible Ihachi follower — or competitor — is Kempō. His *ken* is the same as Kenzan's, but he cleverly obscured the lower half of the *pō* character with a seal, causing the exposed remainder to read *zan.* At a glance, then, his signature reads "Kenzan." His extant works include rectangular or square plates with five- or seven-character inscriptions and simplified motifs like pine, plum, orchid, or mountain hermitage (figs. 128, 129). These attributes, coupled with the floral rosette and short wavy border

126 and 127. (Above) Square plate with design of orchid and rock, painting by Watanabe Soshin; and (right) inscription and signature on verso.

128 and 129. (Above) Kempō: Square plate with design of cherry blossoms, and (right) signature and seal.

130. (Above) Gosuke: Incense container in shape of auspicious mallet with design of pine branches.

131. (Above right) Signature inside cover.

132. Takahashi Dōhachi: Food vessel with design of maple leaves on the Tatsuta River.

133. Nin'ami Dōhachi: Bowl with openwork design of snow-laden bamboo.

patterns, are close to plates by Ihachi, although Kempō's calligraphy and painting are harshly stylized. Around the same time, the Kenzan style was taking root in regions adjacent to Kyoto. The Hira kiln in Shiga Prefecture, reputed to have been started by a disciple of Ninsei, produced Kenzan-style wares with flowers-and grasses decor in underglaze cobalt and iron. The Yanase kiln on Shikoku, operating from the first half of the eighteenth century, produced similar pieces.

Information on Ihachi's successor, the third Kyoto Kenzan, comes mostly from his inscriptions on the boxes containing his pots. They suggest that his personal name was Gosuke, with possible aliases being Miyata Yahei and Zōrokudō. Mentions of Taigadō, the hermitage of Kyoto literati painter Ikeno Taiga (1723–76), and of Kenzan's Narutaki, hint that he was a Kyoto resident. As for his period of activity, one box inscription states that in 1842, the year celebrated as the hundredth anniversary of Kenzan's death, Gosuke produced a series of incense containers fashioned from Narutaki clay. Gosuke's production consists chiefly of small, painted earthenwares like *kawarake* and incense containers, with a variety of decorative schemes (figs. 130, 131). Although some specimens are incised with a pointed instrument, the characteristic "Kenzan" mark used by Gosuke is painted. The first two strokes of the *ken* are thickly brushed and the rest are thin. The fifth stroke is reduced to a dot. The *zan* has a forceful first stroke but as a whole is compressed.

A general economic revival at the very end of the eighteenth century made ceramics production in Kyoto feasible on a larger scale, and the concept of Kenzan style was redefined. *Sencha*, the manner of steeped-tea drinking which had been imported from Ming-dynasty China, and had found a wide following among sinophiles in Japan, stimulated new kinds of production — including porcelain. Although Kenzan had experimented with porcelain early in the eighteenth century, Okuda Eisen (1753–1811) is traditionally credited with producing a viable porcelain product in the Temmei era (1781–89). Eisen's limited production portrays him as a hobbyist, but he produced a group of distinguished students: Aoki Mokubei (1767–1833), Kinkodō Kamesuke (1764–1837), and Nin'ami Dōhachi (1783–1855). Nin'ami's father Takahashi Dōhachi (1740–1804) made at least one Kenzan imitation, a set of *katamukōzuke* with motifs of the Tatsuta River (fig. 132), and Nin'ami left numerous food utensils in a Kenzan style. Most numerous are his large bowls which, in the manner of Kenzan's *sukashibachi*, combined openwork designs with decoration in white slip, underglaze pigments and overglaze enamels (fig. 133). Some of these bear "Kenzan" marks, others "Kenzan" and "Dōhachi" marks, and others just "Dōhachi" alone. In addition to his Kyoto production, Nin'ami made many Kenzan-style pieces during his stay at the Sanuki kilns in Kagawa Prefecture, Shikoku, in 1832 and 1851. We shall also see that Nin'ami's younger brother Ogata Shūhei (1788–1839) came into contact with the Kenzan tradition in 1819 through Edo dilettante Sahara Kikuu.

Slightly younger contemporaries of Dōhachi, such as Kiyomizu Rokubei (1790–1860), Makuzu Kōsai (1796–1851), and Seifū Yohei (1803–61), also focused on highly decorative permutations of Kenzan food vessels (figs. 134–136). In many cases, they used their own kiln marks along with the "Kenzan" signature. This kind of activity demonstrates that Kenzan had become another stock design for the Kyoto stoneware industry. When I worked in the Gojōzaka potters' quarter in the early 1980s, some of my neighbors specialized in these copies, known locally as Kenzan *utsushi*. Although there was no sense of intellectual dishonesty in following the style — indeed, their

134. Seifū Yohei: Bowl with design of chrysanthemums.

135. (Below) Makuzu Kōsai: Bowl with design of peonies.

136. (Right) Impressed seal and signature on verso.

169

products were priced as food vessels and not as "art" — some of them were marked with the "Kenzan" signature alone, prompting the suspicion that they might reappear in the future as newly discovered "original" masterpieces.

In contrast to Kyoto, where Kenzan's legacy was perceived in terms of designs and techniques, the Edo school showed a distinct concern with Kenzan's amateur spirit, and how it might be perpetuated in a series of titleholders. The most complete evidence for a Kenzan succession in Edo is a document called *Kenzan Sedaigaki* (Genealogy of the Kenzan School; fig. 137), compiled in 1836 by Nishimura Myakuan, an Edo landlord, amateur artist, and fifth-generation Kenzan heir.

SAKAI HŌITSU AND THE EDO KENZAN SCHOOL

Kenzan Sedaigaki

First Generation: Ogata Shisui Shinsei; he accompanied Junkō [Prince Kōkan] to Edo;
Disciple, second generation: Kenzan Jirōbei, a person from Iriya;
Disciple, third generation: Miyazaki Tominosuke, also from Iriya;
Fourth generation: Ukean [Sakai] Hōitsu;
Fifth generation: Kasenan Myakuan Sōsen, living in Kinryū-zan [Sensōji in Asakusa, Edo].

1836, sixth month, twenty-fourth day

In Chapter 5, we demonstrated that the Kenzan style was spread from Kyoto to Edo in the early 1730s by Ogata Shinsei himself. The Iriya kiln, where Kenzan is thought to have worked, was within the precincts of the Rinnōji temple and was, according to the early ninteenth-century gazetteer *Shimpen Musashi Fudoki Kō*, manned by farmers who worked part time at making tile and *kawarake* for the temple and shogunate. The new designs from Kyoto must have made a startling impact on the local potters, leading to the emergence of the Kenzan tradition outlined in the genealogy. In the absence of direct evidence that Kenzan himself designated an Edo heir, we turn to Jirōbei, who according to Myakuan's genealogy was Edo Kenzan II. The name Jirōbei appears as Kenzan's landlord in *Ueno Ooku Goyōnin Chū Kampō Watari On Nikki*, a document introduced in the last chapter. Yet there is not a single pot

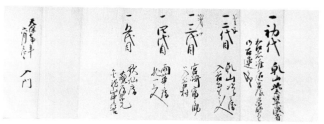

137. Nishimura Myakuan: *Kenzan Sedaigaki* (Genealogy of the Kenzan School).

138. Minzan: Hand warmer with design of chrysanthemums.

139. Signature on base.

bearing the Jirōbei mark, and in a letter (introduced below) transmitting the title from "second-generation Kenzan" to "disciple" Miyazaki Tominosuke, the name Jirōbei is nowhere to be seen.

In contrast to these documentary references, there is artifactual evidence that a potter named Minzan assumed the second-generation Edo title. A pair of hand warmers passed down in the Takizawa collection, Tochigi Prefecture — one marked "This was made by Minzan in imitation of former Kenzan" and the other marked "Third-generation Kenzan" — testify to Minzan's place in the tradition. A similar Minzan piece, whose decor of chrysanthemums is curiously similar to designs by Ihachi, is illustrated here (figs. 138, 139). Yet a number of pieces with the "Minzan" signature in the Morse collection, Museum of Fine Arts, Boston, suggest that Kenzan imitations were only one part of Minzan's production, which seems to have centered on imitations of Delft earthenware. It would all be quite convenient if Minzan were found to be a pseudonym of Jirōbei, but alas, such evidence is wanting. Other works collected around the Edo and Sano areas bearing signatures like "Ōzan," "Chōzan," and "Rokuzan" provide evidence that wealthy hobbyists — possibly Isshian Rankei and Minakami Rosen, who received Kenzan's pottery manuals, or Shōji Dōnusai and Sakamoto Beishū, with whom Kenzan may have enjoyed poetry — had assumed the *zan* character out of admiration for the master. Minzan may have been one of them.

The third-generation Edo successor, according to the genealogy, was Miyazaki Tominosuke, from Iriya village. A letter dated 1766 and published in the painting history *Koga Bikō* provides corroboration: a "second-generation Kenzan" relates that he had received verbal instruction in pottery techniques prior to the master's death, and would pass them to his disciple Miyazaki Tominosuke, who had asked to carry on the tradition. There is one other early mention of Tominosuke on a box

140. Workshop of Miyazaki Tominosuke: Hand warmer with design of cherry blossoms.

141. Signature on base.

142. Era mark on underside of lid.

containing the poems that the original Kenzan wrote in lamentation for his patron, Prince Kōkan: "A letter of transmission from Iriya Kenzan, a hanging scroll and other documents inherited from Haru, the wife of Miyazaki Tominosuke." The front of the box bears the date 1823, first day, twelfth month. It would appear since his wife had the materials as of 1823, Tominosuke himself was already dead. Tominosuke's workshop must have continued making "Third-generation Kenzan" pots after his death, because there are pieces dated to the Tempō era (1830–44), such as a glazed earthenware hand warmer in the Museum of Fine Arts, Boston (figs. 140–142).

Sakai Hōitsu's (1761–1828) brief reign as the fourth Edo Kenzan is shown not only in the *Kenzan Sedaigaki* but in a letter he wrote in 1824. Hōitsu states that he is giving the title and a package of papers (technical manual and Kenzan poems) to Myakuan who, according to the letter, had more interest in ceramics. Hōitsu's fascination for Kenzan's older brother Kōrin is well documented. As far back as 1807, Hōitsu had written to the Konishi, asking for an Ogata-family genealogy. Hōitsu used the material to compile his 1813 *Ogata Ryū Ryaku Impu* (Brief Compendium of Ogata-school Seals), a single-sheet print featuring seals, signatures, and biographical sketches of the Kōrin-school masters. The *Impu* was reproduced in booklet form in 1815, the year celebrated as the hundredth anniversary of Kōrin's death. Around that time Hōitsu also resolved to refurbish Kōrin's grave, and to that end he sent a confidant, Sahara Kikuu, to Kyoto in the autumn of 1819.

Kikuu (1762–1832) was a successful antique dealer turned dilettante who presumably became acquainted with Hōitsu at the Shin Ume Yashiki (New Plum Cottage, later called Hyakkaen, or the Hundred-Verse Garden), Kikuu's retreat in the Mukōjima section of Tokyo. Besides seeing to the installation of a new Kōrin gravestone in Kyoto, Kikuu began to take an interest in Kenzan. His diary, *Umeya Nikki,* records that he obtained from the Konishi three hundred and sixty original Kōrin sketches and a pottery manual passed down from Hon'ami Kōetsu to his grandson Kūchūsai Kōho and on to Kenzan. Kikuu furthermore sought out and studied ceramics with Ogata Shūhei, younger brother of the famous Nin'ami Dōhachi, and when Kikuu returned to Edo in 1820 he brought with him six potters: Shūhei, a "Seiji Kamejirō" (perhaps a pseudonym of Kinkodō Kamesuke), Kiyomizu Rokubei, and three apprentices. In the fifth month of the same year they helped Kikuu open the Sumidagawa kiln in Mukōjima. Was Kikuu not playing Kenzan to Hōitsu's Kōrin? In doing so, Kikuu may have encouraged a Kenzan revival, for Shūhei's brother Dōhachi produced Kenzan copies, with and without his own signature; that also may have been the case with the Sumidagawa ware team. To commemorate the opening of the Mukōjima kiln, Kikuu issued a pamphlet entitled *Sumidagawa Hanayashiki* (Flower-Cottage on the Sumida); the Kenzan genealogy contained therein is important, especially in light of the author's earlier access to the Konishi archive in Kyoto.

Although there is little to attest to Hōitsu's interest in ceramics, it is likely that with the return of Sahara Kikuu from Kyoto in 1820 and the subsequent opening of the Sumidagawa kiln in Mukojima, Hōitsu visited the Shin Ume Yashiki and occasionally painted a few pots. Hōitsu, of course, preferred Kenzan as a painter, as he confessed in his 1823 *Kenzan Iboku* (The Surviving Work of Kenzan; fig. 143), a block-printed catalogue illustrating thirty-four paintings, four calligraphies, and five pots attributed to the master. Having discovered that Kenzan's grave was located at the Zen'yōji temple in Sakamoto, close to his own lodgings in Negishi, Hōitsu decided to commemorate Kenzan, who along with Kōrin was a "great painter." Hōitsu commissioned a memorial tablet, which still stands at Zen'yōji, and used his sketches of Kenzan works as the basis for the commemorative catalogue.

The financial backing for this event came from another Hōitsu acquaintance, Ōsawa Nagayuki (1769–1844), scion of a wealthy family of cotton-goods merchants from Gyōda, present-day Saitama Prefecture. A letter dated 1724 in the Ōsawa family archives, now in the Gyōda Municipal Library, reveals that Hōitsu and Nagayuki consulted closely about the paper for the *Iboku*, the type of stone for a commemorative stele, and the style of calligraphy for its inscription. Nagayuki also purchased a majority of paintings in the *Iboku*, as shown in a 1928 auction catalogue of the Ōsawa collection. One wonders if the production of these paintings had in some way been instigated by Hōitsu himself. A rush of "Kenzan" paintings submitted to the Sumiyoshi family of professional authenticators in Edo also coincides perfectly with Hōitsu's revival. As mentioned in the last chapter, many of the paintings attributed to Kenzan are, in theme and composition, closer to the manner

143. Sakai Hōitsu: Page from the *Kenzan Iboku*.

of Hōitsu than the mid-eighteenth century style. There is, after all, a fine line between a connoisseur and a forger. As Lothar Ledderose has written, "Both try to understand as precisely and completely as possible the creative and technical potential for a formal artist."[2]

Nishimura Myakuan (1784–1853) became Edo Kenzan V upon receiving the title package from Hōitsu on the twenty-eighth day, first month of 1824. He was forty-one. According to an 1837 version of *Kōeki Shoka Jimmeiroku* (Dictionary of Miscellaneous Trades for the Common Weal), Myakuan made his living as a brothel owner in the pleasure district of Yoshiwara. The record states that his proper name was Sahei and he used the art names Saiin Sōsen and Kasen; he was a connoisseur of tea utensils and calligraphy. As the *myaku* in his favorite nom-de-plume hints, he also considered himself an exponent of the Sammyakuin school of calligraphy initiated by courtier Konoe Nobutada (1565–1614).

The motives for Myakuan's involvement in the Kenzan tradition are unknown, but the letter transmitting the title from Hōitsu alludes that the younger man had professed an interest in ceramics. Myakuan probably visited the Kikuu salon and took an interest in the Sumidagawa kiln. While there are no extant pots marked with "fifth generation" or other Myakuan aliases, a few glazed earthenware pieces do bear a Kenzan signature similar to that seen on his *Kenzan Sedaigaki*. In the early 1830s, Myakuan passed his business interests on to his son and retired to a hermitage in Asakusa called Hitomarudō. According to a sequel volume of *Kōeiki Shoka Jimmei Roku* published in 1842, a "sixth-generation Kenzan," pseudonym Gengensai, was the second son of Myakuan. Thus it would appear that Myakuan had passed the title on to his own son. Later, Gengensai was adopted by Yoshiwara landlord Takeshima Nizaemon, and in 1916 a Takeuchi Kyūichi mentions having received "Takeshima Kenzan Raku ware" from his grandfather.[3] Besides this single mention, there is no trace of Gengensai's production; it could be that he too pursued ceramics as a hobby. In terms of sheer production we shall see that Myakuan's real protégés were Ida Kichiroku (1791–1861), Sakune Benjirō (active from 1840–45), and Miura Tōtarō (1821–89), to whom he had granted the respective titles Kensai, Kenzō, and Ken'ya in 1836. The granting of the full

144. Ida Kichiroku (Kensai): Square incense container with design of chrysanthemums.

145. Signature on base.

Kenzan title thus ended with Myakuan or his son, but the Edo Kenzan style was about to undergo a spectacular revival.

Ida Kichiroku was the quintessential wandering artisan — *nagare shokunin*. The 1920 ceramics history *Taisei Tōshi* is the most comprehensive source of information on his career. He is believed to have come from Shimōsa (Chiba Prefecture), Kaijō district, Nunoma village; in 1799 he moved to Edo, where he became an apprentice to an ash and curio merchant named Kobayashi Sōbei. An interest in curios would propel Kichiroku toward opening, in 1825, his own ceramics work-shop in the thriving open-air market of Kuramae. Although plastic has now replaced clay as the preferred material, the place is still a mecca for toy and doll wholesalers. Sometime after 1830, Kichiroku relocated his shop within the precincts of the Sensōji temple in Asakusa. The move was hardly prompted by ecclesiastic yearnings. Asakusa, the geographic locus for the late Edo Kenzan school, began to thrive as an amusement center after the so-called Long Sleeves fire of 1657, when it became a midpoint between the city proper and the newly situated Yoshiwara pleasure district. The kabuki the-atres were exiled there in 1841 in the wake of the moralistic Tempō reforms. The booths along Shin Nakamise, the avenue leading up to the Sensōji gate, continue to purvey exotic (as well as tawdry) curiosities similar to those of Kichiroku's era. Kichiroku had the opportunity to display his skills before eleventh Tokugawa shogun Ienari (1773–1841), and conse-quently his reputation soared.

A certificate from the hand of Nishimura Myakuan, now in the collection of the Ishii family, reveals that in 1836 Myakuan, who had retired to his Hitomarudō in Asakusa, gave Kichiroku the art name Kensai and instruction in Kenzan's pottery techniques. This honor, along with the shogunal audience, would seem a prelude to a successful and stable career. Yet Kichiroku left Edo in the twelfth month of that year. Traces of employment at Sano (Tochigi Prefecture), Nagasaki (Nagasaki Prefecture), Izawa (Mie Prefecture), and Bushū (Saitama Prefecture) portray him as a wanderer. Extant wares by Kichiroku, variously marked "Kensai," "Kichiroku," and "Kitsuroku," range from finely crafted glazed earthenware figurines and incense boxes to rather coarse stonewares, many of them in a Kenzan style (figs. 144, 145). After some three decades on the road, Kichiroku made his final return to Edo in

1859. He stayed with Ken'ya, who at that time had lodgings in the Date clan retainers' quarters in Asakusa, and died on the twenty-fifth day, fifth month, in 1861.

The second person who received a name from Myakuan in 1836 was Sakune Benjirō, or Kenzō, an Imado potter who was active from 1840 to 1845, according to Edward S. Morse.[4] A report by Takeuchi Kyūichi maintains that Kenzō started out working in a tradition of lacquerware known as the Ritsuō style, famed for its attention to detail and rich vocabulary of decorative materials, including shell, gold and silver, and glazed ceramics.[5] The originator of this skill, Ogawa Haritsu (Ritsuō; 1663–1747), was a disinherited samurai from Kuwana, Ise (Mie Prefecture). After moving to Edo, Haritsu developed skills in lacquer, inlay, and painting; he joined the Bashō poetry circle and, according to the 1878 *Kōgei Shiryō*, he even studied ceramics with Kenzan.

Little more is known of Kenzō except that he worked with third *ken* recipient Ken'ya at the Hatano kiln in Odawara. A number of pots passed down in the Kajiyama family, whose ancestor Ryōsuke (1836–1920) started the Hatano enterprise, attest to the Kenzō style. They include sensitively modeled celadons and white wares as well as Raku and Kenzan-style pieces. Besides signatures such as "Made by potter Kenzō," he also used the mark "Shōkoen Shun Shijō." Shōkoen was the name of the Kajiyama villa that was adjacent to a central market called Shun Shijō.[6] This provides identification for a spouted bowl decorated with a Kenzan-style water pattern in the Morse collection in Boston, marked "Made at Shōkoen at Shun Shijō" (figs. 146, 147). When Ken'ya moved to Yokosuka in 1871, Kenzō was not with him. He appears to have stayed in Hatano, and may have died sometime before the kiln was destroyed by fire in 1877. According to Ken'ya's daughter Yone (1861–ca. 1945), Kenzō was a likeable character, fond of food and drink, and like Ken'ya's family, he lived in perpetual poverty.

Ken'ya, or Miura Totarō, was the third and most famous *ken* recipient. For sheer drama, his career rivals if not surpasses that of the original Kenzan. The major sources on Ken'ya are the recollections of his daughter Yone and the diary of Ken'ya's adopted son Ishii Kenko as related by his son, the well-known painter Ishii Hakutei (1882–1958).[7] An illegitimate child, Ken'ya was adopted by an aunt, Take, and from the age of

146. Sakune Benjirō (Kenzō): Spouted bowl with design of flowing water.

147. Signature on side panel.

twelve assisted Take's husband Kichiroku with ceramics. This led to the encounter with Nishimura Myakuan; in 1836 Ken'ya received a title along with his two fellow potters. When Kichiroku left at the end of that year, however, Ken'ya was pressed into supporting the family. He made figurines and small vessels during the day and peddled them in the evenings. Late in life Ken'ya showed his daughter Yone a huge callus on his shoulder, saying that this was the souvenir of his days toting the peddler's bag.

Ken'ya's early struggles in Asakusa were alleviated around 1840 through an encounter with accessory merchant Maruya Rihei, of nearby Ningyōchō. Impressed with Ken'ya's skill in crafting small objects, Rihei urged Ken'ya to study under a Ritsuō-style lacquerer named Kanjirō; Ken'ya also practiced painting under Fujimori Bunkaku, a disciple of the more famous master Tani Bunchō (1763–1840). Fellow painting students included Suzuki Gako (1816–70), whose son Ken'ya would later adopt, and Kajiyama Ryōsuke, whose Hatano kiln would later employ Ken'ya. Ken'ya's fortunes improved, and he began to receive orders from tea practitioners and even daimyo.

In 1845 Ken'ya married Ei, a daughter of the Ishii family of Fukagawa, and was adopted into the family as a male heir. The Ishii, known by their business name Nigenjaya, had become wealthy in the thriving Fukagawa restaurant trade; one of their properties, the Iseya, catered to the crowds drawn to the Tomioka Hachiman Shrine, the cultural nucleus of the district. By the time of Ken'ya's adoption, the Tempō sumptuary laws had slowed the restaurant business, and Ken'ya's father-in-law Yasuemon had retired to collect and recreate the folk painting known as Ōtsu *e* under the name Busshin. Ken'ya constructed a kiln in Busshin's garden, and printed an opening flyer:

> Sets of tea-ceremony utensils, decorative objects, writing implements, personal accessories and Ritsuō lacquerware; or I will make items to your order; I will also fire these objects at a venue of your choosing. Ishii Ken'ya, Kenzan-style potter located at Fukagawa Tomioka Shrine.[8]

Despite Ken'ya's surging career, attested to in ledgers preserved in the Kajiyama family, Ken'ya fell out with his mother-in-law, Tsuma, renounced the Ishii name in favor of his original Miura, and in 1847 moved with Ei to Sangemmachi, Asakusa. His work continued at that location until 1853, when it was interrupted by two important events: the death of supporter Nishimura Myakuan, and the arrival of the American "black ships," commanded by William Matthew Perry. Ken'ya went to Uraga to view the foreign visitors, and was so overwhelmed by this glimpse of Western technology that he seems to have secured from his daimyo patrons an opportunity to study two radically new fields: shore defense and naval architecture. In 1854 he was sent to Nagasaki along with the naval hero Katsu Kaishū (1823–99) to study Western shipbuilding and navigation techniques. He returned to Edo a year later to petition the shogunate of the necessity of building a Western-style ship. Since Ken'ya could neither write nor draft, he explained his plans to scribes, who copied them down. To satisfy skeptics who maintained that an ironclad would immediately sink, Ken'ya floated a saucepan in a basin of water.[9]

While pleas to the shogunate went unheeded, the Date clan invited Ken'ya to Sendai (Miyagi Prefecture), where in 1856 he began construction of Japan's first ironclad steamship, the *Kaisei Maru*. In the seventh month of the following year, with the clan lord in attendance, the ship was successfully launched. As a reward, Ken'ya received a one-hundred-twenty-share rice stipend, a house in Sendai, and a place in the clan lodgings in Asakusa, Edo. This was Ken'ya's finest hour. He spent the rest of 1857 working as an industrial consultant in Hokkaido and Sendai. In the course of assisting enterprises in the latter, Ken'ya granted Tsutsumi-ware potter Shōji Genhichirō Yoshitada (1822–95) the name Kemba (*Ken*, pronounced *Kem* when combined with *ba*, the character for horse), along with a pottery manual and other items still preserved in the Hariō family of Tsutsumi-ware potters. Part of the inheritance is a scroll entitled *Tezukuri Chawan Kokoroe* (Hints on Handmade Tea Bowls), inscribed:

> "My student requested this so I will copy it out. A tea bowl should be neither heavy nor light; it should have form yet also be formless. It should, however, always be naturally rounded; it is not objectionable if it becomes deformed in the process of making. Allow it to move freely, like a gourd dangling in the wind; [sealed] Ken'ya."[10]

These words were not without relevance to Ken'ya's own life. He had risen from penury to the position of domain advisor, but like the metaphoric gourd, he too would dangle in the winds of fortune. The Tokugawa shogunate was falling, its many weaknesses exposed by the foreign incursions. Unstable conditions — some of the more recalcitrant domains were now in open revolt against the central government — made further modernization nearly impossible. In the twelfth month of 1865, Ken'ya was suddenly released from his position with the Date clan. He borrowed heavily from the Ishii family and invested one thousand *ryō*, a huge sum, in an attempt to corner the silver market. As a result of the panic attending the Toba-Fushimi battle in Kyoto in 1868, however, the silver market collapsed. Ruined, Ken'ya boarded a foreign ship in Yokohama and fled back to Sendai. For reasons unknown (although his Date-clan affiliation and boarding a foreign vessel may have been a liability in restoration politics), in 1868 he was imprisoned for treason. This was a crime generally punishable by death, but he was allegedly saved by his son Kenko, whom he had adopted from the family of painter-friend Suzuki Gako in 1859. Kenko is said to have visited the jail every day to beg for his father's release. Moved by this display of piety, the warden granted Ken'ya a pardon.

Just when Ken'ya's fortunes seemed to be at their worst, his old painting companion Suzuki Gako prevailed upon Kaji-yama Ryōsuke to open a kiln for Ken'ya in Odawara. Ken'ya visited this Hatano kiln over thirty times in a two-year period. In an article on Ryōsuke and the Hatano kiln, Nakano Keijirō maintains that the potters used a dark gritty clay from Togawa, north Hatano, and a good number of surviving Ken'ya stone-wares have just such a clay. The kiln made not only decorated vessels but kitchen mortars and even electric insulators.[11]

Information on Ken'ya's post-Hatano movements comes from his daughter Yone. In 1871 the Meiji government requested Ken'ya to open an electric insulator factory in Izumi, Yokosuka (Yokohama). It employed fifty workers, and while Ken'ya was away his wife Ei acted as supervisor. The factory was unable to fill orders promptly, however, and went bankrupt after one year. Then Ken'ya moved to Kosuge, Senjū (now part of Tokyo), where he opened a factory that produced brick and glass. That too quickly went out of business. Finally, Ken'ya secured space in a samurai residence at Takahashi, Fukagawa,

148. Miura Ken'ya: *Inrō* with design of iris bridges (*yatsuhashi*).

149. Signature on base.

and attempted to make enameled porcelain for export. He went bankrupt within six months. All of these projects were underwritten by the Ishii family, which sold its extensive real estate holdings to support Ken'ya's pipe dreams. Ishii Kenko, by then family head, refused to bankroll Ken'ya any longer and in 1875 set him up at Chōmeiji, Mukōjima, with a minimal stipend. Ken'ya was fifty-five.

Ken'ya's daughter Yone recalled her father saying the following about ceramics: "I couldn't have endured this poor life had I known that all I was going to become was a potter." His stipend was insufficient to support frequent bouts of drinking, and to obtain some cash Ken'ya even pawned the Kenzan materials that he had inherited from his early mentor, Mya-kuan. These included a pottery manual, Kenzan's lamentation poems for Kōkan, Kenzan's death poems, and letters of transmission from successive Edo Kenzan title holders. Incidentally, if the contents of the manual that Ken'ya granted his Sendai disciple Kemba are any indication, the techniques passed down in the Edo Kenzan line stem not from the original master, but from Ihachi. The Kemba manual is a perfect match with Ihachi's *Toki Mippōsho*. In any case, Ken'ya never assumed the title. His apparent lack of interest reflects his broader aspirations — aspirations that were never fulfilled. One is reminded of other visionaries of the era, like painters Shiba Kōkan (1747–1818) and Watanabe Kazan (1793–1841), and potter-painter-inventor Hiraga Gennai (1726–79), whose Westernizing dreams variously ended in despair, insanity, and premature death. The space between two worlds is a lonely one.

Ken'ya's ceramics, which survive in considerable numbers, exhibit a distinctive "Edo mood." Fine ceramic vessels were always available from well-established pottery centers, so the small-scale Edo workshop had to focus on other items. Potters turned to production of figurines and lead-glazed earthenware facsimiles of expensive lacquer and metal accessories. This suited the raffish Edo townspeople, who found humor and a certain coquettishness in the copies. A scarcity of dated Ken'ya wares relegates his stylistic development to the realm of conjecture. I have not encountered dated works from the years at Asakusa and Fukagawa, but since Ken'ya had trained in a precision technique like Ritsuō lacquer and had attracted daimyo patrons, it might be surmised that some of the

150. Miura Ken'ya: Spouted bowl with design of spring and autumn foliage.

151. Signature inside foot ring.

152. Miura Ken'ya: Figurine representing auspicious female, *otafuku*.

153. Signature on back of figure.

medicine containers (*inrō*) and portable ink and brush holders (*yatate*) executed in non-Kenzan styles may be from that 1832–53 period (figs. 148, 149). Consistent with the craftsmanship is the style of the "Ken'ya" signature, written in a fine line without the mannerism of the later signature. The only pottery known to have been made by Ken'ya during his entrepreneurial period was at the Hatano kiln between 1869 and 1871. We have already identified some of the Hatano stoneware as a dark, gritty material, which matches a Ken'ya spouted bowl in the collection of the Metropolitan Museum of Art (figs. 150, 151). Dated pieces occur only in Ken'ya's final period at Chōmeiji, 1875–89. Here he continued to manufacture small glazed earthenware items such as *inrō, netsuke*, figurines (figs. 152, 153), toggles (*ojime*), ornamental hairpins, and a decorated bead called Ken'ya *dama*. Ken'ya's grandson Hakutei remarked that no matter how small the object was, Ken'ya would give it exquisite attention. Kanezaki Shimbi identifies *ojime* the size of a single rice grain that contain a "Ken'ya" signature.[12] Tea utensils and food vessels were decorated in the original Kenzan manner, frequently the broken field or *katamigawari* design seen in all of the Edo Kenzan masters. These works typically contain a thickly brushed, idiosyncratic "Ken'ya" signature, although some of them bear "Kenzan" marks as well (figs. 154, 155). While Ken'ya was surely the most dynamic figure in the Kenzan succession, his work shows little growth, suggesting that despite his considerable technical skills, the craft was pursued out of necessity.

Ken'ya left a large number of disciples, all of whom received the *Ken* prefix. According to Ken'ya's daughter Yone, Itō Sadabumi, or Kenkoku, was Ken'ya's assistant in his early days as a maker of Ritsuō-style lacquer. It is said that Ken'ya passed his Ritsuō designs, including one of a book shelf made for ill-fated government councillor Ii Naosuke, on to Kenkoku.[13]

Another Ken'ya disciple was Kemba (not to be confused with the Sendai Kemba mentioned earlier), originally Tsukamoto Torakichi, who joined Ken'ya at the electric insulator workshop in Yokosuka and remained with him until his death. The *ba* character of his name was written as Ken'ya's *ya*, but with one stroke removed — apparently because Kemba's painting was one level inferior to his master! In his later work, Kemba made the forms (figs. 156, 157) and occasionally hired Rimpa-style painter Nozawa Teiu to decorate.[14] Kemba also

154. Miura Ken'ya: Lobed food dish with design of pine in snow.

155. Signature inside foot ring.

signed some of his work with his master's name, and these pieces can be differentiated from Ken'ya's by the thickness of the form and crudity of the signature. Sometime after Ken'ya's death in 1889, Kemba moved to Seto, and then on to Kyoto. At the end of his life Kemba was in Inuyama, Gifu Prefecture, working for kiln owner Ōzeki Sakujūrō.[15] This Inuyama kiln had already achieved some fame for its Kenzan imitations, based not on any particular skill but for the fact that the characters for "Inuyama" can also be read as "Kenzan"; many Inuyama plates, bowls, and covered dishes decorated in a characteristic cherry and maple pattern bear a "Kenzan" signature (figs. 158, 159).

In a June 23, 1890, issue of the newspaper *Yamato Shimbun*, antiquarian Ōtsuki Joden (1844–1931) mentions three more Kenzan disciples: Kenzui, Kenshō, and Kensai. Of Kenzui nothing is known. Ken'ya and Okumura Kenshō worked together at the house of a wealthy merchant named Negishi in Kabutoyama, Yoshimi Village, Ōzato County, present Saitama Prefecture. The Negishi family preserved a few Kenshō designs and a pottery manual called *Kenzan Rakuyaki Hisho* (Kenzan Secret Manual for Raku Ware).[16] Kenshō also appears as the Kenzan-line representative in a one-hundred-fifty-year commemoration ceremony conducted by Ōtsuki Joden at the master's grave at Zen'yōji on June 2, 1892. Minami Shinji, who reported the event thirteen days later in *Yamato Shimbun*, related that Kenshō, initially from a samurai house in Daishōji fief, present Ishikawa Prefecture, was living in Sasanoyuki no Yokochō, Negishi. Ōtsuki Joden is said to have opposed Kenshō's aspiration to the Ken'ya title, which may have spurred the latter's move to Kyoto, where he worked under potter Miyanaga Tōzan (1842–1916).[17]

Kensai (written with a different *sai* from Kichiroku's Kensai) was Urano Shigekichi (1851–1923), known to posterity as the teacher of British potter Bernard Leach (1887–1979). According to *Hasu no Mi* (Seed of the Lotus), a 1981 memoir by his daughter Nami, Urano began training in glazed earthenware techniques in 1872 under one Kimbei, a pupil of Kenzō. A year later, he studied slip-casting — then a revolutionary forming technique — under German chemist Gottfried Wagener (1831–92). Kimbei introduced Urano to Miura Ken'ya in 1877. After his wife, Kenzō's granddaughter Ise, died, Urano married Yoshi, the daughter of pioneer Japanese pho-

156. Tsukamoto Torakichi (Kemba): Tea bowl with design of spring foliage.

157. Signature inside foot ring.

158 and 159. Inuyama ware: Dish with design of cherry blossoms and autumn foliage (above), and signature inside foot ring (right).

tographer Shimaoka Renjō (1823–1914). It was apparently Renjō who arranged to have Urano adopted by one Ogata Keisuke in 1901. Backed by a necrology preserved in the Empukuji temple in the Tokyo suburb Zushi in present Kanagawa Prefecture, Keisuke claimed familial descent from an Ogata Kenzan, whose son had moved to Edo. In all likelihood Keisuke's direct Kenzan ancestor was not Ogata Shinsei but Ihachi. It will be recalled that in his 1820 *Sumidagawa Hanayashiki*, Sahara Kikuu stated that Ihachi's son moved to Edo to serve a samurai, bringing the Kenzan line to an end. That would correlate with Keisuke's genealogy. After the adoption Urano used the name "Sixth-generation Kenzan."

Accompanied by Ogata Keisuke and his wife, Urano moved from his longtime home in Imado to Shin Sakamoto (Iriya) near Ueno Park in 1902. There he built a small earthenware kiln and a three-chamber climbing kiln for stoneware. In 1911, he began to tutor famous potters-to-be Bernard Leach and Tomimoto Kenkichi (1886–1963). Flood damage in that year forced Urano to abandon the large kiln in favor of a Western-style single-domed device with flanking square fireboxes. Five years later that kiln was moved to the estate of aesthetician and folk art doyen Yanagi Sōetsu in Abiko, Ibaraki Prefecture, for Leach's exclusive use. Over the next few years, Urano built a stoneware kiln at Kanami for a hobbyist named Andō Keizaburō, worked at the Hokuraian kiln in Mishima, visited Tomimoto Kenkichi in Ando, Nara, and worked at the Inuyama workshop of Ozeki Sakujūrō. He died in 1923, shortly after the disastrous Kanto earthquake.

Urano's production mirrors that of his master Ken'ya: *inrō*, figurines, and decorative objects, as well as food dishes and occasionally tea utensils in a Kenzan style (figs. 160, 161). His signatures include "Sixth-generation Kenzan," "Kenzan," and "Hokkei Kenzan." Hokkei, meaning "northern valley," probably refers to the Shin Sakamoto production, since the area constituted, at least in metaphor, a valley north of the palace.

Urano's daughter Nami (born 1899), with the backing of Bernard Leach, also produced limited amounts of wares signed "Kenjo" in the 1950s and 1960s. The distance between the first Kenzan and a latter-day follower such as Nami in the eyes of a Japanese connoisseur was revealed to me during a visit to Ōkōchi Kimitake (Fūsenshi), the aristocratic scion who once owned the famed Kōrin-Kenzan plate with a design of plovers over waves (now in the Cleveland Museum). As we chatted in Fūsenshi's cluttered study, I noticed a number of Ogata Nami tea-ceremony bowls on the windowsill — planted with geraniums. Nami has declared to have retired the Kenzan name, but if the last two centuries have been any indication, future generations will produce new aspirants to the title.

The Edo Kenzan revival was played out by the early twentieth century, but among all the participants Sakai Hōitsu emerges as the central figure. From a handful of clues, he assembled a corpus of information that would inform all future studies. He crafted an image of Kenzan the painter, and his followers kept that image alive through reproductions and commemorative activities. His dispatch of Kikuu to Kyoto would result in the organization of the Konishi archive and may have helped to fan the Kenzan ceramics revival in Kyoto. In Ōsawa Nagayuki, Hōitsu established the first major Kenzan collector. Hōitsu and Myakuan also revived the Edo Kenzan ceramics tradition, serving as a bridge between earlier practicing potters like Miyazaki Tominosuke and later ones like Miura Ken'ya. For all these contributions, only a few historical notes on Kenzan occur between Hōitsu's death and the end of the Edo period in 1868; the most important is *Koga Bikō*, compiled by Asaoka Okisada (1800–56). Although he does repeat materials from earlier publications, Okisada introduced testimony from a friend, Kan Kōgetsu, concerning Kenzan's last years: the master was alleged to have lived in the boarding house of timber merchant Sakamoto Beishū at Chikushimaya Rokkembori in the Honjō section of Edo.[18] After *Koga Bikō*,

160. Urano Shigekichi (Kensai; Kenzan VI): Water jar with design of willow.

161. Signature on opposite side.

however, the Kenzan notices are progressively brief and inaccurate, but the confusion speaks for the times. Foreigners had arrived in 1853 — Perry from America and Putiatin from Russia — with mandates to open the country. Treaties with England and America were concluded in 1854, followed by accords with Russia (1855), Holland (1856), and France (1858). Japan found itself thrust into global politics, which further imperiled stability at home. And "Kenzan" — by now very much a larger-than-life tradition — would go international.

JAPONISTES AND SCHOLARS

For all his revival activities, Sakai Hōitsu could never dream that Kenzan would be resurrected as an Impressionist. Yet that is precisely what happened as an enthusiasm for things Japanese — *Japonisme* — bloomed on the other side of the world. The signing of trade agreements in the late 1850s between Japan and the West meant that audiences in America and Europe could now see more than export-standard wares. Following exhibitions of strictly commercial Japanese products at world's fairs in London (1862) and Paris (1867), the Meiji government made its debut in Vienna in 1873 in a special pavilion that included samples of antique arts.

Vienna also marked a new era for Japanese crafts, especially those of Kyoto. From 1869, the Kyoto craft industry had lost both prestige and patronage with the removal of the emperor and the dissolution of the court nobility and the feudal domains. Unemployment in the pottery quarters exceeded fifty percent. The Vienna Exposition was seen as a place to learn new techniques and cultivate new markets; in 1873, potter Tanzan Mutsuo accompanied chemist Gottfried Wagener as part of a government-sponsored delegation to the exhibition. Upon his return to Kyoto, Tanzan instructed local potters in new techniques like slip casting and European-style overglaze enamels. As a result, Kyoto potters such as Tanzan Seikai (Mutsuo's father), Takahashi Dōhachi, and Kiyomizu Rokubei surged forward, winning prizes in the 1876 and 1878 world exhibitions. In a few short years, then, Kyoto had acquired an international reputation for ornate polychrome and gilded ceramics, a style congenial with European tastes during the first two decades of expanded relations. The frenzied, wholesale shift to export products may also mean that for the first time since Kenzan opened his workshop in 1699, wares after his style were not being fired in the Kyoto kilns. The hiatus, however, would be brief.

In 1876, the International Exposition was held in Philadelphia. Through the initiative of Augustus W. Franks (1826–97), the South Kensington Museum (now the Victoria and Albert Museum) asked Japan to send both antique and contemporary ceramics to Philadelphia; the museum would purchase the lot after the exposition. Considering the lush neo-rococo export standard that had prevailed, it was a bold step. Shioda Makoto (1837–1917) drafted a catalogue, which was translated by Asami Tadamasa. Presumably copies were available in Philadelphia in 1876, but the report was not compiled into book form until Franks issued an adaptation in 1880. Nevertheless, it was probably the Western reader's first taste of Kenzan:

> The kiln in Narutaki was erected by a brother of the famous painter Ogata Kōrin, named Shinsho [sic], who amused himself in his leisure hours by making tea utensils in imitation of Ninsei ware. The village of Narutaki, where was his residence, is situated at the foot of the hill of Atago, to the north-west of the Emperor's palace, or in the direction called "ken" in Chinese. On this account he was named "Shisui Kenzan," meaning "beautiful blue hill in northwest part." He died in 1742, in his eighty-second year, and his work is much esteemed by tea drinkers.[19]

The catalogue included three pieces attributed to Kenzan: a brazier (furo), a charcoal container (hiire), and a bowl for sweets; they can still be found in the storeroom of the Victoria and Albert Museum. In addition to the Philadelphia group, Franks exhibited and catalogued seven Kenzan wares for a show at the Bethnal Green branch of the South Kensington Museum in 1878; some of them are now in the collection of the British Museum. James Lord Bowes (1834–99) and George Ashdown Audsley (1838–1925) ventured a few comments about Kenzan in their 1879 Keramic [sic] Art of Japan.[20]

If the British had broken new ground in exhibiting Kenzan, it was the French who ventured criticism. Their contribution first appears in Samuel Bing's (1838–1905) chapter on ceramics for L'Art Japonais, the pioneering survey published by Louis Gonse (1846–1921) in 1883. Bing's source of information (and

of ceramic merchandise which he resold for immense profit)
was Japanese antiquarian Ninagawa Noritane (1835–82),
whose *Kankō Zusetsu* (Illustrated Discourse on Antiquities) was
circulating in Europe in a French translation. Bing himself was
quick to identify in Kenzan ware an expressive style marked by
richness of color and power of design — a power that, according to the author, distinguished originals from the many
copies.[21] Illustrated are four Kenzan wares; one of them, an
incense container, is on display in the Musée Guimet as of this
writing. The Impressionist flavor in Bing's essay also emerges
in an abridged version of *L'Art Japonais* published in 1886.
Author Gonse maintains that Kōrin freed Kyoto lacquerware
from the yoke of Tosa design and, together with Kenzan,
liberated the ceramics world of emulation of Chinese models.
Kenzan possessed a freedom of patternmaking with great
masses of strong shades, showing "the advantages of simplification." What "seems to be artlessness is really Kenzan's
solid talent."[22] Considering that French painters and designers
were studying the bold designs and fields of ungraded color in
Japanese woodblock prints, finding in them an alternative to
the allegedly lifeless standards of the official salon, Gonse's
remarks assume greater meaning. The link between Kenzan
and Impressionism was made explicit by Charles C. Holme in
a chapter on ceramics in *Japan and its Art:*

> [Kenzan] was a true impressionist, who sought in decoration
> for effects beyond mere mechanical detail of form — effects
> resulting from contrast or from harmony of color or material,
> from balance of composition and distribution of parts, or
> which exhibited power and freedom of the hand; and above
> all, in which there was ever-present the exalted poetic feeling
> characteristic of the master Art-work of Japan.[23]

In the years immediately following Holme's article,
Western-language notices on Kenzan were little more than
translated passages from Japanese sources. Then, in 1897, came
Kenzan: Beiträge zur Geschichte der japanischen Töpferkunst (Kenzan:
Commentaries on the History of the Japanese Ceramic Art),
arguably the most important publication on Kenzan in any
language prior to the postwar period. Dr. Justus Brinckmann
(1843–1915), first director of the Museum für Kunst und
Gewerbe in Hamburg and a champion of art and design

reform, conceived his book with the hope that Japanese craft traditions would serve as a model for a declining industrial art in the West. The book itself is something of a craft work, with thick green crepe on the cover and fine vellum and tissue papers within; the illustrations are executed from Japanese-style woodcuts. In seven chapters, Brinckmann exposed the state of the field in Europe and Japan and surveyed Kenzan's endeavors in tea ceremony, painting, poetry, and ceramics. These labors did not go unnoticed by the Japanese; the first chapter of *Kenzan: Beiträge* was translated by Sakiyama Gen-kichi and published in *Shoga Kyōkai Zasshi* (Painting and Calligraphy Society Magazine) in 1899. Brinckmann never visited Japan, and had to build his thesis around the question-able works then circulating in Europe, but he gracefully con-fessed that only "after many disappointments in regard to the value of our property will we obtain the knowledge of truth."

In counterpoint to Brinckmann's deepening of nineteenth-century Kenzan studies are the expansive efforts of American Edward S. Morse (1838–1925). Morse arrived in Japan in 1877, unmindful of the role he was to play in preserving the history of Japanese ceramics. His fateful encounter with pottery came about through his professional interest in marine zoology. During the long daily walks that a physician had prescribed for a digestive ailment, Morse began to stop at antique shops, attracted by the shell-shaped saucers used for serving sashimi. For Morse, the byzantine world of Japanese ceramics pre-sented a taxonomic challenge. Not that this was a completely new undertaking; whether it was Japanese ceramics or marine brachiopods, nineteenth-century scientists were ardent in their quest of evidence for a universal evolution of both biology and society. Japan and other cultures provided evidence for a lost heritage of the West — which of course was thought to repre-sent the highest stage of that universal development.

Morse soon entered a connoisseur's group both to enhance and exhibit his prowess. A favorite contest involved identifying the age and origin of a specimen while blindfolded. A desire for further instruction led him to antiquarian and dealer Ninagawa Noritane, whose oft-consulted *Kanko Zusetsu* we have already mentioned. Through Ninagawa's guidance (and to his profit, as he was the usual intermediary), Morse began to build a collection that would total nearly five thousand pieces, each classified according to Ninagawa's division of region (genus) and workshop or kiln (species). The entire group was sold to the Museum of Fine Arts, Boston, in 1892, and Morse's painstaking research was brought to a summation in a stupendous collection catalogue, published by the Riverside Press in 1901. The encyclopedic nature of Morse's collection is reflected in his Kenzan acquisitions, which are divided, in Ninagawa fashion, into groups from Yamashiro (Kyoto) and Musashi (Edo). In addition to the dozens of wares attributed to the original master, the inclusion and identification of Kenzan followers (e.g., Kenzan III, Ken'ya) and imitators (e.g., Seifū Yōhei, Kiyomizu Rokubei) offer the broadest range of comparative material in any collection in the world.

The mission of preserving Japanese culture through Western-style empirical scholarship — a trend abetted by Japonistes like Brinckmann and Morse — would continue to inform Kenzan studies in Japan in the first half of the twentieth century. The dedication to amassing tangible evidence is particularly apparent between 1913 and 1942, when almost all the primary sources for Kenzan's life and work were brought to light: the Konishi archive, the Narutaki kiln excavations, the Ninnaji and Nijō diaries, the Kyoto municipal record, and Kenzan's pottery manuals. These finds were organized and summarized by Fukui Rikichirō in a 1942 article entitled "Kōhon Kenzan Nempyō" (Tentative Kenzan Chronology).

In 1948, Kobayashi Taichirō embroidered Fukui's chronology into an interpretive biography entitled *Kenzan Kyoto Hen* (Kyoto Kenzan). Kobayashi cast a warm light on his subject. From his early years of immersion in belles lettres and Buddhist meditation, Kenzan embarked on a journey through the potter's world — one first marked by bold experimentation, but gradually descending into mass production, poverty, and obscurity. Kenzan's spirit, however, grew in inverse proportion to those declining material fortunes. This skillful blend of East Asian spiritual ethos and Western artistic angst attracted a broad following; *Kenzan Kyoto Hen* became the classic Kenzan, locking the field into a sentimental straitjacket for the next three decades. Publications from the decade following Kobayashi also show a narrowing of focus, as if to suggest that the broader issues had been resolved; they deal with specific topics such as Kenzan's milieu in a given period, his pottery techniques, or analyses of specific works. In each writing there is a deference, overt or subtle, to the Kobayashi version.

With so much of the Kenzan biography accessible, an increased interest in his oeuvre was to be expected; that trend was abetted by the volume of Kenzan wares trading hands and gaining media exposure. The number and type of objects attributed to Ogata Kenzan swelled dramatically during a Kenzan boom in the 1950s. Art exhibitions included Kenzan works in a spirit of de facto authentication: If the objects did not attract undue criticism or violate the Kobayashi "mood," they would become part of the orthodox corpus. The varieties of Kenzan wares that emerged — many never seen before — were adroitly fitted into the fable. Technically inferior or stylistically anomalous works were seen to express Kenzan's emphasis on "inner values"; more refined pieces reflected his inheritance of the Ninsei tradition or collaboration with the talented Kōrin. This spirit of compromise and fantasy formed the background for the even more fantastic development that would become known as "New Sano Kenzan." Few would deny that by the 1960s many imitations had penetrated the market, yet no one expected the sudden inundation of hundreds of pots and dozens of diaries claimed to be made by a seventy-five-year-old Kenzan during one year in the Japanese countryside.

1. R.A.B. Ponsonby-Fane, *Kyoto, The Old Capital of Japan 794–1869* (Kyoto: The Ponsonby-Fane Memorial Society, 1956), 360.

2. Lothar Ledderose, *Mi Fu and the Classical Tradition of Chinese Calligraphy* (Princeton: Princeton University Press, 1979), 58–59.

3. Quoted in Hancha, "Godai Kenzan Nishimura Myakuan — Part 5," *Tōsetsu* 60 (1958), 48–49.

4. Morse 1901, 304.

5. Quoted in Hancha, "Godai Kenzan . . . -5," *Tōsetsu* 60 (1958), 48–49.

6. Nakano Keijirō, "Miura Ken'ya no Hatano Gama to Kajiyama Ryōsuke" [Miura Ken'ya's Hatano Kiln and Kajiyama Ryōsuke], *Yakimono Shumi* VI:9 (1941), 8; the piece is in Morse 1901, no. 3771.

7. See Miura Yone, "Chichi Ken'ya o Kataru: Sono Ichi, Ni" [Talking about my Father Ken'ya: Parts One, Two], *Yakimono Shumi* 7:6 (1941), 3–6, 7:7 (1941), 12–15. For Hakutei's accounts, see Ishii Hakutei, "Miura Ken'ya," *Tōki Kōza* 5 (1935), 1–18; "Miura Ken'ya," *Tōji* 7:4 (1935), 13–17; "Tōkō Ken'ya no Hanashi" [Discussion of Potter Ken'ya], *Gasetsu* 28 (1939), 341–349.

8. Quoted in Nakano 1961, 26.

9. Leach, 1966, 160.

10. See Masui Kuniō, "Hakodate Ken'ya no Dembun o Jisshō Suru" [Hearsay Reports of Hakodate Ken'ya Proven], *Me no Me* 109 (1985), 78–84.

11. Nakano, 26.

12. Kanezaki Shimbi, "Miura Ken'ya," *Tōsetsu* 139 (1964), n.p.

13. From Takeuchi Kyūichi, "Ritsuō Zaiku Seisaku no Kōkeisha," quoted in Hancha, "Godai Kenzan . . . -Part 5," *Tōsetsu* 60 (1958), 48–49.

14. Ishii Hakutei, "Miura Ken'ya," *Tōki Kōza* IV (1935), 15.

15. Ōno Masato and Katō Tōkurō, "Kemba Monogatari" [Tale of Kemba] *Kobijutsu* 189 (1948), 3.

16. "Kenzan Rakuyaki Hisho Hakken no Kei-i" [Background of the Discovery of the Kenzan Rakuyaki Hisho], *Me no Me* 83 (1983), 38–39.

17. Ishii Hakutei, "Miura Ken'ya," *Tōki Kōza* IV (1935), 17.

18. *Koga Bikō*, vol. 35, 1558–59. By *Koga Bikō* we refer to Ōta Kin's revised and published edition of 1905 entitled *Zōtei Koga Bikō*.

19. Augustus Franks, ed., *Japanese Pottery — Being a Native Report* (London: Chapman and Hall, Ltd., 1880), 60.

20. For the Franks exhibition, see *A Collection of Oriental Porcelain and Pottery*, Lent for Collection by A. W. Franks (London: South Kensington Museum, 1878); For Audsley-Bowes, see *The Keramic Art of Japan* (London: Henry Sotheran and Co., 1879).

21. Samuel Bing, "La Ceramique" [Ceramics], in Louis Gonse, *L'Art Japonais* [Japanese Art] (Paris: A. Quantin, 1883), 288.

22. Gonse, *L'Art Japonais* [Japanese art] (Paris: Maison Quantin, 1886), 268–69.

23. Charles Holme, "Pottery and Porcelain," in Marcus B. Huish, *Japan and its Art* (London: Fine Arts Society, 2nd ed,. 1892), 237–38.

Chapter Seven
THE SANO KENZAN SCANDAL AND BEYOND

In early 1962, the Japanese art world was astonished to learn that several diaries and dozens of pots by Ogata Kenzan had been discovered in Sano, a village in what is now Tochigi Prefecture, north of Tokyo. An impressive array of authorities stood behind the finds, and for a short time it seemed as if an entire new chapter had opened on one of Japan's major artists. By mid-year, however, as the objects were exhibited and more details of their provenance became known, objections were raised from many quarters. As suspicions mounted, it became clear that New Sano Kenzan, as the affair came to be called, was a scandal of unprecedented proportions.

This concluding chapter will outline the genesis and development of the New Sano Kenzan scandal, introducing its personalities and products, and discussing why the latter should be regarded as recent fakes. More important, it will demonstrate how the scandal is symptomatic of larger issues that affect Kenzan studies: the impact of social hierarchies on art criticism; the tendency to favor external evidence in pronouncements of authenticity; the influence of scholarly and popular media on reproductions; and the general inaccessibility of art works in Japan. Finally, there is Kenzan himself. Is he a blameless object of appropriation, or is he in some way responsible for the many products issued in his name?

THE SCANDAL

Most Westerners know of Kenzan, and indeed of the Sano affair, through a book by Bernard Leach called *Kenzan and His Tradition* (1966). Leach relates that while visiting Japan in late 1961, he received an urgent message from a former assistant, Mizuo Hiroshi: over a hundred pots and three diaries by Kenzan had just come to light, and the anxious new owner, Morikawa Isamu, wanted an opinion. Leach hurried to Kyoto in January 1962 where, at a luncheon party, he viewed the finds — three bound diaries and a hundred twenty low-fired, lead-glazed wares with overglaze and underglaze decoration in Rimpa-derived themes of flowers and grasses. Sympathetic guests at the luncheon included Fujioka Ryōichi and Hayashiya Seizō, respective curators of the Kyoto and Tokyo National Museums. Leach described the moment:

> While we were eating the pots began to be brought in. Their beauty and breadth quite astounded me. As more and more pots, and the notebooks appeared, I stopped eating and Mr. Morikawa looked at me across the table and said, "Well?" I looked back at him and replied, "Not only do I think that they are genuine at first sight, but also that they are the finest group of Kenzan pots that I have ever seen." Mr. Morikawa jumped up from the floor and came round and shook my hand with tears in his eyes, for it turned out that he had been met with blank discouragement on the part of most dealers.[1]

Leach's endorsement provided an enormous boost for the Sano finds. His views were published in the *Asahi* newspaper, and other print and broadcast media, particularly the art magazine *Geijutsu Shinchō,* assiduously courted the public over the next six months. The genesis of the discovery was reported thus: some two years before the 1962 debut Hayashiya Seizō alerted Morikawa to a new cache of Kenzan wares at Yonemasa, a Tokyo art gallery; Morikawa visited the dealer and bought his entire stock of about forty pieces. Upon learning that the source was dealer Saitō Mototeru, who claimed to have purchased the pieces from old families in the Sano area, Morikawa proceeded to Sano to make direct purchases of pots and diaries from the same sources.[2] The notion of forgotten country heirlooms, coupled with the backing of Hayashiya, Fujioka, and Leach, was extremely persuasive. The movement for acceptance reached its apogee in June of that year, when

162. New Sano Kenzan ware: Rectangular plate with design of narcissus.

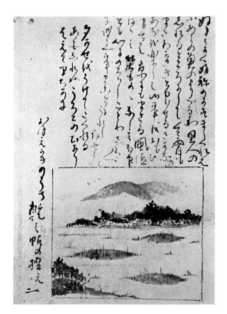

163. Page from New Sano Kenzan diary.

Morikawa's New Sano Kenzans were exhibited at the Tokyo branch of the Shirokiya Department Store; enormous crowds gathered there and at a second venue at the Daimaru Department Store, Osaka, one month later.

But opponents were also emerging. The first public objection was raised in January 1962 by Ashiya (Hyōgo Prefecture) collector Yamada Kōan, who denounced Morikawa for selling four New Sano Kenzan pots for seven million yen. This sum was comparable to those quoted for the finest Kenzan wares, arousing the ire of dealers who knew that Morikawa had obtained the pots for a mere fraction of the sale price.[3]

The Nihon Tōji Kyōkai (Japan Ceramics Society), an association of collectors, dealers, and enthusiasts whose monthly journal, *Tōsetsu* (Ceramics Explained), carried numerous articles denouncing New Sano Kenzan, formed the nucleus of the opposition. On March 12, 1962, this group held an open meeting at which four major questions were raised. First, there were simply too many pieces — by this time more than three hundred pots (fig. 162) and seven diaries had been found (fig. 163). Second, the provenance was dubious. No pieces in the New Sano style had ever been found in previous years, and there were inconsistencies in the testimony of former owners. Third, there were anomalies in the contents of the diaries — for example, seasonal references accorded with the Western solar calendar rather than the lunisolar calendar of Kenzan's day. Fourth, the style of calligraphy on the pots and in the diaries did not at all match accepted standards of Kenzan's writing.[4]

A painter, Kase Tōho, was the most strident critic; from pots and paintings widely accepted as authentic Kenzan products he compiled a table establishing which ideograms Kenzan preferred to use in phonetic Japanese writing, and contrasted those choices with selections in the New Sano diaries. He also questioned the paper used for the diaries — *gasenshi,* a fine artist's paper and an unusual choice given that common *hanshi* was the usual choice for diaries and sketches.[5] Yamaguchi Guro expressed doubts about the worm holes (*mushikui*) in the Sano diaries, observing that since each trail began with a scorch mark, they were probably burned through the paper.[6]

The New Sano supporters pluckily volleyed back, even producing technical evidence for their treasures. They quoted a finding by a physics seminar at Chiba University that the soiling of the pottery showed antiquity, and potter and testing institute specialist Yoshitake Eijirō testified that the pots were of the same clays used by "Kenzan's teacher, Ninsei."[7] This was seen to match a passage in the Sano diaries stating that some of the clays were ordered from Kyoto.

Such claims were apparently unconvincing. As Idegawa Naoki observed in his recent review of the Sano affair, by the end of 1962 the initiative belonged to the critics; the supporters had fallen silent. Over the following years, the whispered but near-unanimous opinion was that the New Sano Kenzans were recent forgeries.[8] The once-celebrated discoveries gradually fell prey to that peculiarly Japanese form of conflict resolution: *mokusatsu*, or "murder by silence."

Silence may have been an effective antidote in 1962, but in the past decade New Sano Kenzan documents and pots have begun to circulate again, and in greater numbers than ever before.[9] It should be clearly stated that, like the pieces from the 1960s, these recent issues are patent forgeries. The question remains, however, why authorities were seduced by the obviously false Sano Kenzan materials. How could trained specialists ignore the objections raised by the opponents? How could they overlook the modern materials like chrome oxide in the pottery pigments, or an influence from the contemporary *nihonga* style in the paintings on the pots and in the diaries? Who, or what, is authoritative in the domain of Kenzan studies? In addressing these questions, we single out four factors that have shaped the Kenzan field as a whole.

First, the initial support for New Sano Kenzan was based on the reputations of its supporters. Fujioka and Hayashiya were respected museum officials, and Bernard Leach was an heir to the Edo Kenzan line. In Japan, the art object is perceived not as autonomous, but as an inseparable part of a historical and social nexus. "Intrinsic" qualities of beauty or genuineness are secondary in importance to the authority of past and present owners and admirers — an authority believed to be vested in the objects that these persons own or otherwise champion. This is why art criticism as we know it in the West (although Western art criticism is certainly not immune to these forces) has not taken root in Japan. As Kōmoto Shinji recently stated, "[in Japan] a critical statement [about art] is often understood as an attack on a person's humanity. The safest way to express a critical view is to go around a subject."[10]

164. Sakai Hōitsu: Detail from sequel edition of *Kōrin Hyakuzu* (A Hundred Kōrin Pictures).

165. Square plate with design of heron.

In light of its apologists' renown, *mokusatsu* was the only effective treatment for New Sano Kenzan.

Second, if historical and social contexts are important, it only follows that materials that establish and sustain those connections will be carefully regarded. In the case of Japanese ceramics, box inscriptions, certificates of connoisseurship, and other accoutrements play such a role. The New Sano diaries performed this function; since the handwriting in the New Sano diaries matches that on the New Sano pots (both supporters and detractors agreed on this), the former conveniently becomes proof for the latter; indeed, sketches of many New Sano pots appear in the diaries.[11] The emphasis on peripheral items is also reflected in the boxes that accompanied the New Sano finds; dealer Saitō Mototeru recently alleged that Morikawa had brought him Kenzan writing samples and asked him to inscribe boxes with similar writing; Saitō was also to "antiquate" the boxes with birch resin.[12]

Third, the New Sano Kenzan pots and diaries capitalized on preconceptions of Kenzan established in scholarly and popular media. Kenzan imitations displayed a modest and predictable nature until the early Meiji Period, when there was a precipitous decline of interest in traditional Japanese ceramics. When production started again in the late 1880s, the old workshop traditions were lost; many potters turned to illustrated books for inspiration (figs. 164, 165). These new imitations, so brazenly different from earlier versions, are most visible in Western collections begun in the last decade of the nineteenth century, for example in the collections assembled by Charles Freer (Freer Gallery of Art, Washington, DC) and Justus Brinckmann (Museum für Kunst und Gewerbe, Hamburg). The dictatorial opinions of wealthy collectors like Ōkōchi Masatoshi, who proclaimed that only a few authentic Kenzans existed, meant that few such forgeries were made in the first half of this century; but that authority was shattered with World War II, and once again new fakes began to appear. For example, *Kenzan,* an exhibition and sales catalogue published by Atarashii Me Sha in 1960, offered Kenzan pots whose designs seemed to derive from publications of the decade just passed. As it turned out, at least half of these were made by a contemporary potter from Inuyama named Yamamoto Kiichi (Nyōsen; born 1916).[13] New Sano Kenzan followed this trend as well. In Chapter 5, we related how Shinozaki Genzō uncovered evidence that Kenzan had made a short visit to Sano in the autumn of 1737. The New Sano diaries read like an extrapolation of the facts uncovered by Shinozaki: Kenzan is hosted in Sano by three local dilettantes, but instead of a short visit he lingers for over a year, assisted by a host of new players. The sketches in the diaries and paintings on the pots in many instances conform to Kenzan wares and other Rimpa designs published during the postwar boom period. A rectangular plate first published by Kobayashi in 1948 (fig. 166) is the obvious source for the New Sano Kenzan plate illustrated here.

166. Rectangular plate with design of narcissus.

Fourth, the New Sano Kenzan initially benefited from an aura of mystery and inaccessibility, one perhaps legitimized by the traditional Japanese discretion over use and display of art objects. From the beginning, New Sano owners played a cat-and-mouse game with their opponents, citing evidence for their finds but never producing that evidence. It is telling that support for the objects began to wane as soon as they were exhibited publicly. Until quite recently it has been difficult to see a systematic selection of Kenzan wares in one exhibition or publication. Institutions as well as private collectors guard their treasures carefully, for they have the real stake in reassessments that a critical study might produce. Curators and scholars adroitly juggle objects in their exhibitions and publications so that no single party is offended. Consequently, a total picture of the artist's work can be little more than vague and intuitive, and there is always room for a few new entries. The New Sano Kenzan wares might have been accommodated as well, but they appeared too suddenly, in too great a number, and, as was later observed, in an excessively florid style. They threatened a carefully built consensus, and that was quietly unacceptable.

New Sano Kenzan followed on the heels of the equally infamous Einin-Era Jar incident, in which modern potter Katō Tōkurō confessed to making a jar that had received official status as an Important Cultural Property — from the Kamakura period (1185–1333). The deception was exquisite: Tōkurō made dozens of pottery shards, which he claimed to have dug from the ancient Matsudome kiln site in Seto; when the jar itself was "excavated," it matched the shards so well that recognition was instant. Then, to the great embarrassment of expert Koyama Fujio and other government authorities who supported the finds, a local historian from Seto stepped forward to declare the piece a patent fraud; soon afterward Tōkurō blithely admitted that he had made the piece himself a few decades earlier.[14] Just as the Einin Jar scandal was cooling, New Sano Kenzan emerged, and now instead of Koyama, two national museum officials, Fujioka and Hayashiya, were involved. But who were the real victims of New Sano Kenzan? Besides the collectors who paid huge sums for the pieces, it is tempting to sympathize with the people of Sano, who were besieged by opportunistic dealers and prying reporters for months in 1962. All is apparently forgotten, however; in early 1989 the town held an exhibition showcasing New Sano Kenzan-type wares as an embodiment of the local heritage. *Caveat emptor!*

AND BEYOND...

Are murder by silence or the intuitive pronouncements of the Japanese art establishment our only possible approaches to Ogata Kenzan? This book has attempted to demonstrate that through the careful study of documents and remaining works one can locate Kenzan's real work, and identify contexts in which it operated. Nonetheless, in his life and work, Kenzan assumed a number of seemingly contradictory postures, guaranteeing a diversity of interpretation. We conclude with another look at the name Kenzan which, in its connotations as a person, pottery workshop, and a tradition, embodies those contradictions.

Consideration of Kenzan the person might begin with his membership in the urban merchant class. In response to government policies limiting their commercial opportunities and ostracizing them socially, wealthy merchants avidly pursued leisure activities, particularly those that conferred a sense of legitimacy. Whether it was a pottery manual, a corpus of poems, or procedures for a tea ceremony, what had in the medieval period been the domain of a single class or kinship line became accessible to anyone with the means to buy it. In this movement Kenzan was both a recipient and a propagator. His early life was filled with opportunities for Confucian study, poetry composition, and Zen meditation. His penchant for seclusion was not a rejection of the world but one of many cultural postures that moneyed merchants could adopt.

Not every wealthy merchant pursued a contemplative life, or at least its appointments, with the dedication of Kenzan, telling us something more about Kenzan himself — that he was studious and energetic, with a yearning for a synthesis of the spiritual and material. He built a secluded villa, and furnished it with a garden, tea hut, and library. Designing utensils for that life was only a step away, and the nearby Ninsei potters had the requisite tools. To be sure, finances played a role in his decision to open a kiln in 1699, but the move would be unthinkable without Kenzan's productive instincts and the incentive provided by the collapse of the Ninsei kiln.

The Kenzan workshop represented a new approach to making ceramics. In earlier Japanese kilns, including those in Kyoto, there was a structural division between management and workshop. No matter how brilliant, designs conceived by absentee patrons and carried out by workshop specialists tend toward professional mannerism — the kind seen, for example, in Ninsei wares. Kenzan also depended on specialists, and in that sense he was different from later artist-potters that established him as a forerunner. His staff included potters Nonomura Seiemon and Magobei, painters like Kōrin and Watanabe Soshin, his own son Ihachi, and a host of unnamed personnel. Nonetheless, the personal inscriptions and signatures on his wares, as well as the expertise manifested in his pottery manuals, signify that Kenzan was a *physical* presence in his workshop. Because of that intimate contact, technique never overwhelmed the expressive element in his wares. At a glance Kenzan seems to have taken the craft out of ceramics and replaced it with pure personal expression. These pots, like some of the great tea wares of a century earlier, suggest that beauty and technical proficiency were not necessarily synonymous. This casual, unfinished flavor has endeared Kenzan to countless generations of admirers.

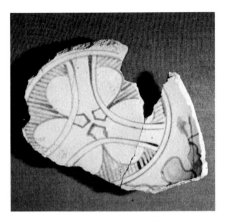

167. Ogata Ihachi: Fragment of a bowl.

168. Signature inside foot ring.

Whether or not the sense of amateurism in early Kenzan wares was an inevitable by-product of his cultivation or simply a new entrepreneurial stratagem is an interesting question. In fashioning himself as a "Hermit Potter," and using that name on mass-produced ceramics, he played a part in the professionalization of amateurism. Indeed, if sheer amateurism was his métier, he would never have had to leave his villa, where he could have made pots in a back yard kiln. But Kenzan ware was not the first ceramic to exhibit this kind of value-adding. The personalization of Japanese ceramics received much of its initial impetus from the late sixteenth-century tea masters, and within several decades of that we see object naming, box inscribing, and other peripheral activities transforming lumps of clay into lumps of taste. To find productive possibilities in all aspects of culture — even in expressive hobbies — was natural for urban merchants.

If we assume that professionalization did not pose a conflict for Kenzan, the decision to forsake his mountain kiln at Narutaki for a place in the downtown ceramics industry becomes more comprehensible. His new Chōjiyamachi location offered direct access to raw materials, to a national distribution system, and to his brother Kōrin, who had already made a mark in urban fashion. This was, of course, a different arena. Clever manipulation of easily recognized motifs counted more than erudite poetry or skillful painting. Kenzan's fashion wares have been disparaged by critics, but as we have seen, they quote from a different but equally rich set of texts. And despite advancing age and acclaim, Kenzan continued to grow artistically. He achieved a transition from the lidded tea bowls and *kawarake*, which brought together traditional forms with new designs, to a more complete interaction of vessel shape and painting in the *katamukōzuke* and *sukashibachi*. Charges of artistic decline can stem only from the notion that since Narutaki wares approximated the "high art" of painting, they represent a standard that no other Kenzan wares could match. As integrated statements of the potter's art, however, the Chōjiyamachi pieces are without parallel.

The prospect of princely patronage, as well as the opportunity to trace the footsteps of his late brothers, were the probable factors that tempted Kenzan to move to Edo. Even though our scenario suggests a semi-retirement, Kenzan responded with vigor to his new surroundings. He adapted to the unfamiliar materials and rustic workmanship and explored new venues in Nagasaki and Sano. In his painting, he produced new Rimpa permutations and a personal style in which he reworked the relationship of calligraphy to painted image. Befriended by princes, poets, and wealthy merchants, he was hardly a neglected old man in an alien city.

Finally, there is the Kenzan tradition — the interpreters and their interpretations. It is impossible to leave these out of any Kenzan study, for they constitute the lens through which the founder has been customarily perceived. The hitherto unacknowledged role of Kenzan's adopted son Ihachi is a case in point. We have revealed how it was Ihachi's pottery manual, not Kenzan's, that was passed from generation to generation in Edo; Ihachi's style seems to have influenced Minzan and indeed all of the Edo Kenzans; and it was Ihachi's descendants in Edo who were identified as blood ancestors by Urano Shigekichi and his successors. Finally, the first Kenzan ware excavated scientifically appears to be, on the basis of its signature, a product of Ihachi (figs. 167, 168). Until more evidence like this is found, formal analysis and comparison of all extant works will be essential, and Kenzan's followers and imitators — many of whom we have now identified — offer the most useful platform for comparison with the original.

Regardless of all his followers, imitators, and apologists, the central role of Ogata Shinsei in the Kenzan tradition is beyond dispute. As a potter, he was certainly a new species, one who brought surface design into the foreground, in place of forming, glazing, and firing. His fusion of painting and calligraphy with ceramics has been frequently imitated, but never surpassed. He also took a keen interest in techniques, especially in new strategies for pigments, slips, and enamels. Kenzan's triumphs encouraged Kyoto potters to organize around master decorators, and names like Rokubei and Dōhachi carry on that legacy today. Leaders of the twentieth century artist-potter movement, particularly Bernard Leach and Tomimoto Kenkichi, have looked to Kenzan for inspiration. More idiosyncratic figures, notably Kitaōji Rōsanjin (1883–1959), have taken a cue from Kenzan's versatility and expressiveness.

Mindful of how each part of an object might contribute to communication, Kenzan the designer created a universe of allusions. Yet in his synthesis of ceramics and design, the whole always seems greater than its constituent parts. For this triumph, many would consider Kenzan a "fine" artist, but he seems to have sensed one thing all along — that pottery could summon a range of emotional responses every bit as rich and complex as the so-called high arts. Indeed, he seems to demonstrate how, in the Japanese tradition, such divisions fall short of meaning.

We have made our analytical arguments. Kenzan, too, thought about his mark in history, and how that might be enhanced. But can mental calculations alone drive an artist to produce images of compelling freshness for over four decades? In those late works, one senses that Kenzan's dedication to the craft outlived conceptions such as professionalism or art-as-play. Clay had become clay, and brush was brush. For most of us, life is a series of half-digested moments. Kenzan, in his own words, had eaten the entire world.

1. Leach 1966, 96.

2. Matsuzaki Shōichi, "Sano Kenzan Mondai no Kei-i" [The Background of the Sano Kenzan Problem], *Me no Me* 103 (1985), 11–12.

3. For Kōan's denunciation see interview in "Nisemono? Hommono? Meitō 'Kenzan' Zoku Zoku Deru" [Fake? Genuine? Work by the Master Potter "Kenzan" Pours Out], *Mainichi Shimbun*, 28 January, 1962; for news of Morikawa's transaction, see " 'Sano Kenzan' Hakken no Hamon" [Repercussions of the "Sano Kenzan" Discovery], *Geijutsu Shinchō* (March 1962), 99; the dealers' reaction is reported in Idegawa Naoki, "Imada ni Nazo o Haramu 'Shin Hakken Sano Kenzan' " [The Still-Unresolved New Sano Kenzan], *Geijutsu Shinchō* (July 1985), 54.

4. Nihon Tōji Kyōkai, eds., "Zadankai: Sano Kenzan o Kataru" [Roundtable on Sano Kenzan], *Tōsetsu* 109 (1962), 11–19.

5. Kase Tōho, "Kenzan no Jibohyō ni tsuite" [On the Roots of Kenzan's Orthography], *Tōsetsu* 113–14 (1962); for comments about the paper, see Kase Tōho, "Shin Hakken Sano Kenzan ni tsuite (2)" [Concerning New Sano Kenzan (2)], *Tōsetsu* 113 (1962), 33.

6. Yamaguchi Guro, "Tokyo no Tsuchi Nado: Shin Kenzan o Tsuku" [Tokyo Clays, etc.: Pointing at New Sano Kenzan], *Nihon Bijutsu Kōgei* 287 (1962), 40.

7. Reported in Matsumoto Seichō, "Doro no Naka no Sano Kenzan" [Sano Kenzan in the Mire], *Geijutsu Shinchō* (October 1962), 160–61.

8. Idegawa, 57.

9. The still-active promoters of New Sano Kenzan include art historian Mizuo Hiroshi, painter and former Sano Historical Society staffer Ishizuka Seiga, and collector Sumitomo Shin'ichi. Their opinions are most recently aired in Matsuzaki Shōichi, ed., "Ano 'Sano Kenzan' o Nijūsan Nen Oimotometa Shūnen Shinjutsu" [The Real Story of a Twenty-Three-Year Quest for "Sano Kenzan"], *Me no Me* 103 (1985). Sumitomo Shin'ichi has published three books illustrating New Sano Kenzan type wares, including *Kenzan Miyako Wasure no Ki* [Kenzan's Miyako Wasure Diary] (Tokyo: Ribun Shuppan, 1983); *Nijō Ke Oniwa Yaki to Kōrin-Kenzan* [The Garden Kiln of the

Nijō Family and Kōrin and Kenzan], (Tokyo: Ribun Shuppan, 1984); *Kenzan Rokujūkyūsai no Tabidachi* [Kenzan's Departure at Age Sixty Nine], (Tokyo: Ribun Shuppan, 1985).

10. Kōmoto Shinji et al., "Against Nature," a roundtable discussion recorded in April, 1988, and published in *Against Nature: Japanese Art in the Eighties* (New York: Grey Art Gallery and Study Center, 1990), 22.

11. Parts of the diaries are translated and illustrated in Leach 1966, 113–35.

12. See " 'Sano Kenzan' o Tsukutta to Iu Giwaku no Hito Saitō Mototeru Hajimete Kataru" [Saitō Mototeru, the Man Accused of Making "Sano Kenzan," Speaks Out], *Me no Me* 103 (1985), 41–44.

13. " 'Genuine or False' Debate Again Flares Up Over Kenzan's Works," *Mainichi Daily News*, 5 March, 1962.

14. See Idegawa Naoki, "Jūbun Shitei o Torikesareta 'Einin no Tsubo' " [The "Einin Era Jar" Whose Important Cultural Property Status Was Retracted], *Geijutsu Shinchō* (July 1983), 58–60.

Appendix One
ANNOTATED CHRONOLOGY

This chronology, covering the Kenzan tradition from the birth of Ogata Kenzan through the Sano Kenzan scandal of the early 1960s, is intended as a reference to sources, both primary and secondary, and as a guide to further study. After each entry, sources are listed in parentheses. Whenever appropriate I have made brief comments. References cited here in abbreviated form are listed in full in the bibliography. Abbreviations used in the chronology include:

Hinamiki: Nijō Ke Nainai Gobansho Hinamiki, a private diary kept by the clerk for the Nijō family. The Nijō diary entries pertinent to the Ogata are published in Jintsu Setsuko, "*Nijō Ke Nainai Gobansho Hinamiki* ni okeru Kōrin Shiryō" (Kōrin Materials in the *Nijō Ke Nainai Gobansho Hinamiki*), *Yamato Bunka* 33 (1960), 44–69.

KKM: *Konishi Ke Monjo*, an archive passed down in the Konishi family, into which Kōrin's heir Juichirō was adopted ca. 1708. The numbers follow the classification system used in Yamane Yūzō's typeset transcription of the entire archive (Yamane 1962).

KKM supplement: Reports of now-missing Konishi documents made by Aimi Kōu, Fukui Rikichirō, and Tanaka Kisaku and compiled in Part VII in Yamane 1962. The numbers follow the classification system used in Yamane 1962.

1663   Kenzan is born. His grave at Zen'yōji, Tokyo, provides the death date of Kampō 3 (1743) at age eighty-one; his pottery manual *Tōji Seihō* bears inscriptions to the effect that it was written in Gembun 2 (1737) by Kenzan at the age of seventy-five. Counting back (and subtracting the year traditionally assigned at birth), we arrive at 1663.

1671   Grandmother Akiba Ichijūin dies (KKM supplement 8); one younger sister dies (KKM supplement 5).

1676   Mother Okatsu (posthumous name Jishōin) dies (KKM supplement 8); two more younger sisters die (KKM supplement 5).

1678   From this period Kenzan's father Sōken begins to lend money to daimyo (KKM 46, 47).

1679   Two more sisters die (KKM supplement 5).

1680   Seventh month: Sōken donates land to a temple in Fukakusa, Kyoto, in the name of his mother, wife, and daughters (KKM 48, 49).

1681   Hon'ami Kōho dies; if Kenzan studied ceramics

with Kōho, as suggested by his receipt of a Hon'ami family pottery manual recorded in *Umeya Nikki* (Aimi 1928, 12–13), it would have had to take place before this time.

1683   First month, second day: "Ogata Gompei and Shinzaburō" pay New Year's greetings to philosopher Itō Jinsai (*Itō Jinsai Nikki*, quoted in Ishida 1960, 202).

1687   Kenzan writes out an inheritance receipt upon the death of his father (KKM 63):

Written Promise
According to my father's writing, a house at Muromachi Hanatatechō, a house at Jōkaimmachi, a house at Takagamine, a calligraphy by Yin Yuejiang, and a set of books was willed to me. Also family assets and other miscellaneous utensils are split between Ichinojō [Kōrin] and myself according to my father's wishes. I am satisfied with this disposition and have no further cause for complaint.

Jōkyō 2 [1687]
Ogata Gompei
Koremitsu [monogram added]

1688   Kenzan changes his name from the original Gompei to Shinsei. That change can be detected in the form of a "Shinsei" signature on a now-lost document dated sixth month, twenty-seventh day, 1688, formerly in the Konishi archive. We know of its existence through a memorandum left by Konishi Hōshu called *Ogata Ke Yuisho Oboegaki* (KKM 185). As Kenzan had signed his eighth-month, 1687, inheritance receipt as "Gompei," the date of the name change can thus be estimated.

1689   Third month: The Ninnaji official diary (*Onki*) records that "Gomonzen Ogata Shinsei" (Ogata Shinsei from in front of the temple) paid his respects to the prince-abbot Kanryū (1672–1707). This is seen as evidence of Kenzan's move to Omuro.

Why did Kenzan choose Omuro? Kenzan's inheritance receipt lists three Kyoto houses (see map, Chapter 2). One was located at Jōkaimmachi, one block south of the Ogata family home at Nakatachiuri. A second house at Muromachi Hanatatechō would have been a half-block east in present-day Honjō, near the intersection of Karasuma and Kamichōjamachi. The third house was located at Takagamine, and is commonly thought to be the same plot allotted to grandfather Sōhaku on Kōetsu's Takagamine village map. But Takagamine had changed. It had hardly grown rank and wild with the decline and eventual disappearance of the Hon'ami (they departed for Edo in 1697), but rather had become a resort for intellectually inclined merchants such as Naba Yūei (1652–99), Mitsui Shūfū (1646–1717), and Noma Sanchiku (1608–76); interestingly, none of these names appears on the early seventeenth-century Takagamine map kept at Kōetsuji.

The Ogata family may have in fact owned two Taka-gamine houses. *Jōju Sensei Monshū* (Collected Students of Master Jōju), a collection of anecdotes about Itō Jinsai assembled by son Tōgai, mentions a literati gathering hosted by Ogata Genshin at a villa called Hanzantei, thought to be located at Takagamine. Genshin was the proper heir of Sōho who was in turn the first son of Sōhaku, so the original branch of the Ogata may have kept their Takagamine land. It is possible that Kenzan's plot was a later purchase by Sōken, who was sufficiently wealthy to buy such an item himself. In fact a letter in the Konishi archive from calligrapher Kojima Sōshin thanking Sōken for a special invitation to Takagamine (KKM 66, sheet 11) suggests that such a purchase had been made. The Hazan-tei gathering is mentioned in Ōtsuki Mikio, "Kenzan no Jikishian Dokushō Sanzen ni Tsuite" (Concerning Ken-zan's Study of Zen Under the Priest Dokushō), *Bukkyō Geijutsu* 77 (1970) 58; the gathering is recorded in volume 22 of Togai's compendium. See also Odaka Toshirō, "Naba Yūei no Den to sono Monji" [Naba Yūei — His Life and his Writing], *Kokusai Kuristokyō Daigaku Jimbun Kagaku Kiyō* (1963), 23.

Seventh month: Kenzan and Kōrin make their first recorded visits to the Nijō family (*Hinamiki*).

1690   Ninth month: Ōbaku monks Dokushō and Gettan visit Kenzan at his retreat, the Shūseidō; Dokushō proba-bly grants Kenzan the name Reikai (*Gazankō, Jikishi Dokushō Zenji Kōroku*). *Gankyokō*, a collection of Gettan poems com-piled in 1698 and published in 1704, also features three poems dedicated to Kenzan at the time of that visit:

From early in life, rejecting the world in
   seclusion,
Beginning anew a retirement afar from the
   capital.
From the house, veils of mist shroud the Twin
   Peaks,
Flowers and trees flourish along three garden
   paths.
He contemplates Buddha's tranquil face in his
   shrine,
He purifies his heart by reading a sutra hung
   there.
The temple bell awakens us from the illusion,
   and invites self-discovery;
A person with real talent should not surrender to
   fame's lure.

Here we can see a virtue like that of [poet] Wei
   Ye of Song.
Bush clover blooms in the garden, flirting with
   the sunlight;
On a bamboo fence, chrysanthemums open their
   petals to the dew;
Soaking in the orchid-scented bath of the
   hermitage,
Our quiet words are punctuated by water drip-
   ping from the eaves.
As a guest my satisfaction was complete,
Causing me to linger on the sunset road home.

Building Shūseidō at an early age,
Your thatched hut nestles against Narabigaoka;
If you sow the seed, the flower of real peace will
   open.
The plaited bamboo door adds to the sense of
   detachment;
With books piled high on the floor, and no sign
   of vulgar amusement.
The aroma of tea hovers in the room — monk's
   pleasure.
Leaving the dusty world for the way of a recluse
   is praiseworthy.

1692   Spring: Visits Ishikawa Jōzan's retreat Shisendō, writes *Ōtotsuka o Yogiru no Ki* (Kumida coll., Tokyo).

Ninth month: Priest Dokushō visits Shūseidō again (*Jikishi Dokushō Zenji Kōroku*).

Ninth month, nineteenth day: Participates in an outing with Naba Yūei (*Shōsō Yōgin*). See Kawasaki Hiroshi, "*Shōsō Yōgin* ni Arawareru Kōrin to Kenzan" [Kōrin and Kenzan as Revealed in the *Shōsō Yōgin*], *Kobijutsu* 81–82, 1987.

1694   Eighth month: Kenzan receives a tract of land in Narutaki, northwest Kyoto, from Nijō Tsunahira (deed in Hōzōji collection).

1696   Kenzan writes a letter to Kōrin (KKM 90). Yamane Yūzō has coordinated the dates mentioned in the letter and memorandum with specific events in Kōrin's life to arrive at the 1696 date (see Yamane 1973, 116). Text of the letter:

It has been some time since we've seen each other. I have been talking to Miyake Jikōan, and [he says] that since the other two are village elders, if in-quiries are made here a reply will come in a few days. I have also told the elder Dōjū that the details will go through Sōin. Tomorrow I shall proceed to Takagamine, and I shall ask Yasusuke. Regarding Zeze, I met with Jizaemon. Since there are some unusual circumstances, I will take note of future developments [before doing anything].

[item:] After deducting what you have borrowed, the money remaining is shown here. The amounts are set down in the accompanying memorandum; if you disagree with this, please let me know. The present circumstances are trying. In any case I am in possession of the original four-*kamme* note, which you may inspect. I want to know your answer in a few days. This memorandum is important so please don't lose it.

Third month, eleventh day
Shinsei [monogram added]

[attached note:] Adding up the money you have borrowed from me over the past three years, and accounting for the amount returned last winter, the total is seven *kamme* nine hundred eighty-three *momme* of silver. At the beginning of this year I received from you promissory notes from [daimyo] Nagato, Tōsa, and Chōkūrōzaemon in the equivalent of one hundred ten *momme*. Even though this lowers the sum on paper, in fact my cash is reduced in amount. There is also the promissory note from Nagai Ichinojō, but here too the prospects are uncertain. Their inaction [on repayment] is causing me inconvenience. If only this cash were in my possession, I could put it to work, but there is the above misfortune [daimyo failure to repay]. At least you should make some return on this loan.

I do understand that it is difficult for you to pay me back in your present circumstances. Therefore you should bring your receipts to the pawn shop and redeem the items you have consigned there. Then you should sell them yourself [rather than letting the pawnbroker profit on them]. Since I myself have been borrowing a lot from Hinoya, I can't be of any assistance to you in redeeming them. If you could only pay me back, I would return the promissory notes to you and you could put them to work. If you redeem the items later [when more interest will be due the pawnbroker] it will be of little use. I understand that now [finding the money to redeem the pawned items] may be difficult.

[item:] The folding screen you left last winter with the old gentleman Jihei to sell in exchange for the money I lent you is still for sale. I will visit Jihei soon, but there is still no word of him selling it. You should take matters into your own hands and return the money you owe me.
[item:] The *tekagami* [album of calligraphies] that you left with Sagami can be redeemed for four hundred *momme*. You should also attempt to sell this yourself.

[item:] As for the art objects left with Hiranoya, I went to see Tōzō [eldest brother Tōzaburō?] but he doesn't have any money either. It seems better to redeem these objects and sell them, and divide whatever profit remains.

In addition to the above, there are things left with Uzaemon and others. But I have no other idea but that suggested above. I will listen if you have some alternative. I myself have no further latitude in this matter.

Third month, eleventh day
[to] Kōrin
[from] Shinsei [monogram added]

1697   Eleventh month, twenty-first day: Sends a condolence gift to Naba Yūei (*Shōsō Yōgin*).

1698   Eighth month, nineteenth day: Hosts Naba Yūei and friends at Narutaki (*Shōsō Yōgin*).

1699   Second month, fourth day: Nonomura Seiemon makes a final appearance in the Ninnaji record, *Onki*. All *Onki* references on Ninsei are listed in Kawahara, *Ninsei*, Nihon no Yakimono, no. 22 (Tokyo: Kōdansha, 1976), 28.
   Third month, eighth day: "Ogata Shinsei, who lives in front of this temple, has brought along the Fukuōji village headman and is petitioning the local bailiff to build a kiln at a house near Izumidani within these precincts" (*Onki*). All Onki references on Kenzan are from Kobayashi 1948, 210−12.
   Third month, ninth day: "The petition of Ogata Shinsei has been handled as a routine request" (*Onki*).
   Third month, twelfth day: "Ogata Shinsei came to pay his thanks for the granting of his request" (*Onki*).
   Seventh month, first day: "For some time Ogata Shinsei has been asking for firewood; Jibu informed him that his request had been granted" (*Onki*).
   Seventh month, twenty-first day: Returns to thank the temple authorities for the fuel (*Onki*).
   Eighth month, thirteenth day: Receives the manual of Ninsei's pottery notes (*Tōkō Hitsuyō*).
   There has been some debate as to the identity of the grantor of these notes, who signed the dedication "Nonomura Harima Daijō" and sealed it with the name "Fujiyoshi." In February, 1942, a large *shishi* (Chinese lion-dog) figurine was submitted for auction at the Tokyo Bijutsu Club. An incised dedication on the object read "first son Nonomura Masanobu, second son Seijirō Fujiyoshi, and third son Seihachi Masasada," and was signed by "Fujiyoshi Daijō Ninsei." That inscription has prompted speculation that this second son Fujiyoshi is the grantor of the pottery manual to Kenzan and the heir to the Ninsei title. Yet Seijirō is never mentioned in the Ninnaji records;

he only appears as a co-borrower in those promissory notes from the 1670s. The probable heir to the Ninsei workshop and the grantor of the manual was Seiemon. The cordial relationship with the Ninnaji prince in the *Onki* underlines Seiemon's status; there is no real evidence for leadership by Seijirō.

Ninth month, sixth day: "Ogata Shinsei came and reported to the bailiff that the kiln was finished and that he wanted to fire soon. He promised to report to the city authorities as soon as he obtained local approval. He stated that there were no further difficulties, and that he would take extra precautions with fire" (*Onki*).

Eleventh month, twentieth day: Presents "for the first time" a *tezukuri* (personally made) tea bowl to Kanryū, the Ninnaji prince-priest (*Onki*).

Twelfth month, seventh day: Back at Ninnaji asking permission to fire again (*Onki*).

1700 Third month, eleventh day: Presents a "Kenzan ware" incense burner to Nijō Tsunahira (*Hinamiki*).

1703 First month: Presents a pair of dishes to Nijō Tsunahira (*Hinamiki*).

1704 Eighth month: Presents a tea bowl to Nijō Tsunahira (*Hinamiki*).

1705 Eleventh month: Presents a pair of dishes to Nijō Tsunahira (*Hinamiki*).

1708 First month: Presents tea bowls to Nijō Tsunahira (*Hinamiki*).

1710 Eighth month: Presents a tea bowl to Nijō Tsunahira (*Hinamiki*).

1711 First month: Presents a *hiire* to Nijō Tsunahira (*Hinamiki*).

Kenzan copies out a group of signature specimens for Kōrin (KKM 142). The sheets are undated, but Yamane argues for a date of ca. 1711 based on the following evidence: these sheets are part of a book kept by Kōrin. On the page immediately following the Kenzan writing in this Kōrin book there is inscribed, in Kōrin's hand, his late-life pseudonym "Masatoki." "Masatoki" first appears in a congratulatory letter to mint official Konishi Hikokurō, who had just built a new house. Now this letter is undated, but it must have been written between 1708, when Hikokurō had adopted Kōrin's son (he presumably built the house in anticipation of the new heir), and 1712, the year of Hikokurō's death. To further narrow the possibilities, Yamane suggests that the superstitious Kōrin changed his name to Masatoki with the construction of his house at Shimmachi, Nijō Sagaru, in 1711. The "Masatoki" page of the Kōrin memorandum also bears the names of two Nijō family officials who assumed their jobs in 1713, providing a

terminus ad quem for the Kenzan sheets. See Yamane Yūzō, "Konishike Monjo Chū no Kenzan Kenkyū Shiryō" [Kenzan Research Materials in the Konishi Archive], Yamato Bunkakan 1963, 123–29, also Yamane, "Kōrin-Kenzan Nidai" [Two Themes on Kōrin and Kenzan], *Kokka* 1037 (1980), 17.

1712 Kenzan's move from Narutaki to Chōjiyamachi, in downtown Kyoto, is recorded in the municipal record *Kyoto Oyakusho Muki Taigai Oboegaki*:

Kenzan Shinsei of Nijō, west of Teramachi on the north side [Chōjiyamachi]: Regarding the matter of Kenzan ware, to the west of Omuro, in a forested mountain within the precincts of bailiff Kobori Jin'emon, Ogata Shinsei owned a house; with the intention of building a kiln and making a living there, he successfully petitioned Takigawa Yamashiro no Kami and Andō Suruga no Kami of this office in 1699. Since the place was located northwest of the capital, he called the pottery Kenzan, and that is where he operated his ceramics business. In 1712, stating that this place was inconvenient, he dismantled his kiln, granted the land to another person, and came to live in Kyoto, where he now operates a ceramics business. Regarding his kiln, since there are many in the area of Awataguchi and Gojōzaka, he is borrowing from them for his work.

1713 Kōrin borrows cash from the Myōkenji temple in Kenzan's name (KKM 91). The Myōkenji temple had a long tradition of Ogata family support.

Kenzan ware appears as an important regional product in the encyclopedia *Wakan Sansai Zue*. For a typeset transcription, see Terashima Ryōan, ed., *Wakan Sansai Zue*, fascicle no. 72 (reprinted Tokyo: Heibonsha, 1987).

1714 Kōrin's patron Nakamura Kuranosuke, along with four other colleagues at the Kyoto silver mint, is exiled to remote Miyake Island.

1715 First month: Presents a tea bowl and flower vase to Nijō Tsunahira (*Hinamiki*).

Fifth month: Kenzan ware is mentioned in *Ikutama Shinjū*, a puppet play by Chikamatsu Monzaemon, performed for the first time at the Takemotoza, Osaka.

1716 Sixth month, second day: Kōrin dies (KKM supplement 5).

Eleventh month: Together with Kōrin's widow, Tayo, Kenzan signs the back of a *Moon and Plum* painting, formerly in the collection of the Myōkenji temple. This painting, now in a private collection, is illustrated in Yamane 1978–80 (Kōrin school v. 1), no. 97; the inscription is illustrated on p. 17 of the same volume.

1717   Third month: Kenzan, on behalf of Kōrin's widow Tayo, acts as guarantor for the sale of Kōrin's house (KKM 124):

Regarding permanent sale of residence:
One lot, covering three house parcels, [at] Kamigoryō Yabunouchi, frontage seven *ken* two *shaku*, as far east as the waterway, depth twenty-four *ken*, west neighbor is Jūichiya Tōbei. Regarding the residence, it was occupied by us, but due to certain matters, we hereby deed it permanently to said person for the price of five *kan*, four hundred fifty *me*, and we certify the receipt of that amount. Regarding this house, there is not the slightest problem with family members or from other quarters. If some kind of quarrel should arise, present this and it will be settled quickly. For future sake I execute the aforementioned deed.
Kyōhō 2 (1716),
third month
Owner: Shotei
Intermediary: Hachimonjiya Kambei
Headman: Kahei
Receiver: Nijō Chōjiyamachi Ogata Shinsei [Kenzan]

[on a separate piece of paper, probably as a sample:]
Written promise:
one place in this *chō* owned by Shotei, agreed sale price one *kan* five hundred fifty *me*
content: same as attached; certain year and month
Kamigoryō Nakamachi
Headman: Lacquerer Heibei
group of five: Carpenter Shōbei
Clothier Shirōbei
Carpenter Jirōbei
Intermediary: Carpenter Kichibei
Owner: Shotei
Receiver: Nijō Chōjiyamachi Shinsei

ca. 1720   Around this time Kenzan adopted Ihachi, a descendant of Ninsei. He was not listed in an Ogata-family genealogy copied out by Kōrin's son Konishi Hikoemon in 1714 (KKM 146), so he may have been absent through the early years at Chōjiyamachi. In a genealogy copied by Hikoemon in 1750 (KKM 151), he is listed with characters connoting "younger cousin" (*jū* and *tei*), suggesting that he was a near-contemporary of the author, who was born in 1700. If Ihachi's name was inspired by the zodiacal circumstances of his birth (*i* = [year of the] boar and *hachi* = eighth [month]), he may have been born in boar years 1695 or 1707. In *Tōki Mippōsho*, an Ihachi pottery manual discussed in Chapter 6, the author states that he "learned the pottery wheel in four days when he was twenty-one." Thus if Ihachi

was born in 1695, he would (by Japanese count) have undertaken pottery training in 1715; if he was born in 1707, he would have begun in 1727. Since all of these dates are speculative and somewhat inconsistent, we suggest that Ihachi joined Kenzan around 1720. Perhaps Kenzan, out of gratitude to his assistant Seiemon (Ninsei II), provided training and a secure future for Ihachi. This was quite in character for Kenzan, who was helping Kōrin's survivors in the same period.

1723   Eleventh month: Visits the Kasuga Shrine together with Nijō Tsunahira (*Hinamiki*).

1724   Third month: Kenzan-ware *suzuributa* (tray for sweets) used in exchange of gifts between courtiers (*Hinamiki*).

1725   Eleventh month: Kenzan-ware food vessels used at a tea ceremony attended by Konoe Iehiro (*Kaiki*).

ca. 1730   Itō Tōgai's *Kasei Shiki* (History of the Family) mentions that his mother, Kana, was descended from Ogata Koremoto, and her great-grandfather was Dōhaku; grandfather Sōhaku was a rich merchant in the service of Tōfukumon'in; Kana's father Gen'an received the *hokkyō* title for his practice in the Nakarai school of medicine (Ishida 1960, 196–97).

1731   Tenth month: Rinnōji abbot Kōkan departs for Edo (*Rinnōji Nempu*); Kenzan is thought to have accompanied him. May have made pottery in the Iriya section of Edo from this time (*Koga Bikō*).

1732   Ninth month, twenty-second day: Kenzan writes Ōkawa Kendō a letter from Edo listing glaze recipes; this was preserved in transcribed form in Kendō's diary. See Shinozaki Genzō, "Sano Kenzan Monogatari-5" [The story of Sano Kenzan — Part 5], *Tōsetsu* 189 (1968), 44.
    The Ōbaku Zen temple Hōzōji was built on Kenzan's former kiln site at Narutaki. Funds were provided by noble Konoe Iehiro for a friend, Hyakusetsu Genryō (1667–1736), who became the first abbot. According to the *Kaiun Daiichi Hyakusetsu Zenji Gyōjō* (Record of First-generation Kaiun Zen Priest Hyakusetsu), kept by follower Gessen Jōtan, the site for the temple was suggested by Hyakusetsu's friend Kuwahara Kūdo (1673–1744), who was at that time occupying the land. Hyakusetsu then approached Iehiro, who arranged to have the Hōzōji moved (creation of new temples was forbidden by the shogunate) from its old location at Takeda village, Fushimi district, Kyoto. Plans for the new complex, drawn up in 1732, are still preserved, and they show that the Hōzōji land, a narrow plot with its long axis inclined up the mountain, coincides with that granted to Kenzan in the 1694 deed. A request for construction drafted by Hyakusetsu in 1734 mentions a few existing buildings, one of them resembling

a tea house; they may have been built by Kenzan for his own occupation some three decades earlier. The Hōzōji history is narrated in Ōtsuki Mikio, "Gasō Hyakusetsu ni Tsuite" (Concerning Painter-Priest Hyakusetsu), *Shiseki to Bijutsu* 370 (1966), 366–84.

1733   Kenzan is mentioned in the second fascicle of *Kindai Seji Dan*, a gazetteer compiled by haiku enthusiast Kikuoka Senryō. See Kobayashi 1962, 164.

1737   First month, twenty-eighth day: Writes a letter to Kōrin's son Konishi Hikoemon (KKM 148):

Greetings for the New Year. Thank you for the fragrance of your New Year's ink as well. I am happy that you and your family are starting the season in health and peace. I too am hoping for good health this year. Last year, when I was ill, I was grateful to visit [and stay] at your dormitory [the Ginza residence in Edo]. This was the greatest difficulty I have ever had, so I am all the more grateful. Since your return to Kyoto, I have been well.

Your letter has been received at Junkō's [Prince Kōkan's] office. Since Kemmotsu had to travel to Kyoto to fetch Shingū, there hasn't been time to write a reply. You should get one after Kemmotsu comes back.

The audience that Hasagawa Chōbei had on the twenty-sixth of this month with Junkō went well. A gift was arranged just as it was for your visit [to the prince] last year. Then [in return] Chōbei placed orders for ceramics. Please thank him upon his return to Kyoto. Please know I will be glad to similarly oblige visitors in the future.

My best regards to all of you — to your wife and to Shotei [Kōrin's widow Tayo]. I regret not having met them for a long time.

[in postscript] Please give my very best New Year's greetings to Nagao. I hope that I will have the pleasure of meeting him again in Edo.

first month, twenty-eighth day
[signed] Ogata Shinsei Furiku [monogram added]
[to] Hikoemon

Third month: Kenzan writes his pottery manual *Tōkō Hitsuyō*, now preserved in the Yamato Bunkakan, Nara. The manual is published in typeset transcription in Yamato Bunkakan 1963 (also see Appendix 2).

Fifth month: Fire ravages Iriya (Kobayashi 1962, 163).

Ninth month: Kenzan travels to Sano, Tochigi Prefecture; writes a second pottery manual, the *Tōji Seihō*, now in the collection of the Takizawa family, Ujiie, Tochigi. *Tōji*

Seihō is published in typeset transcription in Kawahara 1979. The seminal work on the real Sano Kenzan is found in Shinozaki 1942; Shinozaki 1968–69. In those sources, Shinozaki introduces Kenzan's Sano patrons: Sudō Tosen, Matsumura Kosei Eitei, and Ōkawa Kendō. Tosen (given name Riemon; art-name, Chinyrūsai; 1701–79) headed a wealthy merchant family in Koena, near Sano. Tosen himself had been adopted into the Sudō, and was by birth the younger brother of the bailiff Kosei Eitei (given name, Hikokurō; dates unknown). Kendō (given name, Tobei; 1675–1750) was a cultured Sano doctor. Having no heir, he adopted the second son of Sudō Tosen. Ōkawa's first wife was a Matsumura, and his second wife was from the Maruyama, still another Sano family in which a few Kenzan materials were passed down.

Sections of Ōkawa Kendō's diary, now preserved in the Takizawa family collection, mention preparations for Kenzan's visit to Sano: Kendō had placed a large order for bisqueware and materials to an Iriya potter, Kyūsaku, which included forty-six cylindrical vessels, thirty-two cylindrical vessels, forty-two large dishes, eighty large and small *kawarake* (flat dishes), seven incense containers, five *hiire* (ember pot for igniting pipes), a small portable kiln and a quantity of *shiroko* (lead carbonate). Appended to the order is a list of other pottery-related enterprises in the city:

glaze wholesaler: Konoikeya Kichiemon at
   Ryōgokubashi Yoshikawachō;
potters: Tetsuya Jirōbei at Toshimachō 2-chōme;
   Totomiya Bunnojō at Minami Demmachō
   2-chōme; Setosuke at Sukiyabashi;
glass frit supply: at Nippombashi 4-chōme
   higashigawa, next to the store that sells
   Daiōgan medicine.

See Shinozaki Genzō, "Sano Kenzan Monogatari-5" [The Story of Sano Kenzan — part 5], *Tōsetsu* 189 (1968), 44.

1738   Third month, fifteenth day: Prince Kōkan dies (*Rinnōji Nempu*).

Ninth month: Kenzan presents a scroll of fans painted by Kōrin in the manner of Sōtatsu to Tatebayashi Kagei (*Kōrin Hyakuzu*).

Kenzan's Chinese and Japanese poetry mentioned in first fascicle of literary anthology *Dōhōgoenshū*, edited by Shōji Dōnusai. See Suzuki Hancha, "Godai Kenzan Nishimura Myakuan-1" [Fifth-generation Nishimura Myakuan — Part 1], *Tōsetsu* 55 (1957), 47.

It was probably around this time that Kenzan visited Fukagawa where, according to *Koga Bikō*, he was sponsored by the wealthy timberman Sakamoto Beishū. The *Koga Bikō* states that Kenzan lived at Beishū's *nagaya*, and the present connotations of that word as a tenement have prompted the suggestion that Kenzan had sunk into poverty. But in

Kenzan's day, a *nagaya* was simply a long house, usually fronting the street.

According to *Sumidagawa Hanayashiki* (see notes under the year 1820), Kenzan stayed with another wealthy timberman, Naraya Mozaemon. For general information on the Naraya, see Nishiyama Matsunosuke, *Edo Chōnin no Kenkyū* [Research on Edo Townsmen], vol. 1 (Tokyo: Yoshikawa Kōbunkan, 1972), 179–91. Evidence for ceramics production in this neighborhood might be found in an incense box in the Freer Gallery of Art inscribed to the effect that it was made in Nagasaki; there is an area named Nagasaki just a few blocks northeast of the timbermen's villas. For the neighborhood, see Iwai Yoshie, *Edo Machizukushi Kō* [Records on Edo Development] (Tokyo: Seiabō, 1965), 244–45, 347.

There is another top-shaped incense case with an identical inscription illustrated by Mitsuoka Chūsei (Mitsuoka 1973, 96), said to be in the Mitsui Collection; my attempts to locate it in the Mitsui Bunko, Tokyo, have been in vain. One other piece with a Nagasaki inscription is a square incense case decorated with a plum branch in the collection of the Freer Gallery of Art; the technical qualities and calligraphy of the signature are at variance with the one discussed here. The "Kenzan" signature appears to be that of Miura Ken'ya, the Edo Kenzan line potter who actually traveled to Nagasaki, Kyushu, in 1854.

Kenzan has occasionally been linked with a third family of Fukagawa timber merchants, the Fuyuki. The Kōrin *kosode* decorated with autumnal flowers and grasses, now in the collection of the Tokyo National Museum, is said to be a Fuyuki heirloom, prompting speculation that Kōrin was patronized by them. Aside from this one object, however, there is no evidence for a Kōrin-Fuyuki relationship, and no proof whatsoever for Kenzan-Fuyuki contact.

1742 First month, nineteenth day: Kenzan writes to nephew Konishi Hikoemon (KKM 149):

I received a letter from Tomi and Ichisuke that was posted in the old year. But the letter just arrived care of Hikoroku four or five days ago. This accounts for my slow reply, for which I apologize.
First, I am happy that you and your family are well. That your official post in Osaka has been decided is unsurpassingly good news. It is cold there, so please take good care of your health. That you have been chosen from among so many candidates is very auspicious indeed.
I am also glad that you are taking care of Ichisuke. I will write you again.

First month, nineteenth day
Ogata Shinsei Koremitsu [monogram]
[to] Konishi Hikoemon

On the back of that sheet, Kenzan expresses grief over the death of Kōrin's widow:

I was shocked to hear of Shotei's death at the end of last year. I have no words to offer in condolence. I had known her for over forty years. I had hoped to return to Kyoto to meet her again; my regrets are myriad. In prayer I write this. This [condolence gift?] is enclosed.

First month, nineteenth day
Ogata Shinsei Koremitsu [monogram added]
[to] Konishi Hikoemon

Flood in Fukagawa; this may have driven Kenzan back to Iriya.

1743 Sixth month, second day: Kenzan dies. Buried in Zen'yōji at Sakamoto, Ueno (the temple later moved to Nishi Sugamo). Circumstances of death and burial related in *Ueno Oku Goyōnin Chū Kampō Watari On Nikki:*

Shindō Suō no Kami [a local magistrate attached to the Rinnōji] related the following news about Kenzan: A physician who had known him for some time brought the word that Kenzan had been ill and failed to recover; he died this morning. Kenzan had no relatives to see to his funeral; his landlord, Jirōbei, offered to see to the matter but was not so close to Kenzan. Suō no Kami consulted Saemon [apparently a Rinnōji functionary], and together they brought the matter to the secretary of the abbot, who said that since Kenzan enjoyed the favor of former prince-abbot Kōkan, the temple would donate one *ryō* for funeral expenses. Suō no Kami kindly related this to Jirōbei. When the secretary gave the expense money, he stated that the donation was an informal affair and did not constitute an official grant from [the present] prince-abbot Kōjun. Kenzan had no local temple affiliation, so through the good offices of Saemon it was decided to have the burial at Zen'yōji in Sakamoto. Kenzan was duly registered in the temple necrology and services were arranged.

Yamato Shimbun reporter Minami Shinji discovered this passage inscribed into a book owned by one Homma, an official at the Dempōin subtemple, Asakusa. Related in Kobayashi 1948, 15–16.

The date of death and Kenzan's death poems are inscribed on his gravestone at Zen'yōji. It is somewhat unusual that Kenzan is recorded as having died on the same month and day as his brother Kōrin.

1746 *Chajin Kaō Sō* (Grove of Teaman's Monograms)

mentions Kenzan. Subsequent mentions of Kenzan in tea genealogies include: *Yukimagusa Chadō Wakuge* [Tea Meanderings in Snow-laden Grass], by Sakamoto Shūsai, 1747; *Zoku Chajin Kaō Sō* [New Grove of Tea Monograms], 1805; *Chadō Sentei* [Tea Net], by Inagaki Kyūsō, 1816; *Kōgetsu Ō Chake Zuikoshū* [Kōgetsu's Collection of Tea Masters], 1845.

1750 A genealogy in the Konishi archive written by Konishi Hikoemon lists one "Ogata Ihachirō" as a cousin (KKM 151).

1766 Third month: A letter of succession from "second-generation Kenzan" in Edo to Miyazaki Tominosuke:

I copied this [material] from Kenzan shortly before he died. Kenzan hoped that his tradition would be carried on, but through legitimate channels. Following Kenzan's death, we went to the Rinnōji temple office and reported that Kenzan had died of illness. Kenzan's landlord also asked for assistance in the matter. The temple agreed to grant us one *ryō* and told us to proceed. We asked the Zen'yōji temple if Kenzan might be buried there. On the third day [one day after Kenzan's death] we received the money [from the temple]. There is no mistake in this account. Since you have earnestly requested to continue the Kenzan line, I will pass these materials on to you. I record this for the sake of posterity.

Third month, 1766
Second-generation Kenzan [monogram added]
For disciple Miyazaki Tominosuke

Recorded in *Koga Bikō*. See Ōta Kin, ed., *Zōtei Koga Bikō*, vol. 35 (1904) 1559.

1769 A necrology preserved in the Empukuji temple in Tama, Tokyo, mentions that an Ogata Shinhichi, the second son and heir of an "Ogata Kenzan," died in Edo in 1769. As Ihachi's son is said to have moved to Edo (*Sumidagawa Hanayashiki*), Shinhichi may in fact be Ihachi's descendant; if he had become the heir no later than 1769, we have a *terminus ad quem* of 1769 for the death of Ihachi.

1775 Date on a box inscription for a pair of Kenzan-style hand warmers, one with the mark "This made by Minzan after former Kenzan." The box inscription itself identifies Minzan as another name for Ihachi, but Minzan wares as a whole show more affiliation with Delft ware than with Kenzan style.

The name Minzan occurs elsewhere in Japanese ceramics history. In fact, the maker of the Delft and Kenzan-style pieces has been equated with a rather well known Sanuki (Shikoku, Kagawa Prefecture) potter — also named

Minzan. He is said to have been a follower of artist-inventor Hiraga Gennai (1726–79). But there are differences between Sanuki Minzan and the person outlined here. The former uses stamped and incised marks reading "Made by Minzan at Jōshōken in the province of Sanuki" and "Sanuki Shido ware Jōshōken second generation"; his work is typified by molded pieces in the polychrome lead-glaze palette preferred by Gennai. The *min* character of Sanuki Minzan also lacks the jewel (king) radical used in the Minzan signature on the hand warmer.

Other Kenzan-style potters with the *zan* suffix: Ōzan is illustrated in Kushi Takushin, *Kenzan* (Tokyo: Yūzankaku, 1974), no. 167; Chōzan, thought to be connected to Kenzan's Sano trip, is discussed in Suzuki Hancha, "Dai Kenzan kara Leach made — 1" [From the First Kenzan to Leach — Part 1], *Tōsetsu* 76 (1959), 39; Rokuzan is illustrated in Morse 1901, no. 4046.

1792 A dated epilogue in a pottery manual entitled *Tōki Mippōsho* reads:

The above is the ceramics recipe book of Kenzan of Omuro. In addition to his spirit, technique, and refinement, he had divine talent. Late in his life he moved to Edo at the behest of Junkō-sama [Prince Kōkan]; later he came back to Kyoto and died there. He had a late-life disciple named Seigo who was also very skillful, and accordingly Kenzan transferred all his recipes to him. Later, the founder of Banko ware, Nunami Gozaemon, pseudonym Rōzan, conceived an interest in tea and became a disciple of [Omotesenke tea master] Sen Joshinsai [1706–51]. When Nunami was in Kyoto, he found lodgings and was on close terms with Seigo. At his departure from Kyoto, Seigo granted Nunami a pottery manual in Kenzan's own hand. Nunami went on to found the Banko kiln, and now its reputation is spreading far and wide. Three generations have passed since then; as I am old I copy this out and present it to you.

1792, fifth month
Bankodō third generation
Asajisei Recluse San'a [seal added]

The chronology (Joshinsai was the Omotesenke head in the 1730s and 1740s) suggests that the "Kenzan" listed here was not the original but Ihachi. See Suzuki 1942. There are three identical manuals: the *Hongama Uchigama Narabini Kenzan Hihō* in the Wakimoto collection; the *Kenzan Rakuyaki Hisho* in the National Diet Library, Tokyo; and the *Kenzan Hisho* in the collection of Tsutsumi ware potter Hariō Yoshiaki.

1798 Beginning of *Sumiyoshi Ke Koga Tomechō* [Notes on

Painting Connoisseurship of the Sumiyoshi Family] (Coll. Tokyo University of Fine Arts). A total of forty-five Kenzan paintings are recorded and sketched in six volumes, spanning from 1798 to 1863. See Gotoh 1982, 53–58.

1807   Sakai Hōitsu writes to the Konishi family in Kyoto, asking for an Ogata-family genealogy. Hōitsu's original query to Kōrin descendant Konishi Hōshu is lost, but the latter's reply is quoted in the second volume of *Ogata Ryū Hyakuzu* [A Hundred Ogata-School Paintings], published by Nakano Kimei in 1892.

1813   Hōitsu publishes *Ogata Ryū Ryaku Impu,* a single-sheet compendium of Rimpa masters; the *Impu* was republished in booklet form two years later. For illustrations, see Nishimoto Shuko, "Hōitsu no Kōrin Kenshō" [Hōitsu's Kōrin Commemorations], Yamane 1978–80 (Hōitsu school v. 1), 53–58.

1819   Eleventh month: Sahara Kikuu travels to Kyoto to refurbish Kōrin's grave; obtains Kōrin sketches and pottery manual from Konishi family and studies ceramics with Ogata Shūhei. The Kōrin sketches, the Kōetsu-Kūchū-Kenzan manual, and even Kikuu's diary, *Umeya Nikki,* which recorded their existence, are lost. Our knowledge of the contents are based on a report by Aimi Kou, who studied the diary before its disappearance (Aimi 1928). Regarding Kikuu's tutelage under Shūhei, ceramic historians relate that he later assumed the Ogata name out of admiration for Kenzan, but further evidence is wanting.

1820   Fifth month: Kikuu returns to Edo and opens the Sumidagawa kiln at his Shin Ume Yashiki in Mukōjima (*Umeya Nikki;* see Aimi 1928).

    To commemorate the opening, Kikuu printed a pamphlet, *Sumidagawa Hanayashiki.* This mentions the Kōetsu-Kūchū-Kenzan manual, and relates that Kikuu's friend, Yoshimura Kan'a (1764–1848), owned an original pottery manual by Ihachi, Kenzan's adopted son. The *Hanayashiki* also includes a Kenzan genealogy: Kenzan studied the Kōetsu-Kūchū ceramic technique; he pursued Zen under a priest named Dokushō; he never married and took the tonsure; and he adopted Ninsei's son [probably grandson] Ihachi. The document goes on to say that Ihachi's descendants, also named Ihachi, moved to Edo and took employ under a samurai, bringing the Kenzan line to an end. When Kenzan himself lived in Edo he stayed at the resort house of "Naramo" at Honjō Rokkembori [Naramo is the nickname for the wealthy Edo timber merchant Naraya Mozaemon], and also lived east of Tōeizan [Kan'eiji, in present-day Ueno Park] at Iriya village. Finally, the *Hanayashiki* records that after Kōrin's death Kenzan wrote many letters back to the Konishi family [then headed by Kōrin's only legitimate son, who had taken the name Hikoemon]. The *Hanayashiki* is said to exist in the Keiō University

Library, Tokyo, but I have failed to locate it. It is transcribed in Hirotani 1943.

1823   Tenth month: Hōitsu discovers Kenzan's grave at Zen'yōji (*Kenzan Iboku*).

    Twelfth month, first day: A box now containing Kenzan's lamentation poems for Prince Kōkan is inscribed, apparently in the hand of Sakai Hōitsu: "A letter of title transmission from Iriya Kenzan, a hanging scroll, and other documents inherited from Haru, the wife of Miyazaki Tominosuke" (see Gotoh 1982, 164).

    According to a memorandum of Nishimura Myakuan discovered by Kenzan researcher Suzuki Hancha, the lamentation poem scroll was not in the possession of Tominosuke but rather owned by one Hikoemon, a farmer from Sakamoto; this man was also the grandson of a Kenzan disciple named Saizan. See Suzuki Hancha, "Dai Kenzan Kara Leach made — 14" [From the First Kenzan to Leach — Part 14], *Tōsetsu* 114 (1962), p. 68. The scroll and the box are now in the collection of the Yamato Bunkakan, Nara; illustrated and transcribed in Gotoh 1982, 165.

    Late in the year: Hōitsu produces *Kenzan Iboku.* The epilogue reads:

> I have pursued Ogata-style painting for some time, although not to my satisfaction. As the world knows, Kōrin and Kenzan were a pair of great painters. . . . This year, in the tenth month, I was invited to tea by Ryōhan [antiquarian Kohitsu Ryōhan, d. 1853], and by coincidence learned that Kenzan's grave was located near my house, at the Zen'yōji temple on the slopes of Tōeizan [present Ueno Park]. I rushed to the place, found the grave, and offered flowers and incense. Choosing some of the sketches that I had been making of Kenzan painting, I assembled them into a book that would remind posterity of the brilliance of the Ogata school.

The *Kenzan Iboku* is published in full in Tamamushi Satoko, "*Kenzan Iboku* to Genzon Sakuhin" [*Kenzan Iboku* and Extant Works], in Yamane 1978–1980 (Kōrin school v. 2), 57–60.

1824   First month, twenty-eighth day: Sakai Hōitsu passes the Kenzan title to Nishimura Myakuan, as signified in a letter, presently kept with the 1738 lamentation poems in the Yamato Bunkakan, Nara:

> I have held the enclosed pottery manual and scroll for some time, but I will honor your long-standing request. I am busy as a painter, but you have shown a serious interest in ceramics, so I will grant these materials to you. Please pursue the subject with determination.

First month, twenty-eighth day
Ugean [Hōitsu] [monogram added]
[to the] Master of Kasandō [Myakuan]

Illustrated in Gotoh 1982, 165.

1836   Sixth month, twenty-fourth day: Nishimura Myakuan writes *Kenzan Sedaigaki*, a genealogy of the Edo Kenzan line (contents in text). The *Sedaigaki* was first mentioned
by Suzuki Hancha, "Dai Kenzan Kara Leach made-2"
[From the First Kenzan to Leach — Part 2], *Tōsetsu* 79
(1959), 61. I recovered it from a dusty pile of papers in a
closet at Zen'yōji some thirty years later.

Same day: Myakuan also gives art names Kensai, Kenzō,
and Ken'ya to Ida Kichiroku, Sakune Benjirō, and Miura
Ken'ya, respectively. Kichiroku's and Ken'ya's certificates are
in the Ishii family collection. Benjirō's certificate is in the
collection of Ogata Nami, the daughter of Urano Shigekichi, or Edo Kenzan VI. The Urano family obtained the
document from Kenzō's daughter, who visited the Urano as
a ceramics peddler after Kenzō's death in ca. 1878.

Twelfth month: Ida Kichiroku vanishes from Edo, possibly visiting Sano and Bushū, and most surely visiting
Nagasaki and Izawa. Speculation on Kichiroku's employment in Sano is based on two Kichiroku-signed copies of a
Sano Kenzan handwarmer, one in the Morse collection of
the Museum of Fine Arts, Boston (Morse 1901, no. 1350),
and one in the Osaka Municipal Museum. Kichiroku also
matches local descriptions of a nineteenth-century potter
who stayed in the district (see Shinozaki 1942, 49).
Kichiroku's spell at the Kameyama kiln in Nagasaki is
attested to in an 1856 entry in the diary of Izawa merchant
Takegawa Chikusai (1809–83); an extant Kameyama bottle
in the Nagasaki Municipal Museum bears the Kichiroku
signature and the date 1856. Work at the Izawa Banko kiln
is substantiated in the diary of its owner, Chikusai. For the
Kameyama and Izawa references, see Masui Kuniō, "Hakodate Ken'ya no Dembun o Jisshō Suru" [Hearsay Reports
of Hakodate Ken'ya Confirmed], *Me no Me* 189 (1985),
80–84. After Izawa, Kichiroku is rumored to have worked
at the Hanno kiln, in Bushū, Saitama, but further evidence
is lacking.

1837   The biographical dictionary *Kōeki Shoka Jimmei Roku*
contains an entry on Nishimura Myakuan. Quoted in
Suzuki Hancha, "Godai Kenzan Nishimura Myakuan — 1"
[Fifth-Generation Kenzan Nishimura Myakuan — Part 1],
Tōsetsu 55 (1957), 45.

1842   100th Kenzan commemoration.
Gosuke, or Kyoto Kenzan III, is active in Kyoto, as
suggested by a box inscription for an incense container
with a *shishi* design: "Made with Narutaki clay for the
hundredth commemoration of my ancestor; made in 1842

[by] third-generation Kenzan heir"; the inside of the lid of
this pot is inscribed, "Made by Japan Gosuke Kenzan."
Other Gosuke-related box inscriptions include:
a) For a tea bowl at the Enshōji, Nara (also mentioned in
the section on Ihachi, Chapter 6): "Made by second-
generation Ihachi, [box] inscribed by third-generation
Kenzan heir"; sealed "Gosuke."
b) For a set of ten earthenware plates: "ten *teshiro* made at
Hateda; Kenzan staying at Taigadō." See Kushi Takushin,
Kenzan (Tokyo: Yūzankaku, 1974), 340.
c) For an incense container with designs of chrysanthemum
and paulownia: "Made with Narutaki clay for the hundredth commemoration of my ancestor; [dated] 1842 [by]
third-generation Kenzan heir." Sealed "Gosuke." The inside of the lid is inscribed, "Made in the Kaiunzan
[Hōzōji]." See Yasuda Kenji, "Ninsei no Haka to Kenzan
no Ido" [Ninsei's Grave and Kenzan's Well], *Tōsetsu* 15
(1954), 23.
d) On the back of one of a set of ten earthenware plates:
"Made in the Bunka era (1804–17) by Miyata Yahei; third-
generation Kenzan Go." The Kenzan-style *ji* monogram
also is inscribed on some pieces in that set. See Nonomura
Shigeharu, "Tōkō Kenzan Dai Su Kō" [Speculations on
the Generations of Kenzan], *Shoga Kottō Zasshi* 55 (1912).
Significantly, the 1878 craft compendium *Kōgei Shiryō* mentions that a "Kenzan Yahei" was a specialist in earthenware
(*uchigama*) firing in Kyoto.
e) For a water jar in the Dutch style: "Third-generation
Zōrokudō Kenzan." The inside of the lid is inscribed,
"Kenzan Go." See Suzuki Hancha, "Kenzan Keifu Shinkō"
[New Thoughts on the Kenzan Genealogy], *Nihon Bijutsu
Kōgei* 151 (1951), 17.
f) A set of earthenware plates with the inscription "Sandai
Zō Bunka Nensei" [Made by third-generation in the
Bunka Era (1804–18)]. Hancha, "Kenzan Keifu Shinkō,"
22.
A sequel version of *Kōeki Shoka Jimmei Roku* states that
Nishjimura Myakuan's second son Gengensai had become
the "sixth-generation Kenzan." According to Mori Dai-
kyō's 1926 *Kinko Geien Sōdan* [Anthology of Stories on Art
Circles Old and New], Gengensai was later adopted by
Yoshiwara landlord Takeshima Nizaemon. See Suzuki
Hancha, "Godai Kenzan . . . — 6," *Tōsetsu* 62 (1958), 36.

1845   Ken'ya marries and is adopted into the Ishii family.
Sets up a small kiln on the Ishii estate in Fukagawa. See
Nakano Keijirō, "Miura Ken'ya to Hatano Gama" [Miura
Ken'ya and the Hatano Kiln], *Yakimono Shumi* 6:10 (1941), 26.

1847   Ledgers in the Kajiyama family, dated 1847 and
signed "Ishii Ken'ya," show that Ken'ya was receiving
orders — mostly for Ritsuō-style inlay ware — from daimyo Sakai Uta no Kami, Mori Sado no Kami, Matsudaira
Ukyō no Kami, Mizuno Oki no Kami, Bitchū no Kami,

Suruga no Kami, and Nambu no Kami. See Nakano, 27.

ca. 1851 Asaoka Kotei publishes Rimpa section of *Koga Bikō*, providing some details of Kenzan's life in Edo. See Ōta Kin, ed., *Zōtei Koga Bikō*, vol. 35 (Kyoto: Shibunkaku, 1970), pp. 1558–59. Less important Kenzan references in the period include: *Fusō Meiga Den* [Record of Famous Painters], vol. 44 (1848), by Kurokawa Shinson (a nephew, incidentally, of Edo Kenzan V Nishimura Myakuan); *Tōkikō* [Thoughts on Ceramics](1854), by Tauchi Baiken; *Honchō Tōki Kōshō* [Research on Japanese Ceramics] (1858), by Kanamori Tokusui.

1854 Ken'ya sent to Nagasaki along with the naval hero Katsu Kaishū (1823–99) to study Western shipbuilding and navigation techniques.

1856 Ken'ya invited to Nagasaki to supervise the building of Japan's first ironclad steamship, the *Kaisei Maru*.

1857 Summer: Ken'ya invited to Hokkaido as an industrial consultant. See Masui Kunio, "Hakodate Ken'ya," 78–84.

1858 Ken'ya grants Tsutsumi-ware potter Shōji Genhichirō Yoshitada the name "Kemba" and some other items: The materials, still in the collection of Tsutsumi-ware potter Hario Yoshiaki, include:
a) A certificate reading "Kemba: This title granted for devotion to Ogata-style ceramics; apply yourself with diligence. [signed] Kenzan Shinsei sixth-generation Ken'ya."
b) A pottery manual entitled *Kenzan Hisho* [Secret Kenzan Manual], which bears an inscription on the back of the cover: "For the Tsutsumi-ware potter Kemba, student of sixth-generation Karaku Shisui Shinsei Ogata Kenzan, Miura Ken'ya."
c) A number of seals variously reading: "Tenrokudō"; "Ken'ya"; one triumphantly reads "Miura Ken'ya, chief shipbuilder and navigation instructor of Ōshu, Sendai, in Great Japan." See Masui Kunio, "Miura Ken'ya: Sono Hito to Kōdō" [Miura Ken'ya: The Person and his Movements], *Me no Me* 94 (1984), 82.

1865 Twelfth month: Ken'ya is released from the Date clan.

1868 Ken'ya is imprisoned for treason.

ca. 1870 Ken'ya begins to work at the Hatano kiln. Its owner, Kajiyama Ryōsuke, was originally from a rich family of Odawara moneylenders called Yoshida. He was adopted into the Kajiyama family in 1869. In his new business as a kimono merchant he used the name Kikuya (which had also been the Yoshida business name). In addition to his interest in painting, Ryōsuke also went to study medicine in Kyushu, but seems to have become enamored of ce-

ramics; upon his return his baggage was found to be stuffed with potshards. He called his grounds Shōkoen, and assumed the art names "Shōkoen," "Kanzan," and "Shōkodō Shūjin." See Nakano 1941.

1871–75 Ken'ya opens, in succession, an electric insulator factory in Yokosuka, a brick and glass factory at Senjū, and an export-ware workshop in Fukagawa. All quickly go bankrupt. See Miura Yone, "Chichi Ken'ya o Kataru — Sono Ni" [Talking About My Father, Ken'ya — Part Two], *Yakimono Shumi* (1941), 13.

1875 Ken'ya sets up his last kiln at Chōmeiji, Mukōjima. See Miura Yone, "Chichi Ken'ya," 13.

1878 Kawasaki Chitora visits the Konishi, living at the intersection of Yanagi no Baba and Nijō streets in Kyoto; examines the family archives. See Kawasaki Chitora, "Kōrin-Hōitsu," *Kokka* 57 (1894), 158–166.

1892 One hundred fiftieth Kenzan commemoration.
June 2: Former Date-clan Confucianist Ōtsuki Joden conducts a one-hundred-fifty-year commemoration at Kenzan's grave at Zen'yōji on June 2, 1892. Okumura Kenshō acts as the Kenzan-line representative. Minami Shinji reported the event thirteen days later in the *Yamato Shimbun*. Unrelated to the ceremony but of importance to Kenzan studies is Minami's quote of a passage from an official record, *Ueno Ooku Goyōnin Chū Kampō Watari On Nikki* (Daily Record of the Kan'eiji Temple for the Kampō Era), dealing with the circumstances of Kenzan's death and burial. Minami had found the passage inscribed into a copy of the *Kenzan Iboku* owned by one Homma, a magistrate from the Dempō-in temple at Asakusa. See Maeda Kōsetsu, "Kenzan to Hakuzan" [Kenzan and Hakuzan], *Shoga Kottō Zasshi* 46 (1912). This was the first document to link Kenzan with the Kan'eiji (Rinnōji) temple. Taken together with the contents of the *Koga Bikō*, the events described in the Kan'eiji diary commonly have been seen as an indication of Kenzan's late-life poverty and obscurity.
June 3: Date-clan Confucianist Ōtsuki Joden acquires a package of Kenzan documents from Ken'ya's nephew, Miura Matusjirō, who wrote a receipt:

Record:
— One Kenzan pottery manual related verbally by the original master and copied down by the second generation;
— One scroll of waka written in lamentation of Sōhōin [Prince Kōkan];
— Chinese and Japanese death poems with a brief genealogy attached;
— Three letters of transmission: second generation to third generation, third generation's widow to Hōitsu, Hōitsu to Nishimura Myakuan;

— Containers for the above: a large and small box. These objects remained in pawn after Ken'ya's death, but you have redeemed them as an expression of your interest. Since you were a friend of Ken'ya's for over thirty years he would have been happy about this. We waive further claims to this material.

1892, sixth month, third day
[to] Ōtsuki Joden
[from] Miura Matsujirō

Quoted in Kobayashi 1948, 9–10. This Matsujirō was the son of Teru, a sister of Ken'ya's wife, Ei. Ken'ya adopted him as a son late in his life, hence the Miura name. With the exception of the poems to Kōkan and the letter of transmission from Hōitsu to Myakuan, all of the above were destroyed in the 1923 Kanto earthquake. I suspect that the "verbally related manual" was really not by Kenzan at all but from the hand of his adopted son Ihachi. The manual given to the Sendai potter Kemba, as well as one left in the Negishi family collection by Ken'ya's disciple Kenshō, have the same contents as the Ihachi manual, *Tōki Mippōsho*, discussed in Chapter 6. It would seem, then, that the documentary basis of the Edo Kenzan line was not Kenzan at all, but Ihachi. The contents of Kenzan's own manuals, *Tōkō Hitsuyō* and *Tōji Seihō*, are completely different.

Sixth month, second day (old lunisolar calendar): The Nippon Bijutsu Kyōkai (Japan Art Society) sponsored an exhibition of Rimpa (Sōtatsu-Kōrin) school works in Ueno, Tokyo. The organizer was Nakano (Seisei) Kimei (1834–92), who had studied painting under Hōitsu-follower Suzuki Kiitsu (1796–1858) and thus was heir to the Edo tradition of Kōrin-school painting and scholarship. Three years earlier, Kimei had published *Ogata Ryū Hyakuzu* (One Hundred Pictures of the Ogata School), which contained three Kenzan works. Kimei's death one month before the 1892 show compelled son Kigyoku to assume sole responsibility for an exhibition of three hundred and fifty works by Tawaraya Sōtatsu, his follower Sōsetsu, Kōrin, Kenzan, Watanabe Shikō, Tatebayashi Kagei, Hōitsu, Kiitsu, and various Hōitsu disciples. The *Hyakuzu* was also republished that year. See Suzuki Hancha, "Kenzan Hyakugojūnen Kinen no Koto Domo" [One Hundred Fiftieth Kenzan Commemoration], *Yakimono Shumi*, VI:9 (1941), 27–36. Of interest is that one hundred twenty of these items were applied art objects.

1897 Justus Brinckmann publishes *Kenzan: Beiträge zur Geschichte der japanischen Töpferkunst.* Brinckmann's survey is a model of scholarship limited only by his generation's lack of exposure to comparative materials. Some important Brinckmann innovations: 1) introduction and translation of

hitherto unknown Japanese sources such as Kawasaki Chitora's "Kōrin-Hōitsu" and *Kenzan Iboku*; 2) a historically accurate description of the tea ceremony based on an 1874 article by German ethnographer Hermann Funk; 3) translation and explication of the poetry on Kenzan wares; 4) a discussion of connoisseurship based on indigenous Japanese criteria such as the nature of the clay body, forming, and firing marks; 5) a roster of Kenzan followers and imitators; 6) scientific analysis of one of the Hamburg Kenzans for tin oxide content to see if Kenzan understood the Delft opacifying agent (results negative). See Brinckmann 1897.

1901 Ken'ya disciple Urano Shigekichi adopted by Ogata Keisuke, who claimed descent from Ogata Kenzan. This "Kenzan's" first son, Chūbei, moved to Kishū (Wakayama Prefecture) and was adopted into the Sakata family, whereupon the second son Shinhichi inherited the family headship. Shinhichi left the family home in Teramachi Sanjō, Kyoto, and settled in Kurosukidani, Akasuka, Edo, where he died in 1769. Ten years later, third-generation Senzaemon (d. 1796) moved the family to Zushi, now part of Kanagawa Prefecture, to take up farming. The fourth- and fifth-generation descendants died in 1843 and 1855, respectively. Keisuke, a third son of the fifth-generation heir, succeeded an older brother in 1882. See Ogata Kensai, "Ogata Kenzan oyobi sono Kakei ni tsuite" [Concerning Ogata Kenzan and his Family Line], *Shoga Kottō Zasshi* 87 (June 1915). According to Urano's daughter Ogata Nami, Keisuke was a doorman for the kabuki actor Ichikawa Ennosuke in Asakusa, and had the unusual talent of painting sarasa textile patterns on leather. Urano's father-in-law Shimaoka Renjō probably met Keisuke through local amateur art circles, and that connection led to the adoption of Urano into Keisuke's family in 1901. Urano used the name Kenzan VI after the adoption. See Ogata Kenjo (Nami), *Hasu no Mi* [The Seed of the Lotus] (Kamakura: Kamakura Shunjūsha, 1981), 46–53.

1912 The Kokka Club holds a one-hundred-seventy-year Kenzan commemorative exhibition in Tokyo. Earlier in 1912, the national railroad had claimed Zen'yōji as a right-of-way, whereupon the temple was moved from Sakamoto to its present location at Nishi Sugamo. Kenzan's remains were moved with the temple, but it was decided that the original gravestone and Hōitsu stele should remain as close as possible to Sakamoto; the Kokka Club identified its own headquarters at Ikaho as the most appropriate place! The inventory for the commemoration shows twenty paintings, fourteen ceramics, four calligraphies, and four other craft objects by Kenzan and Kōrin. The Club also sponsored a reprinting of Hōitsu's *Kenzan Iboku*. See Kimura Sutezō, "Kokka Kurabu no Kenzan Kenshō Jigyō — Jō" [Kokka Club Kenzan Commemoration Project: Part One], *Yakimono*

Shumi 6:8 (1941). Fortunately, grave and gravestone are now reunited at Zenyōji.

1913 Scholars begin to study the Konishi archive. See Aimi 1915; Fukui 1915.

1928 Kasauga Junsei begins to dig Kenzan's kiln site at Narutaki (Kasuga 1930).

1936 Ninagawa Teiichi publishes his discovery of the Ninnaji diary, *Onki* (Ninagawa 1936).

1937–38 Tanaka Kisaku publishes documents establishing Kenzan's life at Shūseidō (Tanaka 1937, Tanaka 1938).

1940 Tamabayashi Haruo introduces details concerning Kenzan's life in Edo (Tamabayashi 1940). This same article reappears with important additions in *Kenzan* [Publication of the Kenzan Society] 3 (1950).

1941 Haga Yoshikiyo publishes parts of *Kyoto Oyakusho Muki Taigai Oboegaki,* which mentions Kenzan's move to Chōjiyamachi in 1712. See Haga 1941.

1942 Two-hundredth Kenzan commemoration; three pottery manuals, *Tōkō Hitsuyō, Tōji Seihō,* and *Tōki Mippōsho* brought to light (Kawakita 1942, Shinozaki 1942, and Suzuki 1942, respectively). Exhibition held at Takashimaya Bijutsu Salon — see *Kenzan Ihō* [Remaining Fragrance of Kenzan] (Tokyo: Kenzan Kai, 1943). Fukui Rikichirō assembles all bibliographical materials in his "Kōhon Kenzan Nempyō" [Tentative Kenzan Chronology] (Fukui 1942).

1948 Kobayashi writes the first scholarly Kenzan monograph, *Kenzan Kyoto Hen* [Kyoto Kenzan] (Kobayashi 1948).

1962 Sano Kenzan scandal breaks. See Leach 1966; Idegawa 1983; Wilson 1987.

Appendix Two
ESSENTIALS FOR THE POTTER

The two pottery manuals that Kenzan wrote in 1737, *Tōkō Hitsuyō* (Essentials for the Potter) and *Tōji Seihō* (Ceramic Techniques) are among the oldest books of their type in Japan, and indeed in all of East Asia. The more comprehensive of the two, *Tōkō Hitsuyō*, is translated in this appendix. Supplements from the *Tōji Seihō* will be included in the annotations.

The *Tōkō Hitsuyō* (fig. 169), now preserved in the Yamato Bunkakan in Nara, is a compendium of three ceramic traditions, and Kenzan organized it accordingly. The first section is a copy of the notes that Kenzan received from Ninsei in 1699, to which Kenzan made annotations in red ink. In the second section, Kenzan relates the low-temperature (*uchigama*) techniques that he learned from Magobei, an artisan that he employed from the Narutaki years. Techniques that Kenzan considered his own comprise the third section.

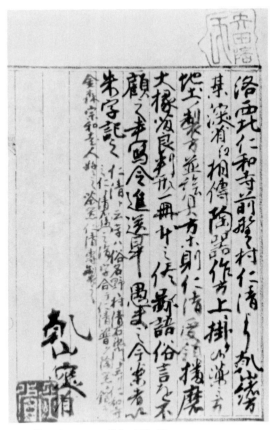

169. Opening page of the *Tōkō Hitsuyō.*

The following conventions are employed in the translation: (a) The notes appear first, followed by Kenzan's annotations in shaded boxes; my additions are in the footnotes; (b) Page numbers (pagination mine; there is no pagination in the original) are bracketed in the left margin; (c) In place of Kenzan's rather inconsistent use of circles and dashes to mark headings, I have used spaces and, for larger divisions, upper-case letters; (d) Ceramic materials are given in Japanese in their first use, with their Western equivalents appended in brackets; wherever possible, the Western equivalents are used thereafter; (e) Standards of measure employed by Kenzan:

Capacity:

1 *gō* = .384 pint (U.S.) = .18 liter
1 *shō* = 10 *gō* = 1.92 quarts (U.S.) = 1.8 liters
1 *to* = 10 *shō* = 4.8 gallons (U.S.) = 18 liters

Weight:

1 *momme* (or *me*) = 1.325 ounces = 3.75 grams
1 *bu* = 1/10 *momme*
1 *kamme* = 1,000 *momme* = 8.72 pounds = 3.75 kilograms

ESSENTIALS FOR THE POTTER

[THE NINSEI RECIPES]

[1] The techniques of pottery fabrication, glaze mixing, and clay formulation that were passed down from Nonomura Ninsei, who lived in front of the Ninnaji temple in northwest Kyoto, to me, Kenzan Ogata Shinsei, are presented here in the form of a book written by Ninsei, signed with the title Harima Daijō, and seal Fujiyoshi, that he was granted. The techniques are copied out in their original form, including even the colloquial terms, as you have requested. The contents are not to be divulged to anyone.

Kenzan Shinsei
[sealed] *Shinsei*

> Ninsei's name was originally Nonomura Seiemon. The name Ninsei came from combining the *Nin* of Ninnaji and the *Sei* of Seiemon; this is the name that he commonly used on his ceramics. Wares in the preference of Kanamori Sōwa were almost entirely made by Ninsei.

[2] CLAYS FOR HIGH-TEMPERATURE CERAMICS

[Base clay:]

> To clay from Kurodani,
> add Yamashina stone
> and levigate. Adjust the
> proportions according
> to specifications.

This clay has been mined for many years in front of the Shiunzan Kinkai Kōmyōji temple in Kurodani. There is an upper layer of white clay, a middle layer of white clay, and a bottom layer used for saggars. There is also a red clay, which is frequently used. The upper layer of Kurodani clay is used for items of high quality, and the middle and lower strata are used according to requirements. Yamashina stone is mined from a mountain called Fuji no O in Yamashina, east Kyoto. The people of Yamashina dig it and sell it to villagers here and there.[1] Ninsei has written a title "Memorandum on Fine and Ordinary Clays" after this, but there is no further qualification. Perhaps he meant that there is a distinction between clay grades, or perhaps it is a title for the following section on clays for the *Goki* style.

Goki-Style Clay:

Kurodani clay:	one *to*, levigated
Yūgyō clay:	five *shō*, dry-sifted
Yamshina stone:	six *shō*, levigated

Mix the above ingredients.

> Goki-style base clays need not be limited to a mixture of Kurodani and Yūgyō clays; if one experiments with clays from any area, I believe that good results can be obtained.[2]

[3] Irabo-Style Clay:

Kurodani red clay:	one *to*, dry-sifted
Yūgyō clay:	five *shō*, dry-sifted
Yamashina stone:	three *shō*, dry-sifted

> This clay formula is not limited to a mixture of Kurodani and Yūgyō clays; if one experiments with clays of any area, I believe that good results can be obtained.

Karatsu-Style Clay:

> Kurodani white clay,
> dry-sifted
> Add a little Kurodani
> red clay to redden the
> body.

> This clay may be formulated from materials of any locale, but especially if one uses the light-red clay body from Karatsu in Hizen, wares comparable to the originals can be produced.
> Rather than blending red and white clays from Kurodani or Yūgyō, one can search for a light-red clay and experiment with it; if the right color emerges in the kiln, it is satisfactory.[3]

Seto *Kwanyū*-Style Clay:

> Kurodani top-grade
> white clay, dry-sifted

> It would appear that *kwanyū* is written with the characters for "ice pattern." This style, commonly called Shino, is a type of ceramics made at Seto in the taste of Oribe. It is really impossible to duplicate [4] the white color of Shino with Kurodani clays; there may be some superficial resemblance, but the disparities are greater. I ordered clay from Seto and worked with it, but any base clay is satisfactory. Formulate a body incorporating ground-up bisqueware [grog], and make a shape. When it is still moist, dip it into a slip made of the aforementioned Seto clay in the same way you would dip a pot into glaze. Let the pot dry, bisque-fire it, and glaze it. Since the slip is from Seto, the fired result will be close to real Shino ware of Seto. Among old Seto wares, there are also vessels of a pale persimmon color that are painted with designs in black and white; these are made of Seto clay, but one can also duplicate the effect with slip in the same manner as described above, and carry out the painting on top of that. The effect will hardly differ from the originals. These styles were made to the taste of Furuta Oribe, and are found in such shapes as incense containers, wine cups, plates, and the like.[4]

Clay for *Benizara*-Style with White Painting:

> Add one part Kurodani
> red clay, dry-sifted, to
> one part Kurodani red
> clay, levigated.

For a pigment [to paint on top of that foundation], dissolve the finest white clay from Kurodani, and use it to paint designs on the raw ware. Since the glaze is transparent with bluish-black mottling, the painting will show up as white.

[5] > The technique for white slip is the greatest secret of the Kenzan kiln, so I will pass it on orally rather than writing it down. I have seen pieces using the above recipe, but the white does not really emerge

as a pure white. Even when it is made of the finest Kurodani white clay, the color is slightly gray. Because I thought it impossible to achieve a good white with this mixture, I attempted to use white clay from Yagi mountain in Bizen and white clay from Satsuma. In particular, I used material from Akaiwa village in Kuzu district, Bungo, which is dug by the villagers and used to whiten paper; using this clay I conceived an original way of painting in white. Recently, many kilns in east Kyoto have imitated this technique, using a material recently introduced to Shimo Awata called Dainichi Yamamoto, mined in Higashi Iwakura. They mix this with Fujio clay, and use it to paint in white. While the color of the material seems white, the pigment piles up on the surface in an unattractive manner. The white pigment used in the Kenzan kiln does not pile up like that. There is a white enamel that protrudes from the surface, but I shall discuss that later.[5]

[6] Ordinary White Clay:

> White Kurodani clay,
> first grade: one *to*
> Yamashina stone: as much as three *shō*
> Levigate the ingredients.

> If ordinary white clay is called for, Kurodani second grade or Yūgyō clay will suffice. Places where good clays can be mined are found everywhere. This fact could have been stated at the beginning of this section, but it might have been misleading.

Clay for Large Vessels:

> Yūgyō clay, sifted fine
> Mix with Kurodani
> second grade, levigated
> The quantity depends on one's specifications.
> This clay is good for making water jars and flower vases. It is also good for kettles, ewers, tea-storage jars, and waste-water jars.

> I am presently contemplating the correct proportions for this mixture.

> Not only these blends of clay, but the red and white clays from anywhere in the world can be used for making ceramics. As to whether the material is good or bad, one has only to put it in the kiln and fire it, and the quality will be readily apparent. If its use in a formula is limited, it is not satisfactory.

[7] *EGUSURI* [UNDERGLAZE PIGMENTS] FOR HIGH-TEMPERATURE CERAMICS

Egusuri means *enogu* [pigment]. This refers to painting after the bisque firing and prior to applying the glaze. Although white pigment should be discussed in this section, I have not included it, for it is already mentioned in the section on *Benizara*-style clay. White pigment and the use of white pigment to cover the surface of the vessel is a technique first devised by me. Now all of the potters in Kyoto use it.

Black pigment:

> *Kane hada* [iron scales],
> finely ground

Kane hada is an iron powder. When a blacksmith forges a tool, the iron scales that fly off the ingot are made up of this material. It may be used by itself, or it may be mixed with *gosu* (asbolite, an impure cobalt) in 5:5 or 10:4 proportions.

Blue pigment:

> The same as *Nankin*
> [Chinese cobalt]

Nankin means the ceramics pigment brought by the Chinese to Nagasaki. There are three grades, which represent a wide spectrum of quality; the very best yields a brilliant blue.

Pale persimmon [colored] pigment:

> Use Fukakusa *mizutare*
> [a hydrated iron dug at
> Fukakusa]; add *funori*
> [seaweed syrup].

It is also advisable to add a little *nikawa* [animal glue]. But when one paints with *mizutare*, the light persimmon color does not always come out. Pale-red clays also work, and I recall that the pale persimmon-colored clay from Seto produces an extraordinarily good color.[6]

[8] GLAZES FOR HIGH-TEMPERATURE CERAMICS

White [transparent] Glaze:

> White stone [feldspar]:   one *to*
> (grind very fine and
> levigate)
> Ash: six *shō*

White stone is a white sand taken from the mountains at Namase village, Arima district, Sesshū. There is a wholesaler of this material near the south end of the Tenjin bridge in Osaka.[7] Sources are not limited to the white sand from Namase. In every place where ceramics are made, suitable white sands exist, so it can hardly be said that ceramics cannot be made without Namase stone. Since this is the material that has long been used by Kyoto potters, however, I shall leave it at that. The above-mentioned ash is wood ash; it is the same material that is used in the dyeing of silk cloth [as a mordant]. After the ash has been used by the dyers, the waste is used by the potter. Generally, if this white glaze turns a greenish-blue in the kiln, the heat is too strong, and if the surface looks like an egg the heat is too weak. How to make the highest quality white glaze using the above formula [is in the next recipe]:

A More Beautiful White [transparent] Glaze:

Feldspar:	one *to*
Ash:	eight *shō*
Process the same as above.	

The meaning of a beautiful glaze is that it has more gloss. The basic ingredients are the same. White stone is the same as the Namase stone above.

Glaze for *Benizara*-Style Wares:

[9]
Feldspar:	one *to*
Ash:	one *to*, eight *shō*
Process the same as above.	

This is a recipe in which the percentage of ash is high and the percentage of stone is low. As a glaze it is rather fluid. The name *benizara* comes from a technique used in Owari-Seto; Ninsei said that it was a local term of the region. The white stone in this recipe is Namase sand. Among old tea bowls, there is a type from Seto known as *Hakuan*. The foundation clay is white, and the fluid glaze turns a bluish color where it pools. This effect is known as *namako*, and is thought to come from using a weak glaze.

Kōrai [Korean Teabowl] Glaze:

Feldspar:	one *to*, levigated
Ash:	one *to*, two *shō*
Shiroko [lead carbonate]:	one *shō*
This is the glaze for *Goki*-style wares.

When this glaze is applied over a foundation of Korean clay, the results will be very good, as I have found.[8]

[10] TEA CADDY GLAZES

Kakitsubata Glaze [base coat]:

Fukakusa *mizutare*:	1 *kamme*
Ash:	360 *momme*
Iron oxide:	60 *momme*

Kakitsubata is a style of Seto tea caddy famous from long ago. Fukakusa *mizutare* is the metallic portion precipitated out of red clay.

Glaze for Pouring over *Kakitsubata* Glaze:

This is called *keiyaku*.	
Fukakusa *mizutare*:	15 *me*
Ash:	30 *me*
Chūdei [brass filings]:	1 *me*

Keiyaku is the glaze used to provide the decorative accent on tea caddies. Generally, among tea caddy glazes there are *kakeyū* [base coats] and *keiyaku*; the latter is applied on top of the former. The glaze that is applied to the body has a high percentage of *mizutare* and a lower percentage of ash, so as a glaze it is refractory and will not run; the glaze on top has a higher percentage of ash, so it is weaker in the heat. When it runs, it creates a decorative accent.

[11] *Kaki* [persimmon] Glaze:

Shigaraki *mizutare*:	a little
Fukakusa *mizutare*:	a lot
Mix the above to make a batch of 2 *kamme*, 500 *me*	
Add ash:	850 *me*

Shigaraki *mizutare* can be found anywhere in the pottery villages of Shigaraki as red clay. This glaze can be used on tea caddies as well as on various other vessels. Where the fire is strong, the glaze will turn red; where the fire is weaker, it will turn black.

[12] *Nogime* [*temmoku*] Glaze:

Shigaraki *mizutare*:	5 cups
Ash:	7 cups
Shōban:	15 *momme*
To make *temmoku*, mix these together.

This is a type of old Seto tea caddy, one esteemed for its quality. *Temmoku* is a tea bowl with a rather strange shape; the name comes from the size of the bowl.[9]

Shunkei Glaze:

Fukakusa *mizutare*:	6 cups
Ash:	3 cups
Kibune purple stone:	1 cup
Kongōsha [carborundum]:	half cup
Gofun (calcium carbonate):	a little
Lead carbonate:	a little
Iron scales:	a little

Kibune stone can be found in quantity in the Kibune River north of Kyoto.[10]

[13] Tea Caddy Glaze:

Mizutare:	10 cups
Calcium carbonate:	3 cups
Kin no ru kasu [gold slag]:	1 cup
Ash:	15 cups
Konjō [smalt]:	half cup

This is one of the techniques learned by Ninsei during his study in Seto, in Owari. *Kin no ru kasu* is the slag left over from gold and silver mining. When gold is smelted this is what is left over. *Konjō* is the same as *hana konjō* and *kara konjō*.

Seto Glaze:

Mizutare:	1 *shō*
Ash:	1 *shō*
Shiroboko:	1 *shō*[11]

Karamono Glaze:

Fukakusa *mizutare*:	1 *kamme*
Ash:	900 *me*
[14] *Kanaguro* stone:	150 *me*
Kaiseki (beach stone):	100 *me*
Purple stone:	200 *me*
Lead carbonate:	50 *me*

Kanaguro, according to Ninsei, can be found in Seto, but I think the purple-black stone from the bed of the Kamo River in Kyoto can be used. *Kaiseki* has a purple-yellow color. Purple stone is the same as *Kibune* stone.

[15] *Kana* Glaze for Tea Caddies:

Fukakusa *mizutare*:	500 *me*
Ash:	300 *me*
Kurohama:	a little

This is a tea caddy glaze where metallic flashes appear on the surface. *Kurohama*, according to

Ninsei, is a product used in Seto, but iron scales may be substituted as well.

Shōi-Style Tea Caddy Glaze:

Fukakusa *mizutare*:	62 *momme*
Shigaraki *mizutare*:	62 *momme*
Iron scales:	7 *momme*
Brass filings:	13 *momme*

Shōi-style is a type of old tea caddy.

[16] *Namako* Glaze:

Mizutare:	194 *momme*
Ash:	90 *momme*
Brass filings:	8 *momme*

Namako is the name of an old style of tea caddy, very fine in quality.

[Another] *Karamono* Glaze:

Fukakusa *mizutare*:	100 *me*
Purple clay:	30 *me*
Lead carbonate:	5 *me*
Ash:	90 *me*
Tobacco ash (use the stalk):	20 *me*
Gin no karami [silver slag]:	10 *momme*

When silver ore is smelted at a silver mine, the *karami* [waste] floats to the top and the silver sinks. The top is discarded. I saw this process at the Tada silver mine in Sesshū. If one applies to the silver mine this can be delivered.[12]

[17] *Asahi*-Style Glaze:

Fukakusa *mizutare*:	150 *me*
Omobai ["heavy" ash]:	85 *momme*
Gold slag:	26 *momme*, 5 *bu*
Purple clay:	40 *me*
Calcium carbonate:	3 *momme*
Iron scales:	5 *momme*

Omobai, according to Ninsei, is the ash that has accumulated in the flue of the kiln over a long period of time. Purple clay is calcined mountain ochre. Kibune stone works better than the purple clay in this recipe.

[18] This concludes the section on tea caddies.

OTHER HIGH-TEMPERATURE GLAZES

Ruri Glaze:

Namase feldspar:	1 *shō*

Ash:	6 *gō*
Gosu:	22 *momme*

Ruri glazed wares are made in China and in Hizen [Arita]. The dark-blue glaze is applied to the entire surface. The shapes include deep bowls and the like. The glaze is made by mixing high-quality *gosu* into the base glaze. This glaze used on a Kyoto clay might not work very well, but I have never tried it.

Celadon Glaze:

Namase feldspar:	1 *shō*
Lead carbonate:	4 *gō*
Ash:	1 *shō* 3 *gō*
Gosu:	a little

In Chinese celadon manufacture, a stone that produces a green color is mixed with ash to produce the glaze. I cannot understand why Ninsei added *gosu*.[13]

[19] Green Seto [Oribe] Glaze:

Feldspar:	1 *shō*
Ash:	1 *shō* 8 *gō*
Brass filings:	5 *momme*

This is a good mixture. This is the green Seto glaze that is applied over a base of transparent Seto glaze on plates and other vessels. When applied in this manner, it produces a good effect. I have tried it many times.[14]

Rust Glaze:

Mizutare:	1 *shō* 5 *gō*
Ash:	3 *shō* 5 *gō*

Dissolve the above in water and apply.

This rust glaze is a persimmon-colored glaze used for various utensils such as cooking pots, kettles, tea-storage jars, water jars, waste-water jars, and large storage jars.

[20] *Irabo* Glaze:

Yamashina stone:	10 cups
Ash:	8 cups

Tea Caddy Glaze:

Mizutare:	10 cups
Ash:	12 cups

Mix the above two glazes in the following proportions:

Irabo Glaze:	8 cups
Tea Caddy Glaze:	10 cups

Apply this mixture with the same thickness as the *Goki*-style glaze.

This *Irabo* mixture is not satisfactory. The *Irabo* preferred by tea enthusiasts has a foundation of white *hakeme*. The Irabo glaze is applied on top of that. In this mixture, however, the red clay in the *mizutare* obscures the *hakeme*, so it is not effective. As an alternative, a good effect can be achieved by applying a regular transparent glaze to a coarse, light-red clay body.

[21] Hakeme and *Ido*-Style Glaze:

Red Fujio stone:	10 cups
Ash:	9 cups

The red stone can be obtained by ordering to Fujio. The mixture is not so good. A plain transparent glaze is probably better.

[22] *NISHIKI*-STYLE [OVERGLAZE ENAMEL] TECHNIQUES

Red Enamel:

Kane dama:	1 *momme*
Fine white *biidoro* [frit]:	2 *momme*
Lead carbonate:	1 *momme*
Hōsha (borax):	3 *bu*

(use transparent borax)
Grind the above and add *funori* (seaweed syrup).

Kane dama is the finest quality *bengara* red clay. White frit is not so good, but there is no choice but to use it. It is better to use *nikawa* instead of *funori* here.[15]

Moegi [light-green] Enamel:

Lead carbonate:	8 *bu*
Light-green frit:	5 *momme*
Iwa rokushō [natural rock copper]:	6 *bu*

Mix the above in the same way as the red formula.

This is a good recipe.

[23] Blue Enamel:

Fine white frit:	5 *momme*
Smalt:	2 *momme* 7 *bu*
Lead carbonate:	2 *momme*

Mix same as above.

This is a satisfactory recipe.

Yellow Enamel:

White frit:	5 *momme*
Kane dama:	7 *bu*
Lead carbonate:	1 *momme* 5 *bu*
Tan [lead oxide]:	7 *bu*

Mix same as above.

This is not a good recipe; I will write about this in detail in my own section.

[24] Purple Enamel:

Frit:	4 *momme*
Kane dama:	5 *rin* [*rin* = ½ *bu*]
Lead oxide:	8 *bu*
Lead carbonate:	2 *bu*
Gosu:	1 *bu*

This purple is also unsatisfactory. For that reason, I researched this glaze for a long time, and I will include the technique I devised in my own section.

White Enamel:

Use white frit

This technique is also unsatisfactory. First of all, it is very difficult to put white enamel on top of a fired stoneware glaze. For this reason, I would look for an alternative.

[25] Gold Enamel:

Gold powder:	1 *momme*
Borax:	2 *bu*

Borax that is calcined (prefired) tends to allow the gold to be rubbed off easily. Thus raw borax must be used. Kyoto potters use calcined borax, but the gold has only a faint gloss; because it is put on thinly, it rubs off easily. With the raw borax mixture there is no gloss if it is applied thinly, so when one paints with it it must be applied thickly.

Black Enamel:

Iron scales
Gosu

Mix these two ingredients in equal parts to achieve the desired color. Add *nikawa*, and apply.

This is the technique that Ninsei used for black enamel, but it has to be used under another glossy enamel, such as green or blue, or it will scale off; also it has no gloss when used by itself. Since this recipe is good only for painting the veins of leaves and the like [under a coat of another translucent enamel], I discuss the black enamel that I devised in my own section.

[26] RAKU GLAZES

Tea Caddy Glaze:

Lead carbonate:	100 *me*
Purple clay:	8 *bu*

This is the base glaze; apply the following cover:

Lead carbonate:	10 *momme*
Akaboko:	1 *momme*

Another covering glaze:

Lead carbonate:	10 *momme*
Gosu:	8 *bu*

These are Raku-glaze techniques. Since Ninsei passed them down, they are recorded here. None of them, however, are of much use. I am familiar with the Kyoto techniques of black and red Raku, but since these have been a secret of the Raku family since the time of Rikyū, I will not write them down here.[16]

White Raku Glaze (also good for red Raku):

Lead carbonate:	100 *me*
Hinooka stone [silica]:	15 *momme*[17]
Frit:	5 *momme*

Pigments for Raku Ware:

Blue:	smalt
[27] Black:	iron scales
Persimmon color:	*mizutare*

The above is what Ninsei recorded in his book of techniques. If you so desire, I will tell you more personally.

Black Raku Glaze:

Lead carbonate:	100 *me*
Frit:	5 *momme*
Akaboko:	15 *momme*
Borax:	5 *momme*
Bronze filings:	4 *momme*

(2 *momme* of this should be iron scales)
The *akaboko* should be well calcined.

Another Black Raku Glaze:

Black frit:	100 *momme*
Iron scales:	30 *momme*
[28] Nara *rokushō* [an impure natural copper]:	20 *momme*

Another Similar Glaze:

Iron scales:	1 *momme*
Fukidama [glass]:	2 *momme*
Lead carbonate:	2 *momme* 5 *bu*
Borax:	8 *bu*

The above are Raku glazes.

[29] The Ninsei Raku techniques are listed above, but these are unsatisfactory and I have no interest in commenting on them; here they are abbreviated.

The aforementioned methods of high-fired glazed ware, Raku ware, underglaze pigments, overglaze enamels, and clay formulation were copied down and handed over by me. As they are the trade secrets of my house, they are not to be divulged. As you have requested, however, I am presenting them to you.
Nomomura Harima Daijō
(sealed) Fujiyoshi
Genroku 12 (1699),
eighth month, thirteenth day
To the gentleman Ogata Shinsei

This is a copy of the notes in which Ninsei transmitted his ceramic techniques to me, Kenzan.

[30] [this page has a single recipe that is crossed out]

[THE OSHIKŌJI RECIPES]

[31] *Uchigama* [earthenware] Ceramics:

[32] In Oshikōji, in the east part of Yanagi no Baba, in Kyoto, there is an Oshikōji-ware potter named Ichimonjiya Sukezaemon; using the techniques he learned from a Chinese, he is making glazed earthenware. It is said that this Oshikōji ware predates Chōjirō, the founder of Raku ware, but I don't know which is earlier. From 1699, I lived at Senkei [Narutaki] northwest of the capital; there I began making ceramics. Since the location was in the northwest quarter of the city, I signed "Kenzan" on the pots that were there. At that time I employed a skilled craftsman, one Magobei, who was related to the Oshikōji family and had trained under them. He was a skilled workman and proficient at firing the kiln; he, along with Seiemon, the eldest son of Ninsei of Omuro, assisted me. From these two men I learned the secret traditions of Oshikōji glazed earthenware as well as those of Ninsei ware of Omuro. I have recorded Ninsei's tradition above; here I shall relate what the Oshikōji potter Magobei taught me by word of mouth.[18]

CLAYS FOR [OSHIKŌJI] EARTHENWARE:

There are no regions in Japan, or even in foreign countries, that do not have clays suitable for making *uchigama* ceramics. When looking for a suitable clay, one should search locally first; for clay recipes consult the first section.

[33] [GLAZES FOR OSHIKŌJI EARTHENWARE:]

Transparent Base Glaze:

Lead carbonate:	100 *me*
Hinooka [silica]:	40 *me*

To mix these, first sift, dissolve, discard excess water, mix with *funori*, screen again. I will tell you how much water to add.

ENOGU [PIGMENTS FOR UNDERGLAZE PAINTING] FOR [OSHIKŌJI] EARTHENWARE:

Black Pigment:

Iron scales:	10 *momme*
Gosu:	5 *momme*

[34] Grind this into a fine powder and dissolve in *funori;* apply.

Green Pigment:

Lead carbonate:	10 *momme*
Silica:	4 *momme*
Rokushō [natural copper carbonate]:	1 *momme* 2 *bu*

Mix same as above.

Blue Pigment:

Lead carbonate:	10 *momme*
Silica:	4 *momme*
Smalt:	6 *momme*

Mix same as above.

Red Pigment:

Mountain ochre
[35] Mix same as above.

Yellow Pigment:

Lead carbonate:	10 *momme*
Silica:	4 *momme*
Tōshirome [a natural antimony oxide]:	3 *bu*

Mix same as above.

Purple Pigment:

Lead carbonate:	10 *momme*
Silica:	4 *momme*
Gosu:	5 *bu*

Take special care with the proportions; use reddish [high manganese] gosu, if possible. The character of the pigment can be observed by immersing it in water.

Mix same as above.
The firing process and the nature of the kiln you can see for yourself, so I will not go into any detail here.
The above was taught to me by Magobei, a relative and [36] worker of the Oshikōji family; he lives at the Bi-

kunizaka reservoir in Awata, east Kyoto. I record the tradition exactly as he taught it to me.

> Regarding the aforementioned glaze techniques, clay formulations, kiln firing, and pigments, since I have been working with them for many years, I have memorized both the general principles and details.

[THE KENZAN RECIPES]

About forty years have passed since I first began making ceramics in the hills northwest of Kyoto. From that time, in addition to the techniques passed on to me from Ninsei and the Oshikōji kiln, I used just about every kind of method; I discarded what I found to be of little use and gradually added my own ideas, creating a unique Kenzan style, which I shall now relate. During these decades, I have yet to attempt making tea caddies, so I will not write about the subject. From this year, however, I will experiment with tea caddies and record the results. But first I want to relate the methods I have used up until the present.

[37] From here on, I will write what I have learned and tried myself. Also I will mention special effects and the like.

[38] CLAYS FOR [KENZAN] CERAMICS AND THEIR FORMULATION:

Whether in Japan or a foreign country, the availability of a local clay is more important than considerations of quality. In the case of low-temperature ceramics, since there is not much heat stress on the body, any clay can be used. Certain clays, however, crack at the base while drying; this kind of material cannot be used alone. In [39] Kyoto, when this occurs, we use a material from Yamashina Fujio — it is neither a clay nor a stone; it is basically a sand. This material should be mixed with the faulty clay in a ratio of five parts clay to one part sand. This mixture should be sieved and left to partially dry, then prepared for forming. When the problem of a faulty clay is encountered in Edo, sand from the Bōshū Peninsula is added — the material is used in the minting industry. If one orders this sand and mixes it into the clay in a ratio of five parts clay to one part sand, there will be no cracking. There are sands in any part of the world where ceramics are made; thus satisfactory clays can be formulated anywhere. The materials, however, must be adjusted according to the kind of object that one is making.

[40] Method for Formulating Non-Cracking Clay

[Porcelain] Similar to Hizen [Arita] and Nankin [Jingdezhen]:

> Blue-and-white porcelain from Jingdezhen (*Nankin kyūki*) has motifs such as pine, bamboo, and plum (*shōchikubai*) and mountain retreats (*unyadai*, or *undō*). These motifs are executed in underglaze blue on tea bowls, incense burners, and wine cups.

White clay from the upper part of Mount Hira in Kōshū has been mined by the villagers and sold to pottery workshops in Kyoto; I bought a considerable amount myself. This clay, however, when used by itself, does not fire to a pure white. The color resembles the unglazed areas of folk porcelain from China and Kyushu. To achieve a pure white, I use a technique which is the most important of the Kenzan kiln. That is, I mix the white clay from Bungo with this Hira clay in equal [41] parts. With this mixture, make a shape, cover it with ordinary stoneware glaze, and put it in the climbing kiln in an area where it will be exposed to high heat, or put it in a saggar. If it is placed near the rear of the kiln chamber where the heat is weaker, the color will not mature.[19] This is a description of how porcelain is made. This recipe is limited to high temperatures; it is useless for low-temperature work. With the low-temperature *uchigama* technique, even the weakest clays seldom crack. In the case of high-temperature work, certain clays may crack in the kiln and prove useless. Accordingly, one must first test the clay in the kiln to determine whether it is good or bad.

[42] Clays, Glazes, and Decorating Techniques for *Kōrai Hakeme* Tea Bowls [Korean tea bowls with brushed white slip designs]:

Use finely crushed red clay; if cracks appear in the bottom, mix in sand in the manner mentioned above; the red sand from Fujio may also be used. In Kyoto, at Kurodani, this red clay can be found anywhere under the ordinary houses. In Edo and Musashi, certain clays will crack at high temperatures. Using a clay from Owari, Kyoto, Kōshū, Shigaraki, or Shidoro — or any clay, be it white or red, that will not fail in the kiln — make the desired shape, and let it dry to a moist hardness. Take mountain ochre, or the equivalent, which can be purchased in any medicine store in Edo, [43] crush it, dissolve it in water, and sift it. Use the material that settles to the bottom. Baste the pot once or twice with this, dry it out, and bisque-fire it. After that, mix together ten parts white clay from Bungo with two parts Hinooka stone (silica) or the white sand mined at Dainichi mountain in Iwakura. Mix together and grind once or twice in a stone mill, making a fine powder. Add a lot of *funori* and a little *nikawa*. Put the pot on the wheel or hold it in your hand, and apply the slip according to your specifications. The results will vary according to where you place the piece in the kiln.

[44] *Kōrai Koyomi* Style [Korean inlaid white slip design]:

This is also known as Mishima style. The other name is *koyomi*, but whether or not it can be called Mishima *koyomi* is a matter for further investigation. *Koyomi*-style pieces were imported as Korean tea bowls from long ago. There are many varieties of design; for example, *shin no te* and *hana* Mishima. To copy this style, form the vessel, and when the piece is firm but still moist, incise designs with a thin bamboo spatula. Using the same [45] white pigment used for *hakeme*, paint over the entire vessel, including the areas just incised. Then, with a fine *hera*, carefully scrape away the slip around the incised areas so that only the inlaid slip remains. There is also an alternative to incising. The designs can be stamped into the piece using stamps of bisqued clay in various shapes. These should be stamped into the body while it is still wet, then inlaid and trimmed. For the *gohon* or *unkaku* [two other variants of Korean tea bowls with slip decoration] motifs, either the incising or stamping [46] method detailed here is used.[20] Whether one is in Japan or a foreign country, when one attempts to copy old ceramics, one should make every effort to use the clay from the original locality and copy straight from the model. If this is not done, one can achieve a superficial resemblance, but upon closer inspection there will be many differences. An exact replica will not be possible using the clay of one's own locality — even disregarding patina. For this reason one must search for the specific [47] clay from a specific country to match the original.

[KENZAN STONEWARE GLAZES:]

Even in the case of glaze, one must study it closely. When making transparent glaze, one should use Namase feldspar from the upper part of the mountain in Arima district, Sesshū; wood ash is added to that. I know of no other way, although I have been researching the problem for many years. The proportions I have [48] recorded above. The high-temperature glazes of Ninsei of Omuro are, on the whole, satisfactory. Regarding the mixture of Namase feldspar and ash, if the proportion of ash is high and stone is low the glaze will be weak, and vice versa. Accordingly, when the pots are put into the kiln they must be placed according to whether their glaze is strong or weak. Regarding the persimmon-color glaze, that is, the glaze used on tea-storage jars, cooking pots, and kettles, Ninsei used a glaze composed only of *mizutare* and ash.

[49] PIGMENTS FOR [KENZAN] HIGH-TEMPERATURE CERAMICS

White Pigment:

Akaiwa stone, a fine white clay from Kuzu district, Bungo:	1 *kamme*
Hinooka or Dainichi mountain stone:	200 *me*

Crush these in a stone mill while adding water; sift and let settle; add *funori* or *nikawa*, apply to the surface.

The white clay called for in this recipe is not limited to the white clay of Akaiwa, Kuzu district, Bungo; a fine white clay of any locality, be it from Japan or from abroad, will suffice. I have recorded what I have used up until the present, although I am sure that there are other types that, upon testing, will be found to be good.

[50] Black Pigment:

Lowest grade *gosu*:	5 *momme*
Iron scales:	10 *momme*

Grind these extremely fine; add *funori* and *nikawa*.

Blue Pigment:

Finest Chinese *gosu*
Smalt

These two are mixed together, with the proportions based on testing. If the *gosu* is of the very highest grade, it alone will suffice. It may also be good *gosu* from the Arita kiln in Hizen, in which case smalt will not be necessary. *Funori* and *nikawa* should be added to the above.

Pale Persimmon Pigment:

Add a little bit of mountain ochre to the white pigment.
[51] Add *funori* and *nikawa* to the above.

There are no colors but the above four that can be used for high-temperature underglaze painting.

[52] [KENZAN] OVERGLAZE ENAMELS FOR HIGH-TEMPERATURE CERAMICS:

I have decorated in overglaze enamels on Nankin ware [Chinese porcelain from Jingdezhen], Oranda ware [Delft earthenware], Hizen Arita ware, and on wares from other Kyushu kilns and from kilns in Southeast Asia — working without regard to whether the wares were made by me or not.

Red Enamel (*aka e*):

I have been experimenting for many years, but I have still not found a satisfactory red. First, calcine *ryokuban* [iron sulphate], transforming it into *kōhan* [a pure iron oxide], and rinse it. Mix with transparent borax and fire it until there is a luster. Or use finely levigated *bengara* [53] *tandō* [probably an iron-saturated earth] in the recipe given in the Ninsei section.[21]

Gold Enamel:

To 10 *bu* of gold dust add raw borax in the amount of 2 *bu* 5 *rin* or 3 *bu*. Add only *nikawa*; do not use *funori*.

I have mentioned the use of borax in an earlier section.

Silver Enamel:

The crushed silver used in the preparation of silver leaf is good. When this silver is not available, use silver pigment, 1 *bu*, mixed with borax, 7 *rin*.
Here also use *nikawa*; do not use *funori*.

[54] Blue and Green Enamels:

Ninsei's recipes are satisfactory.
For the colorant in the green enamel, *iwa rokushō* [a variety of natural copper] is best. The color of Nara *rokushō*, when used alone, is not very good. It should be combined with *iwa haku roku* or the finest grade of number two *iwa rokushō*. When these materials are mixed together, it is best to include Nara *rokushō* in the highest percentage. Furthermore, when an enamel containing *rokushō* is mixed with an enamel containing smalt, it can be used for painting; it will become a deeper green. In this way the front and back of leaves, etc., can be differentiated.[22]

[55] Yellow Enamel:

White frit:	10 *momme*
Lead carbonate:	4 *momme*
Natural antimony oxide:	3 *bu*

Grind the antimony very well, and mix it with the frit and lead. Dilute this in *funori* and *nikawa*, and paint it on. This glaze can also be used in for underglaze painting on earthenware.
The formula of:

Lead carbonate:	10 *momme*
Silica:	4 *me*
Natural antimony oxide:	3/10 *bu*

is unsatisfactory as an overglaze yellow. The addition of frit is an essential element in this glaze; Ninsei's formula is less satisfactory.

Dark Yellow Enamel:

Add a little bit of the pure iron oxide, obtained by calcining iron sulphate, to this yellow enamel. Concerning the proportions, the color of the mixture should be a light pink.

[56] Purple Enamel:

The techniques of both Ninsei and Oshikōji are unsatisfactory. To ten parts of purple frit add three parts lead carbonate, add *funori* and *nikawa*, and paint on thickly. This recipe is good for both overglaze and underglaze enamelling. When applied lightly, a wisteria color will result, and when applied thickly, a deeper purple color will emerge.

[57] Black Enamel:

Just as Ninsei has recorded, mix together iron scales and a low-grade *gosu*, add *nikawa*, apply, and over this put on a purple, green, or blue enamel. This can be used to represent the veins in leaves and grasses, over which the colored enamels are applied; the black will appear as a gloss. It cannot, however, be used by itself.

[58] Black Enamel for Overglaze:

This is the technique I researched for many years; it allows one to paint Chinese characters, figures, Japanese script, birds, animals, and the like in a glossy black. This recipe is good for what painters call *tsuketate* [free brushwork without outlines], and it is made with:

White or green frit:	10 *momme*
Lead carbonate:	5 *momme*
[59] *Iwa hakuroku* [an impure rock copper]:	7 *momme*

The *hakuroku* which is Nara *rokushō* mixed with calcium carbonate is not very useful. When *iwa rokushō* is crushed and immersed in water, that which precipitates to the top is *hakuroku*. The pure-green material is not so good; rather a tea color is preferred. These enamels should be mixed with *funori* and *nikawa*.

[Firing the low-temperature kiln:]
When firing the enamel kiln, the gloss will not appear if the heat is cut off prematurely. Fire the pots thoroughly, [60] let cool, and take them out of the kiln. *Iromi* (test pieces) are small fragments upon which various colors are painted; they should be placed just inside the spy hole of the kiln so that they can be easily extracted; when the color of the kiln is just right, they should be pulled out and inspected. Generally, these test pieces can also be

used for high-temperature work. Make a small jar shape, bisque-fire it, and glaze it with the same glaze as the regular pots in the kiln. When packing the kiln, put as many as three of them opposite the spy hole on a saggar. Then, when the kiln has achieved the proper temperature, take them out and check them; if the glaze has not yet melted, put them back in. At this point, the kiln can be stoked with thin pieces of wood called [61] *sashiki*. Take the test pieces out once again, and if the glaze has melted, the stoking may be stopped. The same process may be carried out for the successive chambers of the kiln. The same method is used for the enamel kiln. The color of the inside of the kiln alone is not a reliable indication. I describe the firing process for enamels (*nishiki*-style) in the next section.

[62] Tea caddy glazes are described in detail in the section on Ninsei's technique.

I have been in this trade for many years, but there are few people who want tea caddies. Since there is little interest, I am not going to bother with it. I hope that you experiment with the techniques of Ninsei. As for myself, I will record the good glaze recipes, fabrication techniques, etc., that I have tried myself.

[63] EXCLUSIVE KENZAN-STYLE FIRING TECHNIQUE AND GLAZES FOR EARTHENWARE

[CLAYS FOR KENZAN EARTHENWARE]:

Regarding clays, as I wrote earlier, any kind of clay from any location can serve as a foundation; if one applies the appropriate slip over that, any style of pot can be made. The formulation of base clays is recorded above.

GLAZES FOR [KENZAN] EARTHENWARE

The formula used by the Oshikōji kiln is satisfactory. That is, to 10 parts of lead carbonate add 4 parts of [64] silica; this is the traditional technique. If these proportions are adjusted to 3½ parts silica, the glaze will melt more quickly, which is desirable for gatherings or for a hobbyist.

[Firing:]

When one fires glazed earthenware in a small muffle kiln, even if the glaze has not completely dried when the wares are first put into the kiln there will be no breakage if the heat of the kiln is not yet strong. From [65] the second loading, however, both the inside and outside of the kiln are at a higher temperature. Any pieces

that are still moist will explode when put into the kiln. Therefore, from the second firing on, the pots should be preheated. If the pots are not bisque-fired thoroughly, they will have a scorched appearance; even if the bisque kiln should require more wood, do not be stingy with fuel — it is important that the pots are fired well. If the bisqueware is underfired, fire it again. If moisture is absorbed into the kiln in the course of the firing, the results will be bad, with a strange color. Therefore, when the kiln is being built, find a place free of water that has good drainage. A foundation should be dug [66] and lined with sheets of iron or copper; sand is laid over that. A layer of loosely placed stones or tiles should be put on top. The kiln is built over that. If the space between the muffle and the kiln wall is too wide, the flame will be too strong and the glaze will become discolored. The space should be about two fingers in breadth. To see whether or not the wares are being properly fired, look through the spy hole; if there is a white color and the outlines of the wares are indistinguishable, the temperature is right. Also, as I wrote [67] above, the pigments and glazes used in the kiln should be painted on small fragments and placed so that they can be easily extracted from the kiln. When they have melted, take them out. If the firing is not thorough enough, the whole surface will lack gloss; also it is unsatisfactory if the base glaze and white pigment peel apart from each other. When applying glaze or pigment, add a lot of *funori* and *nikawa*, apply to the vessel, and let dry; if they are not stuck on firmly, they will scale off. So one must exercise great care.

[68] PIGMENTS, SLIPS, AND ENAMELS FOR [KENZAN] EARTHENWARE
White Pigment:

White frit:	100 *me*
Lead carbonate:	30 *me*
White clay:	50 *me*

The white clay may be *akaiwa* from Bungo or any good substitute. Grind extremely fine. Mix with a lot of *funori* and *nikawa*. Dry well. Apply glaze on top. Whether the pigment is applied overall or just to one area, the procedure is the same.

[69] Another White Pigment:

Hiuchi stone mined at Mito:	30 *me*
Lead carbonate:	35 *me*
Enshō [potassium nitrate]:	11 *me*

When mixed together this will amount to 76 *momme*. Add to this 38 *momme* of white clay from Bungo or any other place. The processing is the same as the above.[23]

[70] Black Pigment:

    Nankin *gosu:*   5 *momme*
    Iron scales: 10 *momme*

Finely pulverize, levigate, and add *funori* and *nikawa.*

Red Pigment:

To mountain ochre add a little bit of pure iron oxide, which results from calcining iron sulphate. Finely grind, sift, and add *funori* and *nikawa.*

Blue Pigment:

    Lead carbonate: 10 *momme*
    Silica: 3 *momme,* 5 *bu*
[71]   Smalt: 6 *momme*

This can also be used for overglaze enamels, although a recipe with *biidoro* is preferable. Add *funori* and *nikawa,* same as above.

Green Pigment:

    Lead carbonate: 10 *momme*
    Silica: 4 *momme*
    Rokushō: [see below]

Iwa rokushō, Nara rokushō, and *iwa hakuroku* are all acceptable as colorants, and may be combined as long as the total does not exceed 1 *me* 2 *bu.* The recipes for the blue and green may be used for overglaze or underglaze painting.

[72] Purple Pigment:

    Lead carbonate: 10 *momme*
    Silica: 4 *momme*
    Reddish *gosu:*   5 *momme*

Add *funori* and *nikawa.* Much better than this recipe is one where purple frit is used.

Yellow Pigment:

    Lead carbonate: 10 *momme*
    Silica: 4 *momme*
    Natural antimony
    oxide: 3 *bu*

Add *funori, nikawa,* same as above. This is mentioned in [73] the section on overglaze enamels; a glaze with frit in it is better.

[Blended colors:]
Peach Color:

As I mentioned above, add a little bit of the pure iron oxide obtained through calcining iron sulphate to the white. The resulting color will resemble peach blossoms.

Autumn Leaf Color:

Add a little bit of the pure iron to the yellow.

[74] For the *shuboku* color used by painters, add the good red colorant (pure iron oxide) mentioned in the above two recipes to the black pigment. For a pale persimmon color, add a little bit of mountain ochre to the white. For a pale blue color, mix white pigment with blue pigment. Mix according to the degree of darkness or lightness desired. For a light-green color, mix *rokushō* into the white pigment.

[Painting over other colors:]

[75] When either this light blue or light green is applied to the surface, other colors may be painted on top of it. White, black, red, and the regular green or blue can be used for painting, and they will be distinguishable from the foundation color. The peach-color pigment may also be used as a foundation color in this manner. If one wants to make designs on an overall foundation of green or blue, first paint the designs in the desired color, then apply the blue or green around them. Scrape away the colors from areas that you want to reserve. This is the same for yellow and purple.[24] To make an overall black surface, first put down a layer of white, then two layers of black. Paint evenly to avoid irregularities, dry [76] well, and on top of that paint flowers, grasses, trees, and script in white. For regular painting, first paint the patterns in white, and then put the covered enamels on top of that. Black may not be used in this way. Also on red clays or pale-red clays, first paint the patterns in white, and then paint the colors on top of that. If you don't use the white first, the colored enamels cannot be seen clearly. Mountain ochre and similar materials that are used in red and black pigments tend to alter the character of the glaze; it may lose its gloss or peel off [77] the surface. Therefore, the white should be used under these pigments, as it has a strong fluxing power to bond adjacent surfaces. In whatever case, if one first paints the motif in white, and then the various colors on top of that, the black may be painted between them. The black will not adhere to the body if the white is not underneath. Not only with the black, but whenever motifs are painted, it is desirable to apply the white first.[25]

[78] Gold and Silver:

One should first find the thin metallic leaf used for lacquer decoration, gold or silver, cut it to the desired shape — for example, moon or flower — and glue it to the bisqued vessel. The glue should be made from one part borax and three parts white pigment; mix a thick solution of *funori* and *nikawa* and add to that. Let the mixture harden to the consistency of paste. Paste the cut-out metallic leaf to the appropriate place, then paint on colored designs in black, white, purple, blue, green, yellow, peach, etc. Glaze the entire surface twice. The glaze directly on top of the metallic leaf will scale off, leaving it clearly visible. The overall coat of glaze will neatly cover the surface to the edge of the metal, proving that the leaf was not something that was just glued on after. These metallic leafs are difficult to affix to curving or irregular surfaces, but they can be applied to horizontal surfaces of cup stands, lids of incense containers, etc.; in fact, they will adhere whether the surface is vertical or horizontal.

[80] In addition to the above, I will let you know about any special shapes, new experiments, and new techniques.
Third month, fifth day
Kenzan Shinsei [monogram]
[in a different hand:] Autumn, eighth month, Gembun 2 [1737], to Rankei of Edo
[sealed] *Shōnin no in* [intaglio seal]

[81] [blank page]

[82] [in a different hand:] This is Minakami's secret book; it is not to be shown to anyone.
Minakami Rosen
[sealed] *Tōenkyō zō sho ki* [relief seal]²⁶

NOTES

1. The clay from Kurodani was so highly esteemed that it was published as a famous regional product in the *Kefukigusa,* published in 1638. Kurodani clay comes from part of a large vein of decomposed granite that runs from Ginkakuji in eastern Kyoto to Tōji in the south-central part of the city. The deposits were exhausted in the eighteenth century. At present Kyoto potters fabricate an equivalent by adding kaolin and pyrophyllite to an ordinary ball clay. In the *Tōji Seihō,* Kenzan gives a more detailed explanation of clay processing; it accords with the technique used by Japanese potters today.

2. *Goki* is a type of Korean bowl made in the fifteenth and sixteenth centuries; it was prized by Japanese tea men. Yūgyō clay was obtained from the area of present-day Gojō-Higashiōji Streets in Kyoto. During the building of the Gojō Bypass in the 1950s, construction work laid bare a large seam of dark, very plastic clay, which was probably a part of the Yūgyō deposit. I obtained some through the good offices of Pamela Vandiver, Smithsonian Institution, and the Kyocera Corporation, Kyoto, and made some tests; it was very easy to shape on the wheel, but not very refractory. The blotchy effects that Kenzan mentions in his footnotes are now called *gohon* by potters and *kanoko* (deer spots) by tea devotees. The phenomenon occurs when clays of high alumina, high alkali content are exposed to changes of atmosphere in the kiln.

3. Kenzan's personal approach is more sensible than the recipe passed down by Ninsei. The important aspect of this recipe is the texture of the clay, which results from dry sifting rather than levigating (the latter process leaves only fine clay particles and deprives the clay of texture). Following Kenzan's recipe, I prepared a Karatsu-style clay from freshly dug material in the west Kyoto mountains, and achieved a clay body comparable to that of Karatsu. Potters working with industrially processed, levigated clay bodies cannot achieve such an effect.

4. Shino appears from the Tenshō era (1573–91) in tea records, but it is not the style of ceramic referred to as Shino today; the early Shino style was a white or transparent glaze applied to *temmoku*-shaped tea bowls. Kenzan's reference marks the first time that the term Shino is applied to the feldspathic-glazed product made in Mino from the late-sixteenth to early-seventeenth centuries. The style with pale persimmon-colored clay that Kenzan mentions is probably what is now called Narumi Oribe ware. A survey of his shapes and techniques suggests that Kenzan derived more inspiration from Oribe wares than from any other style.

5. The precise nature of this *Benizara* style is difficult to determine. The *Benizara*-style glaze detailed in the next section is a fluid ash glaze, and Kenzan relates it to the glaze on a type of Seto tea bowl known as *Hakuan.* The *Hakuan* bowls, however, do not have underglaze painting in white. A fragment excavated from the Narutaki kiln site has white slip painting on a foundation of red clay; this might represent the *Benizara* style. Kenzan clearly placed high value on his recipe for white slip. He relates here that he tried a number of different clays before finally settling on a material from Bungo (present-day Oita Prefecture). The Bungo clay was probably a form of kaolin. The secret of the white slip formula, which Kenzan reveals in later parts of this manual and in the *Tōji Seihō,* was to bisque the white clay before making up the slip; in that way, the slip could be applied to the bisqueware without the usual problem of scaling caused by excess shrinkage of the slip in relation to the clay body.

6. These four recipes are for underglaze pigments for stoneware. The iron scales will fire black at lower temperatures and rust at higher temperatures. *Nankin* is

gosu, or asbolite, a cobalt-bearing mineral with considerable iron and manganese impurities. These impurities soften the harsh blue of the cobalt. There has never been much *gosu* in Japan; most of it was imported from southern China, from a region called Goshū in Japanese — from which the material may derive its name. *Funori* and *nikawa* are necessary for the pale persimmon pigment because *mizutare* is a clay, which will shrink upon drying and scale off the surface of the pot; it will also resist an application of glaze. *Funori* is a viscous seaweed syrup that retards drying and promotes adhesion. *Nikawa*, an animal glue used by painters and dyers, also promotes adhesion.

7. Namase stone is a feldspar. The original deposits, which served Kyoto potters throughout the Edo Period, are now depleted, but a nearby mine in Hiraki has a comparable product. From testing, I found that when it was used in Kenzan's (Ninsei's) formula of ten parts stone to six parts ash (*kashi*, a kind of oak, is recommended by Kenzan as a source for ash in the *Tōji Seihō*), a good transparent glaze resulted at about 1220–30 degrees C. This very simple feldspathic glaze was probably transmitted to Kyoto by Ofuke-ware potters from Seto in the first half of the seventeenth century, and was used as the staple Kyoto-ware glaze throughout the Edo Period.

8. It is rather unusual to use lead in high-temperature glazes (lead volatizes at high temperatures), but there is some precedent for the practice in Jun ware and copper red wares from China. This glaze has no relation to either. My tests with the formula yielded a soft, slightly cloudy glaze similar to the one seen on a number of Kenzan tea bowls and a few Narutaki shards. The lead lowered the melting point of the glaze; Kenzan probably found it convenient for use on wares fired in the rear of the kiln chamber, where temperatures were relatively low.

9. *Shōban* remains unidentified. Taken separately, the characters now connote saltpeter and alum. Looking at the formula as a whole, it would seem that *shōban* was a high-sodium compound which made the glaze fluid, producing the streaky effects known as "hare's fur." *Nogime* refers to the variety of *temmoku* tea bowl produced at the Jian kilns in China during the Southern Song Dynasty; many of those bowls feature "hare's fur" effects.

10. *Shunkei* is a type of old Seto tea caddy. According to some accounts, it was a style made in the taste of the Muromachi lacquer master Shunkei (active early fifteenth century); Shunkei was also a name assumed by the legendary Seto potter Katō Tōshirō (active early thirteenth century) upon his retirement. *Kongōsha* comes

from deposits of weathered igneous rocks in the Nara basin. *Gofun*, calcium carbonate, is a crushed shell used by painters for white pigment. Kibune stone is a fairly soft red stone that can still be found in great quantities in the Kibune River north of Kyoto; it has high percentages of iron and manganese.

11. In the *Tōji Seihō*, Kenzan writes that he did not understand what was meant by *shiroboko*, but that Ninsei said it was a regional term used by Seto potters. Judging by the proportions, it was probably a high-silica clay; the recipe as a whole suggests an amber glaze.

12. Kenzan's study of the silver smelting process demonstrates the extent of his interest in materials for ceramics.

13. If the *gosu* was an impure one, high in iron, a celadon would have been possible.

14. This is the Oribe copper-green glaze. The copper in the brass powder turns the glaze green in an oxidizing kiln atmosphere. In the *Tōji Seihō*, Kenzan writes, "Apply this mixture on a pot covered with transparent glaze. It [the green] should be applied to half [or a portion] of the vessel. . ."

15. The most critical ingredient in red enamel is a good colorant. The ideal material is a pure iron oxide, but even the finest grades contain some impurities. The *kane dama* used by Ninsei was probably an iron-saturated earth; if one inspects the red enamel on authentic Ninsei wares, it will be found to be a rather dark, rusty red. Ninsei skillfully compensated for the bad color with gold and silver accents. It is of great interest that Ninsei did not understand how to obtain a good red by calcining iron sulphate; the technique was known to the Kakiemon family and, as will be seen below, to Kenzan, too. Kenzan writes to avoid mixing *funori* with red, another trick known to specialists — red will dissolve inside of *funori*.

16. In the *Tōji Seihō*, Kenzan writes: "Since this [the manufacture of the Raku style] is their family trade, I feel it improper to copy their work, and thus I will not write anything about the black Raku glaze. I have been on good terms with the Raku family since the time of Ichinyū, the fourth-generation head of the family, so I don't want to inconvenience them. If someone orders black Raku ceramics from me I will refer them directly to the Raku family, since they have been in the trade since the time of Rikyū.

17. Hinooka stone is silica. The hills around Hinooka (Yamashina Ward, east Kyoto) are full of it.

18. *Uchigama* literally means inner kiln, or muffle kiln, refer-

ring either to the fact that the kiln was small enough to be used indoors or that the wares were fired in a protective muffle. The general connotation here, however, is lead-glazed earthenware.

19. Tomimoto Kenkichi investigated this Hira clay and found it to be a buff stoneware with a high percentage of siliceous and feldspathic sand. See Tomimoto, "Ninsei-Kenzan no Tōhō" [The Techniques of Ninsei and Kenzan], *Sekai Tōji Zenshū*, vol. 5, Edo (Tokyo: Iwade Shobō and the Zauhō Press, 1956), pp. 225–233. If the sand was ground into the body, a degree of vitrification comparable to porcelain may have been achieved.

20. The terms *koyomi* and Mishima derived from the fact that the inlay patterns resembled the patterns on calendars (*koyomi*) from the Mishima Shrine. There is no Kenzan ware which shows a direct attempt to copy either Mishima or *hakeme* styles, but there is some significance in the fact that Kenzan has included these two techniques in the section on his personal innovations. As related in Chapter 4, during the Chōjiyamachi years, Kenzan used his white slip technique to create patches of white to serve as a ground for painted designs. The concept of painting on the white slip may have been inspired by *hakeme*, and it is of special interest that in Kenzan's *hakeme* instructions it is written that the white slip should be applied after the bisque firing — the usual procedure is to paint on the white while the vessel is still moist. The Kenzan *hakeme* technique thus accords with his post-bisquit approach to slip decoration used at Chōjiyamachi.

21. At some point during his career, Kenzan learned the secret of calcining iron sulphate to obtain a pure iron oxide as a colorant in the red enamel. This technique, a secret of the Kakiemon family, was unknown to Ninsei.

22. Kenzan discusses the assets and liabilities of various rock coppers, now largely unobtainable. The quality of the green on authentic Kenzan wares reflects the fastidiousness of the master. The often-used Kenzan dark green was obtained, as hinted here, by adding a bit of blue enamel to the green.

23. This white pigment (really a white enamel) is the key recipe in the Kenzan stable of low-fire glazes. It serves as an adhesive undercoating or as a base for blended colors. Kenzan gives recipes using both Kyoto and Edo materials. *Hiuchi* stone is probably a form of silica.

24. Kenzan's wording in this section is rather imprecise, but it would appear that he is referring to painting contrasting zones of color on a single vessel, in the manner of Kōchi ware.

25. Clay-bearing pigments such as ocher are highly absorbent and contractile, and tend to peel away from other surfaces. The white pigment served as a kind of buffer for these materials. Kenzan also emphasizes that if the white is painted as a foundation, colors painted on top of it will show to their best effect.

26. Isshian Rankei, the recipient of the *Tōkō Hitsuyō*, was a member of the circle of amateur artist-poets that kiln associated with in Edo; later the manual entered the hands of Minakami Rosen, of whom nothing is known save his *Tōenkyo* (Living in Pottery Smoke) seal impressed on the last page of the manual, suggesting that he was an amateur potter. Subsequent ownership is unknown; in the early twentieth century, the manual was purchased by Ikeda Nariakira, who located it in a pawn shop in Otaru, Hokkaidō. Later the book entered the Yamato Bunkakan, where it is presently housed.

There are a number of other pottery manuals connected with the Kenzan tradition: 1) a Kōetsu-Kūchū-Kenzan pottery manual acquired by Sahara Kikuu in 1819 and mentioned in his pamphlet *Sumidagawa Hanayashiki* and his diary *Umeya Nikki*; this manual, probably based on Raku-ware techniques, is now lost; 2) a manual from the hand of Kenzan's adopted son Ihachi; this came into the hands of Kikuu in 1820 from Asakusa dilettante Yoshimura Kana; it too is mentioned in *Sumidagawa Hanayashiki* and is also lost; 3) a manual copied out from Kenzan's oral teachings by one "second generation Kenzan"; this manual, allegedly the one passed down in the Edo Kenzan line, was apparently destroyed in the 1923 Kanto earthquake; 4) a memorandum on Raku glazes sent by Kenzan to the Sano amateur Ōkawa Kendō in 1732 and subsequently recorded in Kendō's diary; the diary is now in the Takizawa collection, Tochigi Prefecture; 5) four copies of the *Tōji Seihō* passed down in the Sano area; 6) *Tōki Mippōsho*, a manual attributed to Kenzan's adopted son Ihachi, and four copies; 7) a *Kenzan Yaki Yaki Hisho* recorded by Edward S. Morse in his collection catalogue, whereabouts unknown (although it may well be a manual called *Kenzan Raku Yaki Hisho*, one of the *Tōki Mippōsho* copies formerly in the Negishi collection [which Morse visited] and now in the National Diet Library); 8) I have just discovered another Kenzan manual written by Miura Kenya in the Ii Bijutsukan, Hikone.

Appendix Three
GUIDE TO CONNOISSEURSHIP

Imitations comprise over ninety-five percent of all ceramics with the Kenzan mark. Connoisseurship — here signifying the identification of authentic specimens — is therefore essential in an understanding of Kenzan. The following paragraphs cover some general criteria useful in connoisseurship. The sixteen pages that follow illustrate groups of Kenzan-style ware, from authentic works to recent fakes. In the context of this book, "authentic" denotes wares made by the workshop of Ogata Kenzan, under his supervision, with varying degrees of participation by the master himself.

SHAPES
Kenzan commissioned skilled artisans to form his works. Skill is especially present in the molded plates. If the walls are over five millimeters thick, or if they are conspicuously warped, the piece is suspect.

TECHNIQUES
Kenzan worked with reddish to buff-colored earthenware clays, with buff stoneware clays, with a little bit of local porcelain, and with glazed blanks brought in from Arita. The typical stoneware clay is a buff material, with small-to-medium grains. Large grains occur only infrequently. The white slip is fine, with a good white color. Since Kenzan seems to have frequently applied it to the bisqueware, it often has fissures or scales off. On earthenware, underglaze iron pigment is blackish or purplish due to the admixture of *gosu* (impure cobalt). Among overglaze enamels, pay attention to the yellow and green; the former will be dirty, the latter should be rich, without blackening.

DECOR
For his underglaze enameled earthenware, Kenzan preferred indigenous literary designs; for earthenwares decorated with underglaze iron, Kenzan used landscapes, "gentleman" subjects (for example pine, plum, orchid), and "lucky gods." For underglaze and overglaze decorated stoneware, Rimpa-style designs are common. If the design is too faithful a copy of a painting or other craft work, it is suspect.

CALLIGRAPHY
Intensive studies of authentic specimens, especially the Konishi archives and Kenzan's pottery manuals, have revealed the following idiosyncrasies. In the illustrations, the characters in bold are abstracted from authentic specimens of Kenzan's calligraphy.

1. Usage

a) A preference for an archaic version of the character *tokoro*, which appears in every Konishi archive sample and in ceramics as well (fig. 170).

b) The character *koe* is written with the final stroke hooking to the right rather than curving down to the left; this is an archaic convention (fig. 171).

c) The character *aki* is written with its stem and radical reversed, another archaic convention (fig. 172).

d) As of 1737 Kenzan changes the way he writes the character *ga*. The change appears in the pottery manuals and ceramics datable to Kenzan's last years in Edo only (fig. 173).

2. Kanji

a) When executing enclosure shapes such as *kunigamae*, Kenzan tends to leave the bottom open and wide. This is a characteristic often seen in *Oieryū* calligraphy, which was the orthodox script style of Kenzan's day (fig. 174).

b) When writing elements such as the *ukammuri*, Kenzan rounds the left corner with an extra breath, pulling the horizontal line up out of its normal path. This is evident from the late Narutaki years (fig. 175).

c) The radical *shinnyū* is executed with the final horizontal stroke pulling downward rather than horizontally (fig. 176).

d) The enclosure *mongamae* is abbreviated with its middle stroke pulled up into a "hill" (fig. 177).

e) When executing right corner strokes such as in the stem of *eda*, the brush retraces its path briefly before pulling downward (fig. 178).

f) The second stroke of *kokoro* is written with a shallow hook (fig. 179).

g) Characters like *ike* are opened up in the middle, with shallow hooking strokes (fig. 180).

h) The character *nari* is vertically attenuated (fig. 181).

i) The right "leg" stroke in characters like *ken* begins convex rather than concave (fig. 182).

j) Kenzan habitually collapses the right side of "box" (mouth) elements (fig. 183).

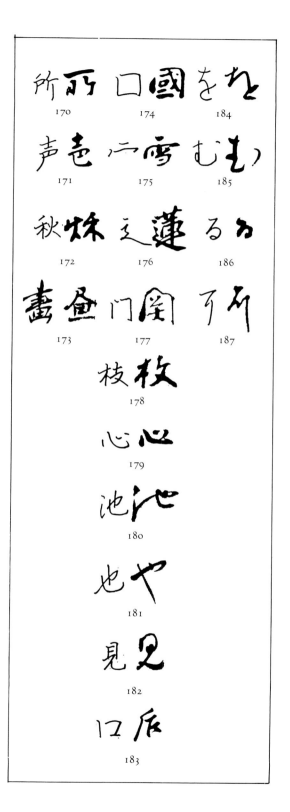

3. Kana:

a) The kana (w)o is written with its upward curve unusually high (fig. 184).

d. The bottom part of the kana *mu* is written differently (fig. 185).

e. The character *ru* is written in smaller scale than other kana (fig. 186).

f. An extra stroke is added to the archaic form of *ni* (fig. 187).

SIGNATURES

As a man of letters, Kenzan was very exacting about the content of his signatures. They should conform to the place of production and the medium. If there is an anomaly, the piece should be regarded with suspicion.

Narutaki production: Kenzan used "Fusō" (Japan) "Yōshū" (an alternative name for Kyoto), "Dai Nippon Koku" (Great Country of Japan), "Tōin," and "Shōkosai." Chōjiyamachi: plain "Kenzan" signatures predominate. Edo: In both painting and ceramics, Kenzan used "Keichō," "Keijō," "Heian Jō," and "Karaku," all allusive names for Kyoto. In painting, he used the pseudonym Shisui. Since Ogata Kenzan himself regarded "Kenzan" as a name related to his ceramics, any painting with that mark is suspicious.

STYLISTIC DEVELOPMENT

The following sixteen pages illustrate, through select pieces, the development of the Kenzan style from 1699 down to the present. Where possible, the signature (or other relevant detail) is illustrated immediately below each respective piece. The pieces were clustered in the manner mentioned in Chapter 3 of the main text, that is, by dividing several thousand Kenzan wares according to such criteria as shapes, techniques, decor styles, border patterns, inscription styles and contents, signature styles and contents, seals, and monograms. In terms of generational change, the following scheme is proposed:

Groups 1–10: Authentic work of the Kenzan workshops at Narutaki, Chōjiyamachi, and Edo, under the direct supervision of and with occasional personal participation by Kenzan himself.

Group 11: Transition from Kenzan to Ihachi in Kyoto.

Groups 12–14: Kenzan-style production in Kyoto, from the mid-eighteenth century through the early twentieth century.

Groups 15–16: Kenzan-style production in Edo and elsewhere, from the mid-eighteenth century through the twentieth century.

Group 17: Kenzan painting, authentic works and later production.

Group 1: Indigenous "classical" themes at Narutaki, 1699–1712. Flat, rectilinear shapes, earthenware, painted in underglaze enamels with themes inspired by Japanese classical literature such as Fujiwara no Teika poems (figs. 189–194) and the Noh drama (figs. 195–198). Border patterns usually stenciled, in a stylized wisteria pattern. Inscriptions in a Japanese-style (*wayō*) calligraphy, inspired by Teika's script style. One shard excavated from Narutaki (fig. 188) seems to be from the bottom of such a piece.

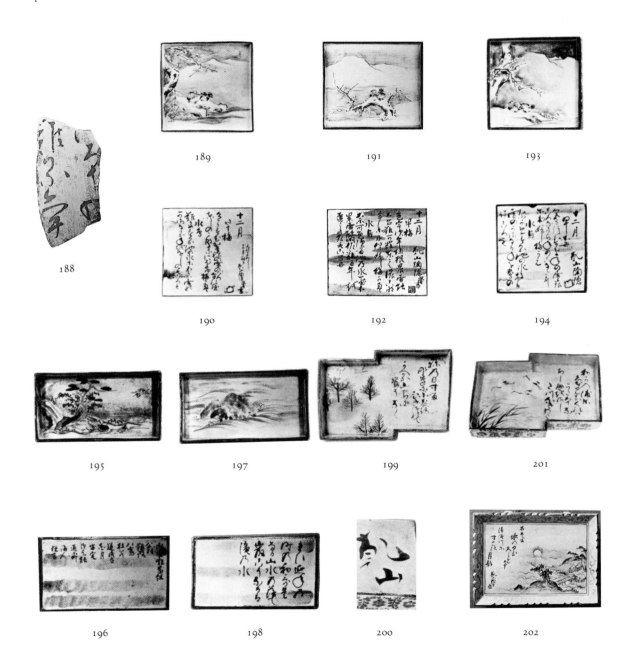

188

189

191

193

190

192

194

195

197

199

201

196

198

200

202

Group 2: Chinese "classical" themes at Narutaki, 1699–1712. Flat, rectilinear shapes, earthenware, painted in underglaze iron with themes inspired by Chinese-style landscape painting and poetry. Border patterns include cloud and palmette scrolls derived from Chinese ceramics. Long inscriptions in Chinese-style (*karayō*) calligraphy. One shard excavated from Narutaki (fig. 203) matches the inscription on an extant piece (fig. 204).

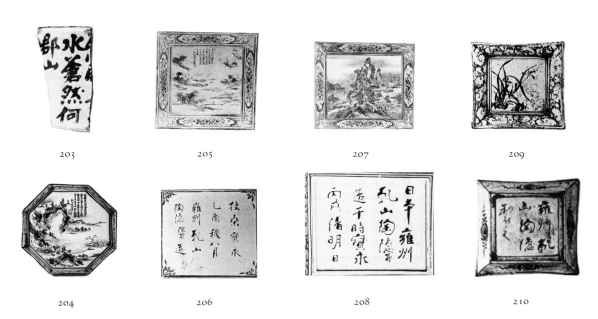

203   205   207   209

204   206   208   210

Group 3: Re-creations (*utsushi*) of foreign styles at Narutaki, 1699–1712. Wheel-thrown and molded forms, decorated in underglaze and overglaze enamels. Decor derived from late Ming-dynasty overglaze-enameled porcelain (figs. 211, 213), Delft ware (fig. 215), and underglaze-decorated stoneware and porcelain from China (fig. 217). Inscriptions, inspired by the reign marks on Chinese ceramics, frequently include Japan ("Nippon" or "Dai Nippon") as the place of origin of the work.

211   213   215   217

212   214   216   218

Group 4: Shards from Narutaki and matching extant pieces, 1699–1712. Wheel-thrown and molded forms, earthenware and stoneware, intended for decoration in underglaze and overglaze enamels. The simple decor on these early wares could have been done by artisans such as Seiemon and Magobei — and that is suggested by the appearance of stamped (figs. 223, 230) and stenciled (figs. 226, 228) signatures.

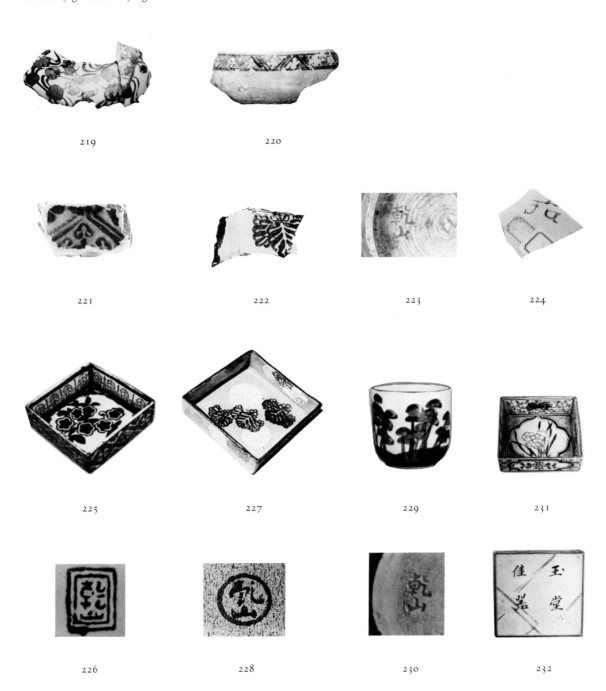

219   220

221   222   223   224

225   227   229   231

226   228   230   232

Group 5: Beginning of a Rimpa style at Narutaki, 1699–1712. Wheel-thrown, molded, and handbuilt forms, earthenware and stoneware, with underglaze pigments, overglaze enamels, and overglaze gold. Decor subjects include quite literal adaptations of paintings and designs from the *Saga Bon,* the early seventeenth century publications connected to Kōetsu and Sōtatsu (fig. 239), and Kōrin-style floral compositions (figs. 245, 247). Noteworthy is the clear division of pictorial motifs and abstract patterns; these tend to combine in later stonewares (e.g., groups 7–8). Simple "Kenzan" signatures on the bases, but dissimilar to types illustrated in the first two groups. Like other stonewares from the Kenzan workshop, these were probably decorated and signed by Kenzan's staff.

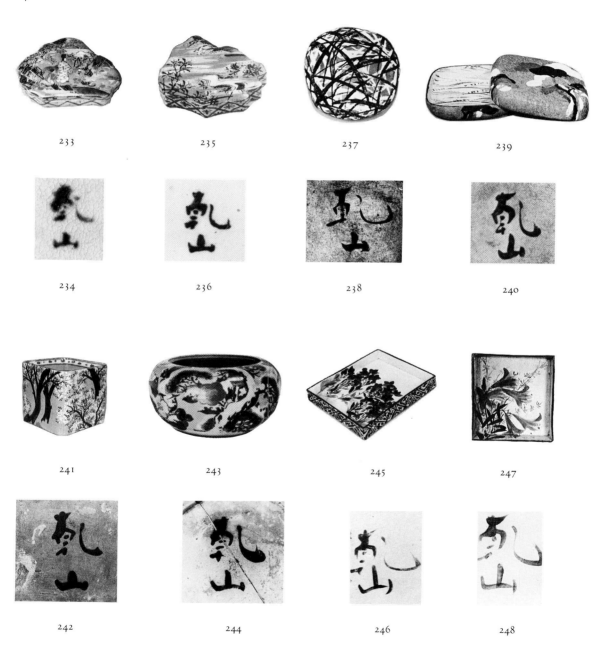

Group 6: Kōrin-Kenzan collaborations, late Narutaki-early Chōjiyamachi, 1709–16 (including possible imitations). Flat square plates, earthenware, with underglaze iron painting of birds, flowers, and auspicious figures. All bear signatures by Kōrin and Kenzan, and most have poetic inscriptions by Kenzan. There are several types, distinguishable by the crispness of the painting and calligraphy, the type of border patterns, and the legibility of the seals. The top row (figs. 249–252) constitutes the most reliable standard.

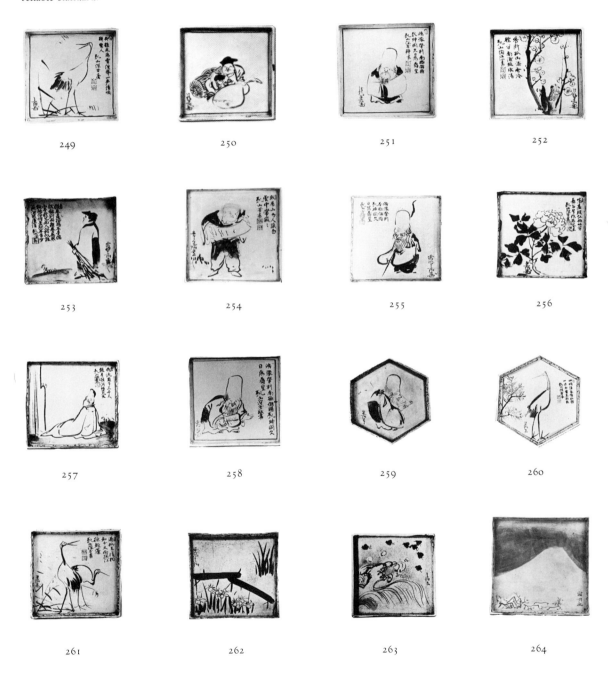

249

250

251

252

253

254

255

256

257

258

259

260

261

262

263

264

Group 7: Food vessels, Chōjiyamachi, 1712–31. Predominantly wheel-thrown forms, made in sets, stoneware, with decoration of Kōrin-inspired flowers-and-grasses in white slip, underglaze iron, and underglaze cobalt (and a lesser amount of work in overglaze enamels). Some painting on porcelain blanks, probably brought in from Arita (fig. 279). Pieces bear a simple "Kenzan" signature.

265

267

269

271

266

268

270

272

273

275

277

279

274

276

278

280

Group 8: Shaped dishes and openwork bowls, Chōjiyamachi, ca. 1720–31. Wheel-thrown and molded forms, stoneware, with decoration of Kōrin-inspired flowers-and-grasses in overglaze enamels. Simple "Kenzan" signature, framed.

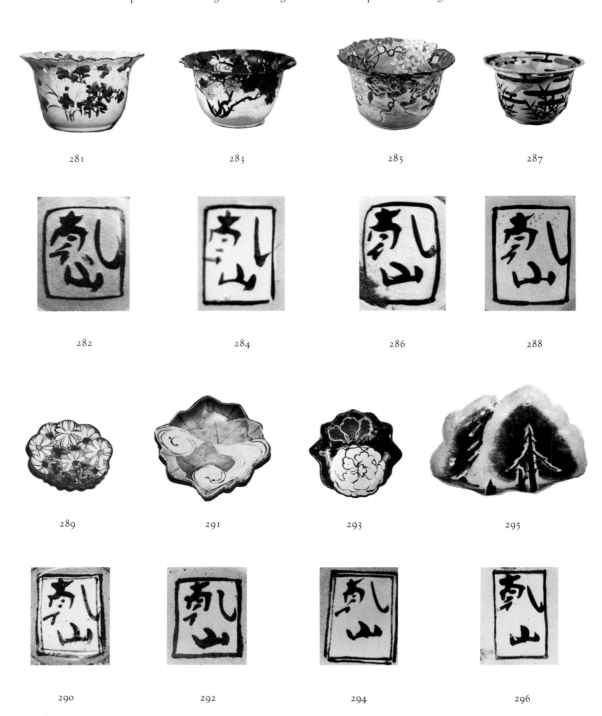

281

283

285

287

282

284

286

288

289

291

293

295

290

292

294

296

Group 9: Continuation of "Chinese classical" themes at Chōjiyamachi, ca. 1712–31. Wheel-thrown and molded forms, earthenware and stoneware, with white slip coating and underglaze iron painting, usually in themes derived from Chinese poetry, painting, and ceramics. Inscriptions and signatures in a very careful Kenzan-style hand, either by the master himself or a close follower like Ihachi, who studied Kenzan's script style. Many pieces inscribed with dates. Some of the seals in this group are executed in sgraffito, a technique not seen in other Kenzan seals.

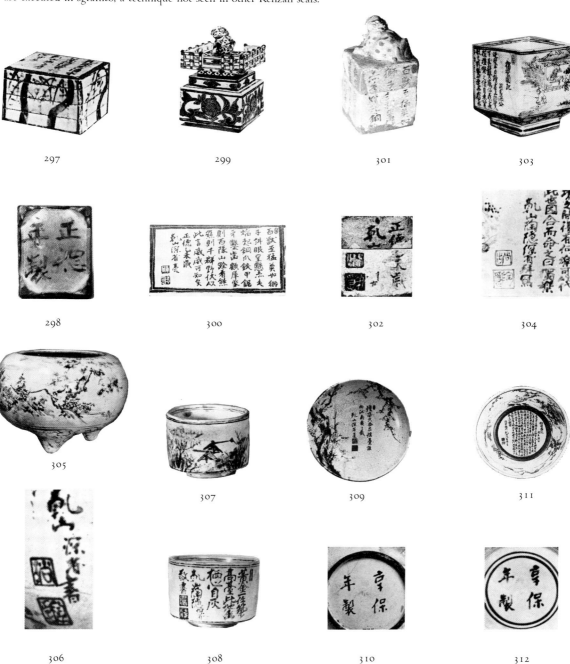

297

299

301

303

298

300

302

304

305

307

309

311

306

308

310

312

Group 10: Edo, Sano, and Nagasaki, 1731–43. Predominantly wheel-thrown, earthenware, with Kōrin-inspired decoration in underglaze and overglaze enamels. Poetic inscriptions and painting in Kenzan's own hand. Some signatures expressly claim Kenzan as the painter (figs. 316, 322, 324), and refer to his Kyoto origins (using terms for Kyoto such as "Heian Jō," "Keichō," and "Karaku"; figs. 314, 316, 320, respectively) and present whereabouts (variously: Edo, Sano, Nagasaki district of Edo; figs. 314, 324, 326, respectively).

313

315

317

319

314

316

318

320

321

323

325

327

322

324

326

328

Group 11: Transition from Kenzan to Ihachi, ca. 1720–50. Molded flat plates, earthenware, many in sets, and some in wheel-thrown forms, principally tea bowls. Decoration is usually "gentleman" subjects (e.g., orchids, peonies, chrysanthemums, plums) in underglaze iron. Border patterns are typically floral rosettes on the outside and short squiggly lines on the inside. Poems are short, occasionally with mistaken characters. Signatures typically read "Written by Kenzan Sei." Seals include a small relief "Tōin" and large relief "Shōko," of a different style than used in works illustrated above.

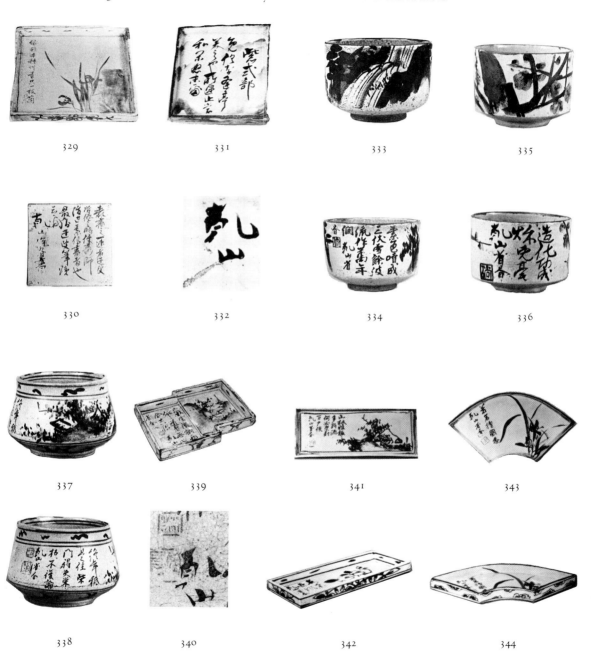

329

331

333

335

330

332

334

336

337

339

341

343

338

340

342

344

Group 12: Ogata Ihachi, ca. 1720–60. Ihachi, whose signature and general style was identified in Chapter 6, worked in four basic modes: flat plates and bowls, earthenware, decorated in underglaze iron (very similar to Group 11 except for the seals, which now read "Kenzan" (relief) and "Shinsei" (intaglio) (figs. 345, 346); food dishes, stoneware, modeled after Kenzan's Chōjiyamachi designs, in underglaze iron and cobalt and in overglaze enamels (fig. 347); foreign designs, stoneware and earthenware, including Delft ware, Kōchi ware, Cizhou ware (figs. 353, 355, 357, respectively); and Raku ware with pictorial designs (figs. 359, 360).

345

347

349

351

346

348

350

352

353

355

357

359

354

356

358

360

Group 13: The Kenzan style in Kyoto, Late eighteenth-early nineteenth century. Kenzan flowers-and-grasses designs in earthenware and stoneware, especially as interpreted by Ihachi, are carried on into the second half of the eighteenth century (figs. 361, 363). "Named" followers, such as Kempō (fig. 365, 366) and Gosuke (fig. 367), work principally in earthenware. From the early nineteenth century, under the influence of potters such as Dōhachi, the designs become more florid (figs. 369–376).

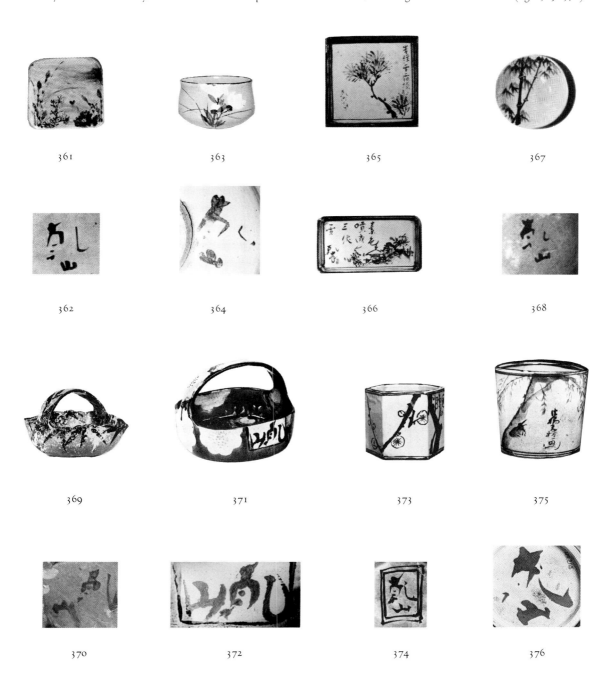

361

363

365

367

362

364

366

368

369

371

373

375

370

372

374

376

Group 14: The Kenzan style in Kyoto, mid-nineteenth-early twentieth century. Principally stoneware, decorated in underglaze iron and overglaze enamels. Designs and signatures become increasingly florid (figs. 377–380), and from the second half of the nineteenth century, there is a shift away from orthodox designs toward freer interpretations derived from illustrated art literature (figs. 385 and 387, derived from early nineteenth century catalogues on Kōrin). Certain design elements repeat, without regard to the vessel shape (figs. 381–391).

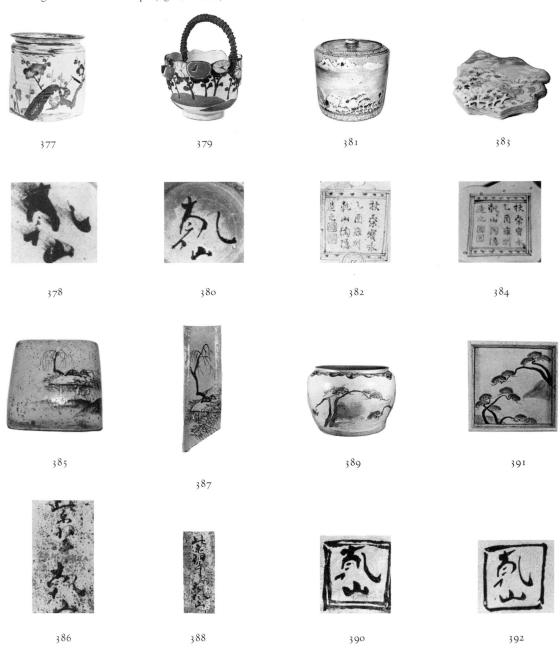

377

379

381

383

378

380

382

384

385

387

389

391

386

388

390

392

Group 15: The Kenzan succession in Edo (Tokyo), mid-eighteenth-late nineteenth century. Principally earthenware, decorated in underglaze enamels. Designs derive from the Ihachi Kenzan style; chrysanthemums are a particular favorite, with a lesser number of Chinese and Delft-inspired designs. Represented here are Minzan (Edo Kenzan II?, figs. 393, 395), Miyazaki Tominosuke (Edo Kenzan III, figs. 397, 399), Kichiroku (Kensai, figs. 401, 403), and Ken'ya (figs. 405, 407).

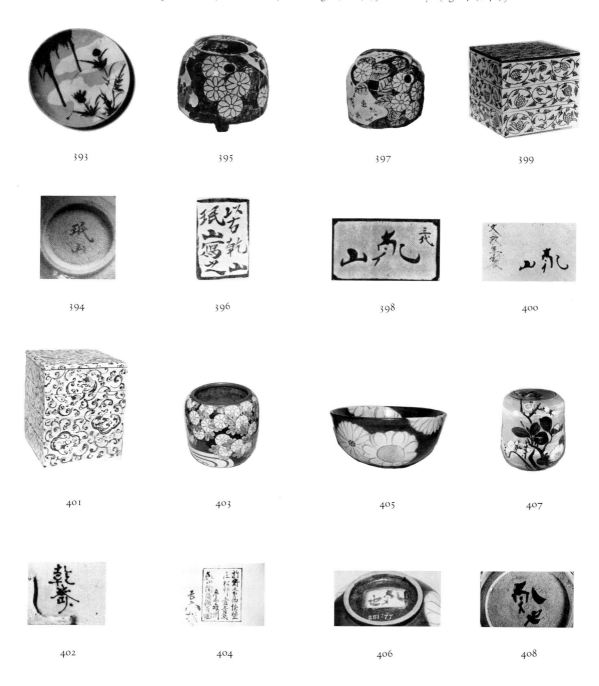

393

395

397

399

394

396

398

400

401

403

405

407

402

404

406

408

Group 16: Kenzan imitations in Tokyo and elsewhere, late nineteenth-twentieth century. Miscellaneous techniques and decor schemes. Figs. 409 and 411 are from a Ken'ya-affiliated potter in Edo, late nineteenth century; figs. 413 and 415 are by Urano Shigekichi (Kenzan VI), the tutor of Bernard Leach; fig. 417 is black Raku ware, probably made in Edo as an "export antique"; fig. 419 is Inuyama ware, from Gifu Prefecture; fig. 421 was probably made in Inuyama in the 1950s by Yamamoto Nyōsen; fig. 423 is New Sano Kenzan ware.

409

411

413

415

410

412

414

416

417

419

421

423

418

420

422

424

Group 17: Kenzan and Kenzan-style paintings, mid-eighteenth to twentieth century, with signature and seal details. Various formats and styles. Figs. 425 and 427 represent a monochrome style, characterized by small formats, bold calligraphy, and the use of the oblong relief seal "Tōzen." Figs. 429 and 431 represent a Rimpa style, characterized by large vertical formats, a more graceful script, and the use of the large square relief seal "Reikai" and a small relief seal "Shinsei." Some of these may well be early nineteenth century products, from the milieu of Sakai Hōitsu. A somewhat different signature and "Reikai" seal can be seen in many fan paintings (figs. 433, 435); here too an early nineteenth century date may be in order. Figs. 437 and 439 represent late nineteenth or even twentieth-century products, outside of the mainstream Kenzan-Rimpa style.

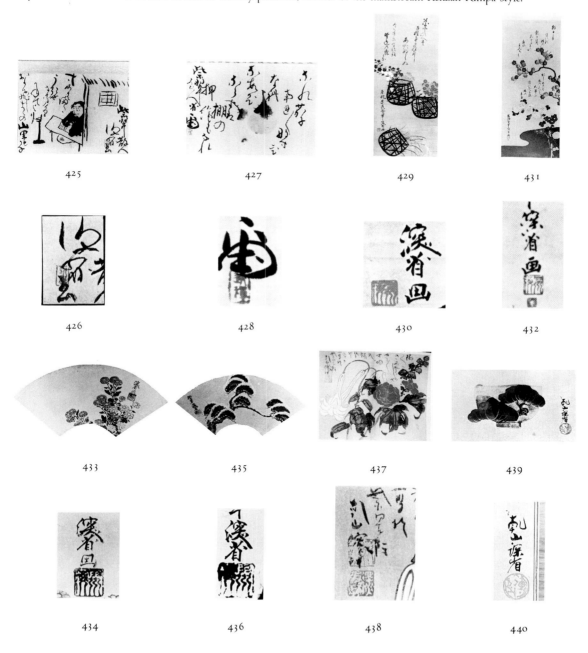

Appendix Four
PLATES AND FIGURES

COLOR PLATES:

1. Square plate with design of willow and bush warbler in underglaze enamels. From a set of twelve plates depicting Fujiwara no Teika's poems of birds and flowers of the twelve months. Dated 1702. H. 2.2 cm., d. 16.8 cm., w. 16.8 cm. MOA Museum of Art, Atami, Shizuoka Prefecture.

2. Incense box with design of geese and bush clover in overglaze enamels, based on Fujiwara no Teika's poems of birds and flowers of the twelve months. H. 3.0 cm., d. 11.5 cm. Museum für Kunst und Gewerbe, Hamburg.

3. Rectangular plates with individual designs in underglaze iron. Set of five. H. 3.5 cm., d. 19.7 cm., w. 17.0 cm. Honolulu Academy of Arts.

4. Charcoal container (hiire) with design of Duluo Yuan Ji (Chinese poet Sima Guang's eleventh-century essay about his Garden of Self-Enjoyment) in underglaze cobalt. H. 10.8 cm., d. 9.8 cm., w. 9.7 cm. Private collection, Japan.

5. Square plate with design of pine branch in underglaze iron. Dated 1711. H. 2.5 cm., d. 21.4 cm., w. 21.4 cm. Private collection, U.S.A.

6. Square plate with design of chrysanthemums in underglaze iron. Painting by Kōrin. H. 2.8 cm., d. 21.8 cm., w. 21.8 cm. Private collection, Japan.

7. Charcoal container (hiire) with design of landscape in underglaze iron. Painting by Kōrin. H. 10.9 cm., d. 11.5 cm., w. 11.6 cm. Yamato Bunkakan, Nara.

8. Lidded bowls with design of crane and reeds in underglaze iron and cobalt. Set of ten. H. 7.0 cm., d. 11.7 cm. Kyoto Folk Art Museum.

9. Sauce pot with design of spring grasses in overglaze enamels. H. 6.2 cm., d. 8.3 cm. Suntory Museum of Art, Tokyo.

10. Food dishes with design of chrysanthemums in overglaze enamels. Set of five. H. 4.1 cm., d. 16.5–19.6 cm. Gotoh Museum, Tokyo.

11. Rectangular plate with design of Chinese bellflowers in underglaze enamels. H. 3.0 cm., d. 31.7 cm., w. 26.2 cm. Private collection, Japan.

12. Bowl with openwork design of chrysanthemums in overglaze enamels. H. 12.0 cm., d. 19.0 cm. Hatakeyama Memorial Museum, Tokyo.

13. Jar with design of maple leaves in overglaze enamels. H. 14.5 cm., d. 15.9 cm. Idemitsu Museum, Tokyo.

14. Tea bowl with design of moonflowers in overglaze enamels. H. 9.0 cm., d. 13.0 cm. Yamato Bunkakan, Nara.

15. Iris Bridges (Yatsuhashi). Hanging scroll, ink and colors on paper. H. 28.6 cm., w. 36.6 cm. Private collection, Japan.

16. Tea bowl with design of horses in underglaze iron. H. 6.4 cm., d. 9.9 cm. Idemitsu Museum, Tokyo.

BLACK AND WHITE FIGURES:

1. Page from the Nishiyama Gire (Fragments from Ishiyama): Poem by Ki no Tsurayuki. Ink, silver, and gold on assembled dyed paper. H. 20.3 cm., w. 16.1 cm. Courtesy of the Freer Gallery of Art, Smithsonian Institution, Washington, D.C. Acc. no. F69.4.

2. Cabinet with design of pampas grass and paulownia crests. Black lacquer on wood with sprinkled gold. H. 50.0 cm., d. 30.5 cm., w. 38.0 cm. Suntory Museum of Art, Tokyo.

3. Att. Hon'ami Kōetsu: Stationery box with design of boat bridge (funabashi). Black lacquer on wood with lead, cut silver, and sprinkled gold. H. 11.8 cm., d. 24.2 cm., w. 22.7 cm. Tokyo National Museum.

4. Hon'ami Kōetsu and Tawaraya Sōtatsu (att.): Sheet from an album of poem cards (shikishi). Ink and colors on paper, each sheet h. 18.1 cm., w. 17.0 cm. Gotoh Museum, Tokyo.

5. Att. Tawaraya Sōtatsu: Detail from a screen decorated with fans. Ink and colors on paper, entire screen h. 155.0 cm., w. 358.0 cm. Private collection, Japan.

6. Att. Hon'ami Kōetsu: Flute case with design of deer. L. 39.7 cm., w. 3.7 cm. Yamato Bunkakan, Nara.

7. Chōjirō: Red Raku ware tea bowl, named Yugure. H. 8.9 cm., d. 10.2 cm. Gotoh Museum, Tokyo.

8. Oshikōji-style ware (att. to Chōjirō): Bowl with design of melons and vines in polychrome glazes. H. 6.0 cm., d. 33.0 cm. Tokyo National Museum.

9. Ninsei ware: Faceted tea caddy with iron glaze. H. 8.9 cm., w. 6.8 cm. Kōzu Museum of Historical Culture, Kyoto.

10. Ninsei ware: Tea-storage jar with design of poppies in overglaze enamels. H. 42.8 cm., d. 14.5 cm. Idemitsu Museum, Tokyo.

11. Nakatachiuri, Kyoto.

12. Reconstruction of Shūseidō compound based on diagram passed down in Kaji family, Kyoto (now preserved in the Nakane Garden Research Center). Drawing by Don Choi.

13. Chang Jizhih: The Diamond Sutra (detail). Dated 1246. Ink on paper. From two albums of text, each leaf h. 29.1 cm., w. 13.4 cm. The Art Museum, Princeton University. Lent by John B. Elliot.

14. Fujiwara no Teika: Page from the Ogura Shikishi. Ink on paper. H. 17.5 cm., w. 15.0 cm. Gotoh Museum, Tokyo.

15. Receipt for inheritance of Ogata Gompei (Kenzan). Dated 1687. Ink on paper. H. 30.4 cm., w. 38.7 cm. Agency for Cultural Affairs, Tokyo.

16. Receipt for inheritance of Ogata Ichinojō (Kōrin). Dated 1687. Ink on paper. H. 30.5 cm., w. 34.3 cm. Agency for Cultural Affairs, Tokyo.

17. "Orthodox" version of character *ji* (self).

18. Kenzan's version of *ji* (from inheritance receipt, line four, eighth character).

19. "Orthodox" version of character *sho* (to write).

20. Kenzan's version of character *sho* (from inheritance receipt, line one, sixth character).

21. *Ōtotsuka o Yogiru no Ki* (A Visit to the Ōtotsuka; detail). Dated 1692. Ink on paper. Overall, h. 30.1 cm., w. 237.2 cm. Private collection, Japan.

22. Letter to Kōrin. Ink on paper. H. 15.9 cm., w. 61.6 cm. Osaka Municipal Museum.

23. Reconstruction of Kenzan's Narutaki workshop, based on building plans preserved in Hōzōji, Kyoto, and on excavations of kiln remains at the site. Drawing by Don Choi.

24. Square plate with design of plum and mandarin duck in underglaze enamels. From a set of twelve plates depicting Fujiwara no Teika's poems of birds and flowers of the twelve months. Dated 1702. H. 2.2 cm., d. 16.8 cm., w. 16.8 cm. MOA Museum of Art, Atami, Shizuoka Prefecture.

25. Inscription on verso.

26. Detail of verso.

27. Rectangular plate with design of landscape in underglaze iron. Painting by Soshin. Dated Hōei era (1704–11). H. 4.0 cm., d. 37.0 cm., w. 33.9 cm. Private collection, Japan.

28. Era mark on verso.

29. Rectangular plate with design of six classical poets in underglaze enamels. Dated 1711. H. 2.6 cm., d. 26.4 cm., w. 34.6 cm. Private collection, Japan.

30. Inscription and signature on verso.

31. Fragment of tea bowl in the style of late Ming-dynasty enameled ware (*gosu aka e*). Underglaze cobalt. H. 7.2 cm., d. 8.7 cm. Kyoto National Museum.

32. Signature inside foot ring.

33. *Gosu aka e* style ware: Bowl with diadem and disc pattern in overglaze enamels. H. 8.3 cm., d. 19.7 cm. Kyoto City Archaeological Museum.

34. Tea bowl with patterns of birds and flowers in underglaze cobalt. H. 12.5 cm., d. 11.0 cm. Hōzōji, Kyoto.

35. Annam ware: Bowl with design of floral scroll in overglaze enamels. H. 8.9 cm., d. 13.3 cm. Tokugawa Art Museum, Nagoya.

36. Bowl with Cizhou-style designs in underglaze iron. Dated 1706. H. 14.9 cm., w. 34.8 cm. Hamamatsu Municipal Museum, Shizuoka Prefecture.

37. Signature and inscription on base.

38. Cizhou ware: Tall jar with design of crane in landscape in underglaze iron. Dated 1541. H. 28.7 cm. Herbert F. Johnson Museum of Art, Cornell University, Collection of George and Mary Rockwell.

39. Fragments of Oribe-style tea bowl in underglaze iron. H. 9.0 cm., d. of original bowl approx. 12.0 cm. Kyoto National Museum.

40. Fragments of Oribe-style square dish in underglaze iron. H. 3.3 cm. each. Hōzōji, Kyoto.

41. Oribe ware: Tea bowl with stripe design in underglaze iron. H. 6.9 cm., d. 14.0 cm. Yamato Bunkakan, Nara.

42. Oribe ware: Square dish with designs in underglaze iron. H. 4.3 cm., d. 19.7 cm., w. 19.7 cm. Tokyo National Museum.

43. Fragment of food dish in lily shape with design in underglaze iron. H. 5.3 cm., w. 5.0 cm. Hōzōji, Kyoto.

44. Food dish in lily shape with design in underglaze iron. From a set of five. H. 5.0 cm., d. 5.5 cm. Private collection, Japan.

45. Karatsu ware: Food dish in shape of split pepper. H. 7.0 cm., d. 11.5 cm. Kyoto City Archaeological Museum.

46. Karatsu-style cylindrical food dish with design of lattices in underglaze iron. H. 7.3 cm., d. 6.2 cm. Private collection, Japan.

47. Impressed seal on base.

48. Karatsu ware: Cylindrical food dish with design of lattices. H. 11.2 cm. Private collection, Japan.

49. Fragment of porcelain decorated in underglaze cobalt. H. 5.2 cm., w. 7.3 cm. Hōzōji, Kyoto.

50. Kyoto urban ceramics workshop, after an 1882 painting by Kōno Bairei (1844–95) in the Peabody Museum, Salem. Drawing by Don Choi.

51. Square plate with design of pine branch in underglaze iron. Dated 1711. H. 2.5 cm., d. 21.4 cm., w. 21.4 cm. Private collection, U.S.A.

52. Signature on verso.

53. Square plate with design of plum branches in underglaze iron. Dated 1711. H. 2.5 cm., d. 21.0 cm., w. 21.0 cm. Private collection, Japan.

54. Signature on verso.

55. Square plate with design of willow in underglaze iron. Painting by Kōrin. H. 2.8 cm., d. 21.8 cm., w. 21.8 cm. Fujita Museum, Osaka.

56. Square plate with design of monk Hotei in underglaze iron. Painting by Kōrin. H. 2.8 cm., d. 21.8 cm., w. 21.8 cm. Fujita Museum, Osaka.

57. Signature on verso.

58. Square plate with design of Chinese calligrapher-poet Huang Shangu watching gulls, in underglaze iron. Painting by Kōrin. H. 2.9 cm., d. 22.2 cm., w. 22.2 cm. Tokyo National Museum.

59. Signature on verso.

60. Detail from five sheets in a book of Kōrin memoranda.

Ink on paper. H. 18.8 cm. Agency for Cultural Affairs, Tokyo.

61. Lidded bowls with design of crane and reeds in underglaze iron and cobalt. Set of ten. H. 7.0 cm., d. 11.7 cm. Kyoto Folk Art Museum.

62. Signature inside foot ring.

63. Ogata Kōrin: Sketch for a stacked food box (jūbako) with design of plum, from Konishi archive. Ink on paper. H. 36.5 cm., w. 63.7 cm. Osaka Municipal Museum.

64. Food wrapper with Korin-style design of cranes. Ink and silver on gold-foiled paper. Approx. 17 cm. square. From Kimono: Rimpa Hyakuzu Ten (exhibition catalogue, Kyoto: Society for Preservation of Traditional Textile Arts, 1982).

65. Att. Hon'ami Kōetsu and Tawaraya Sōtatsu: Elongated poem card (tanzaku) with design of cranes over water. Ink and colors on paper. H. 37.5 cm., w. 6.0 cm. Yamatane Art Museum, Tokyo.

66. Lidded bowls with design of spring grasses in underglaze iron and cobalt. From a set of ten. H. 6.5 cm., d 11.9 cm. Yuki Museum, Osaka.

67. Food dishes with individual designs in underglaze iron and cobalt, and overglaze gold. Set of five. H. 2.4 cm., d. 16.0 cm. Nezu Institute of Fine Arts, Tokyo.

68. Signature on back of rim.

69. Ogata Kōrin: Sketch of blossoming plum. Ink on paper. D. 11.0 cm. Osaka Municipal Museum.

70. Ogata Kōrin: Sketch of flowing water. Ink on paper. D. 11.0 cm. Osaka Municipal Museum.

71. Food dishes with design of maple leaves on the Tatsuta River in overglaze enamels. Set of five. H. 3.0 cm., d. 18.2 cm. Yamato Bunkakan, Nara.

72. Verso with signature.

73. Ogata Kōrin: Sketch of maple leaf from Konishi archive. D. 4.5 cm. Private collection, Japan.

74. Bowl with openwork design of pine in snow in overglaze enamels. H. 11.5 cm., d. 20.4 cm. Private collection, Japan.

75. Verso with signature.

76. Kenzan's commemorative stone in Iriya.

77. Lamentation poems for Prince Kōkan. Ink on paper. H. 31.5 cm., w. 43.2 cm. Yamato Bunkakan, Nara.

78. Kenzan's grave marker (front). Zen'yōji, Nishi Sugamo, Tokyo.

79. Square plate with design of white lily in overglaze enamels. Dated 1736. H. 3.0 cm., d. 22.1 cm., w. 21.2 cm. Ex-Masaki collection, Tokyo.

80. Signature on verso.

81. Dish in the shape of an abalone with design of pine and cherry trees in underglaze enamels. Dated 1737. H. 6.2 cm., d. 24 cm. Private collection, Japan.

82. Inscription on base.

83. Signature on side.

84. Charcoal container (hiire) with motifs of orchid, plum, and narcissus in underglaze enamels. H. 10.5 cm., d. 11.6 cm. Private collection, Japan.

85. Signature inside foot ring.

86. Dish with design of summer landscape in underglaze enamels. H. 3.6 cm., d. 19.8 cm. Private collection, Japan.

87. Poem on back of rim, composed by Sudō Tosen.

88. Signature on back of opposite rim.

89. Dish with design of hollyhock in underglaze enamels. H. 3.6 cm., d. 19.6 cm. Private collection, Japan.

90. Signature on back of rim.

91. Incense container with design of toy top in underglaze and overglaze enamels. H. 5.4 cm., d. 9.6 cm. Freer Gallery of Art, Smithsonian Institution, Washington, D.C.

92. Signature on base.

93. Tea bowl with design of moonflowers in overglaze enamels. H. 9.0 cm., d. 13.0 cm. Yamato Bunkakan, Nara.

94. Signature outside foot ring.

95. Tea bowl with design of horses in underglaze iron. Dated 1741. H. 6.4 cm., d. 9.9 cm. Idemitsu Museum, Tokyo.

96. Att. Ogata Kōrin: Sketches for Kenzan ware. Detail from horizontal scroll, ink on paper. H. 16.6 cm., total w. 206.1 cm. Idemitsu Museum, Tokyo.

97. Rectangular plates in the shape of elongated poem cards (tanzaku), designs in underglaze enamels. Five from a set of ten. Dated 1743. H. 2.6 cm., d. 28.5 cm., w. 6.9 cm. Yuki Museum, Osaka.

98. Signatures and style names on verso.

99. Inscribed box.

100. Tea bowl with design of rose in overglaze enamels. H. 8.0 cm., d. 13.0 cm. Ex-Bishamondō collection, Kyoto.

101. Inscription and signature on opposite side.

102. Wild pinks and cormorant, originally from a set of twelve album leaves depicting Fujiwara no Teika's poems of birds and flowers of the twelve months. Ink and colors on paper. Twelfth-month leaf dated 1743. H. 16.1 cm., w. 23.0 cm. Metropolitan Museum of Art, New York. The Harry G.C. Packard Collection of Asian Art, Gift of Harry G.C. Packard and Purchase, Fletcher, Rodgers, Harris Brisbane Dick and Louis V. Bell Funds, Joseph Pulitzer Bequest and the Annenberg Fund, Inc. Gift, 1975.

103. Ogata Kōrin: Wild pinks and cormorant, from sketches depicting Fujiwara no Teika's poems of birds and flowers of the twelve months. Ink on paper. W. 11.8 cm. Osaka Municipal Museum.

104. Iris Bridges (Yatsuhashi). Hanging scroll, ink and colors on paper. H. 28.6 cm., w. 36.6 cm. Private collection, Japan.

105. Detail.

106. Hollyhocks. Pair of panels, ink and colors on gold-foiled paper. Dated 1742. Each panel h. 94.0 cm., w. 40.3 cm. Musée Cernuschi, Paris.

107. Detail.

108. Willow in Spring. Hanging scroll, ink on paper. H. 24.4 cm., w. 45.4 cm. Yamato Bunkakan, Nara.

109. Detail.

110. Rectangular plate with design of willow in underglaze iron. H. 2.0 cm., d. 10.4 cm., 24.0 cm. Idemitsu Museum, Tokyo.

111. Monk Raizan (Chinese: Laican) Roasting Yams. Hanging scroll, ink on paper. H. 27.4 cm., w. 44.3 cm. Private collection, Japan.

112. Detail.

113. Ogata Ihachi: Water jar (mizusashi) with design of birds, butterflies, and imperial chrysanthemum in overglaze enamels. H. 15.7 cm., d. 16.7 cm. Shōgoin, Kyoto.

114. Signature on base.

115. Ogata Ihachi: Tea bowl with design of pine, bamboo, plum, and imperial chrysanthemum in underglaze cobalt. H. 7.0 cm., d. 9 cm. Shōgoin, Kyoto.

116. Signature inside foot ring.

117. Ogata Ihachi: Black Raku tea bowl with design of flaming jewel in underglaze cobalt. H. 8.0 cm., d. 10.5 cm. Shōgoin, Kyoto.

118. Signature on opposite side.

119. Kenzan signature from Tōkō Hitsuyō.

120. Ogata Ihachi: Tea bowl with design of pine, bamboo, and plum in underglaze cobalt. H. 8.7 cm., d. 9.5 cm. Enshōji, Nara.

121. Signature inside foot ring.

122. Box inscription (signed and sealed third-generation Kenzan, Gosuke).

123. Ogata Ihachi: Cylindrical food dish with floral designs in underglaze cobalt. Dated Enkyō era (1744–1748). H. 8.0 cm., d. 7.0 cm. Private collection, Japan.

124. Signature inside foot ring.

125. Ogata Ihachi: Square plate with design of pine in underglaze iron. One of a set of four, each with individual designs. H. 2.2 cm., d. 14.6 cm., w. 14.6 cm. Eugene Fuller Memorial Collection, Seattle Art Museum.

126. Square plate with design of orchid and rock in underglaze iron. Painting by Watanabe Soshin. H. 2.6 cm., d. 22.5 cm., w. 22.0 cm. Nezu Institute of Fine Arts, Tokyo.

127. Inscription and signature on verso.

128. Kempō: Square plate with design of cherry blossoms in underglaze iron. H. 2.3 cm., d. 14.7 cm., w. 14.8 cm. Reimei Kyōkai, Kyoto.

129. Signature and seal.

130. Gosuke: Incense container in shape of auspicious mallet with design of pine branches in underglaze iron. H. 5.4 cm., w. 4.8 cm. Montreal Museum of Fine Arts.

131. Signature inside cover.

132. Takahashi Dōhachi: Food vessel with design of maple leaves on the Tatsuta River in overglaze enamels. From a set of ten. H. 4.8 cm., d. 15.8 cm. Private collection, Japan.

133. Nin'ami Dōhachi: Handled bowl with openwork

design of snow-laden bamboo in underglaze iron. H. 19.0 cm., d. 23.0 cm. Private collection, Japan.

134. Seifū Yohei: Bowl with design of chrysanthemums. H. 9.0 cm., d. 15.0 cm. Courtesy, Museum of Fine Arts, Boston.

135. Makuzu Kōsai: Bowl with design of peonies in overglaze enamels. H. 8.0 cm., d. 14.6 cm. Metropolitan Museum of Art, New York. Photo by author.

136. Impressed seal and signature. Photo by author.

137. Nishimura Myakuan: Kenzan Sedaigaki (Genealogy of the Kenzan School). Ink on paper. Dated 1836. H. 15.8 cm., w. 36.0 cm. Zen'yōji, Tokyo.

138. Minzan: Hand warmer with design of chrysanthemums in underglaze enamels. H. 16.0 cm., d. 18.5 cm. Private collection, Japan.

139. Signature on base.

140. Workshop of Miyazaki Tominosuke: Hand warmer with design of cherry blossoms in underglaze enamels. Dated Tempō era (1830–44). H. 15.1 cm., d, 19.0 cm. Courtesy Museum of Fine Arts, Boston.

141. Signature on base.

142. Date on underside of lid.

143. Sakai Hōitsu: Page from the Kenzan Iboku. Dated 1823. Ink and colors on paper. H. 26.1 cm., w. 18.1 cm. Private collection, U.S.A.

144. Ida Kichiroku (Kensai): Square incense container with design of chrysanthemums in underglaze enamels. H. 5.8 cm., d. 3.8 cm., w. 5.5 cm. Montreal Museum of Fine Arts.

145. Signature on base.

146. Sakune Benjirō (Kenzō): Spouted bowl with design of flowing water in underglaze cobalt. H. 8.0 cm., d. 17.5 cm. Courtesy, Museum of Fine Arts, Boston.

147. Signature on side panel.

148. Miura Ken'ya: Inrō with design of iris bridges (yatsuhashi) in underglaze enamels. H. 1.2 cm., d. 9.0 cm., w. 6.6 cm. Courtesy of the Freer Gallery of Art, Smithsonian Institution, Washington, D.C. Acc. no. F1984.45 ABC.

149. Signature on base.

150. Miura Ken'ya: Spouted bowl with design of spring and autumn foliage in underglaze iron and cobalt. H. 9.7 cm., d. 17.0 cm. Metropolitan Museum, New York. Photo by author.

151. Signature inside foot ring. Photo by author.

152. Miura Ken'ya: Figurine representing auspicious female, otafuku, in overglaze enamels. H. 18.0 cm. Private collection, Japan.

153. Signature on back of figure.

154. Miura Ken'ya: Lobed food dish with design of pine in snow in underglaze enamels. H. 3.0 cm., d. 15.5 cm. Zen'yōji, Tokyo.

155. Signature inside foot ring.

156. Tsukamoto Torakichi (Kemba): Tea bowl with design

of spring foliage in underglaze iron and cobalt. H. 7.2 cm., d. 13.4 cm. Tokyo National Museum.

157. Signature inside foot ring.

158. Inuyama ware: Dish with design of cherry blossoms and autumn foliage in overglaze enamels. H. 1.6 cm., d. 21.4 cm. British Museum.

159. Signature inside foot ring.

160. Urano Shigekichi (Kensai; Kenzan VI): Water jar with design of willow in underglaze enamels. H. 18.6 cm., d. 12.0 cm. Museum für Kunst und Gewerbe, Hamburg.

161. Signature on opposite side.

162. New Sano Kenzan ware: Rectangular plate with design of narcissus in underglaze enamels. H. 3.5 cm., d. 17.0 cm., w. 20.8 cm. Private collection, Japan.

163. Page from New Sano Kenzan diary. From *Shin Hakken Sano Kenzan Ten* (exhibition catalogue, Shirokiya Department Store).

164. Sakai Hōitsu: Detail from sequel edition of *Kōrin Hyakuzu* (A Hundred Kōrin Pictures). Dated 1826. Each page h. 25.0 cm., w. 16.5 cm. Private collection, Japan.

165. Square plate with design of heron in underglaze iron and cobalt. H. 4.0 cm., d. 24.1 cm., w. 27.5 cm. Museum für Kunst und Gewerbe, Hamburg.

166. Rectangular plate with design of narcissus in underglaze iron. H. 4.2 cm., d. 12.0 cm., w. 20.0 cm. Private collection, Japan.

167. Ogata Ihachi: Fragment of a bowl with design in underglaze cobalt. D. of entire fragment 9.0 cm., d. of foot ring 4.1 cm. Dōshisha University Archaeological Research Center, Kyoto.

168. Signature inside foot ring.

169. Page from the *Tōkō Hitsuyō*. 1737. Ink on paper. H. 26.7 cm., w. 17.9 cm. Yamato Bunkakan, Nara.

170–187. Calligraphy specimens.

188. Shard inscribed with Japanese-style calligraphy in underglaze iron, from the Narutaki kiln site. H. approx. 6.0 cm., w. approx. 3.0 cm. Private collection, Japan.

189. Square plate with design of plum and mandarin ducks in underglaze enamels. From a set of twelve plates depicting Fujiwara no Teika's poems of birds and flowers of the twelve months. Dated 1702. H. 2.2 cm., d. 16.8 cm., w. 16.8 cm. MOA Museum of Art, Atami, Shizuoka Prefecture.

190. Inscription and signature on verso.

191. Square plate with design of plum and mandarin duck in underglaze enamels. From a set of twelve plates depicting Fujiwara no Teika's poems of birds and flowers of the twelve months. H. 2.3 cm., d. 17.9 cm., w. 20.0 cm. Los Angeles County Museum of Art.

192. Inscription and signature on verso.

193. Square plate with design of plum and mandarin duck in underglaze enamels. From a set of twelve plates depicting Fujiwara no Teika's poems of birds and flowers of the

twelve months. H. 2.2 cm., d. 16.7 cm., w. 16.7 cm. Private collection, Japan.

194. Inscription and signature on verso.

195. Rectangular plate with design from theme of Noh drama in underglaze enamels. From a set of ten. H. 2.6 cm., d. 11.4 cm., w. 19.2 cm. Idemitsu Museum, Tokyo.

196. Inscription on verso.

197. Rectangular plate with design from theme of Noh drama in underglaze enamels. H. 2.6 cm., d. 10.8 cm., w. 19.0 cm. Peabody Museum, Salem.

198. Inscription on verso.

199. Plate in the shape of overlapping poem cards (*kasane shikishi*) with design of pines in underglaze enamels. Set of five. Size unknown. From Kobayashi 1948, p. 16.

200. Signature from verso of another plate in above set. From Kobayashi 1948, p. 17.

201. Plate in the shape of overlapping poem cards (*kasane shikishi*) with design of cranes over reeds in underglaze enamels. Set of five. Size unknown. From Kobayashi 1948, p. 16.

202. Rectangular plate with landscape design in underglaze enamels. Dated 1711. D. 26.8 cm., w. 35.0 cm. From Michael Tomkinson, *A Japanese Collection* (London: George Allen, 1898), pl. 88.

203. Fragment of teabowl with Chinese characters in underglaze iron, from Narutaki kiln site. H. approx 5.5 cm., w. approx. 3.0 cm. Hōzōji, Kyoto.

204. Eight-sided plate with design of landscape in underglaze iron. H. 5.5 cm., d. 29.5 cm. Private collection, Japan.

205. Rectangular plate with design of landscape in underglaze iron. Dated 1705. Dimensions unknown. From Kobayashi 1948, p. 20.

206. Signature on verso. From Kobayashi 1948, p. 21.

207. Rectangular plate with design of landscape in underglaze iron. Dated 1706. H. 4.4 cm., d. 25.6 cm., w. 28.1 cm. Private collection, Japan.

208. Signature on verso.

209. Square plate with design of orchid in underglaze iron. Dimensions unknown. From Kobayashi 1948, p. 261.

210. Signature on verso.

211. Square plate with design of cracked ice in underglaze enamels. Dated Genroku era (1688–1704). H. 2.5 cm., d. 14.5 cm., w. 15.5 cm. Private collection, Japan.

212. Signature inside foot ring.

213. Cup stand with design of diadems in overglaze enamels. H. 4.9 cm., d. 11.7 cm. Private collection, Japan.

214. Signature on base.

215. Charcoal container (*hiire*) with Dutch ceramics design in overglaze enamels. H. 9.3 cm., d. 13.3 cm. Freer Gallery of Art, Smithsonian Institution, Washington, D.C.

216. Signature on base.

217. Bowl with crane and scroll design in underglaze iron. Dimensions unknown. From *Tōsetsu* 14 (1954), pl. 40.

218. Signature on base.

219. Shard with design of flowing water and snowflakes in underglaze iron and cobalt, from Narutaki kiln. W. 9.5 cm. Kyoto National Museum.

220. Shard with diaper pattern in underglaze cobalt, from the Narutaki kiln site. W. 9.7 cm. Kyoto National Museum.

221. Shard with lozenge and quatrefoil pattern in underglaze cobalt, from the Narutaki kiln site. W. approx 3.0 cm. Hōzōji, Kyoto.

222. Shard with stenciled design of chrysanthemum and paulownia in underglaze iron and cobalt, from the Narutaki kiln site. H. approx. 4.2 cm.

223. Shard with impressed "Kenzan" mark, from the Narutaki kiln site. W. approx 3.5 cm. Hōzōji, Kyoto.

224. Shard with part of painted character *ki* (vessel) in underglaze iron, from the Narutaki kiln site. W. approx. 2.7 cm. Hōzōji, Kyoto.

225. Square food dish with lozenge and quatrefoil pattern in underglaze cobalt. W. 11.5 cm. Private collection, Japan.

226. Stenciled signature on base.

227. Square food dish with stenciled designs of chrysanthemum and paulownia in underglaze iron and cobalt. H. 4.2 cm., d. 13.6 cm., w. 13.6 cm. Kōzu Museum of Historical Culture, Kyoto.

228. Stenciled signature on base.

229. Food dish with design of pines in underglaze iron. Dimensions unknown. From *Sekai Tōji Zenshū*, vol. 6 (Tokyo: Shōgakkan, 1975), p. 230.

230. Stamped signature on base.

231. Square dish with design of plum in underglaze iron. From a set of five. Dimensions unknown. Private collection, Japan.

232. Inscription on verso.

233. Incense container with design of the Narrow Ivy Road in overglaze enamels. H. 2.5 cm., d. 10.0 cm. Freer Gallery of Art, Smithsonian Institution, Washington, D.C.

234. Signature on base.

235. Incense container with design of deutzia and cuckoo in overglaze enamels. From a set of twelve incense containers depicting Fujiwara no Teika's poems of birds and flowers of the twelve months. H. 2.6 cm., d. 12.2 cm. Private collection, Japan.

236. Signature on base.

237. Lidded box with design of pampas grass in underglaze iron and cobalt, and overglaze gold. H. 7.9 cm., d. 26.7 cm. Suntory Museum of Art, Tokyo.

238. Signature on base.

239. Lidded box with design of pines in underglaze iron and cobalt, and overglaze gold. H. 6.3 cm., d. 23.4 cm. Idemitsu Museum, Tokyo.

240. Signature on base.

241. Charcoal container *(hiire)* with design of cherry in underglaze iron and cobalt. H. 10.6 cm., d. 11.2 cm., w. 11.0 cm. Metropolitan Museum of Art, New York. Photo by author.

242. Signature on base. Photo by author.

243. Water jar *(mizusashi)* with design of snow-laden pines and camellias in overglaze enamels. H. 13.3 cm., d. 24.6 cm. Private collection, Japan.

244. Signature on base.

245. Rectangular plate with design of Chinese bellflowers in underglaze enamels. H. 3.0 cm., d. 31.7 cm., w. 26.2 cm. Private collection, Japan.

246. Signature on base.

247. Rectangular plate with design of lilies in underglaze enamels. H. 4.5 cm., d. 28.0 cm., w. 24.7 cm. Private collection, Japan.

248. Signature on base.

249. Square plate with design of crane and reeds in underglaze iron. H. 2.8 cm., d. 22.0 cm., w. 22.0 cm. Fujita Museum, Osaka.

250. Square plate with design of Daikoku (God of Wealth) in underglaze iron. H. 2.8 cm., d. 22.0 cm., w. 22.0 cm. Fujita Museum, Osaka.

251. Square plate with design of Jurōjin (God of Longevity) in underglaze iron. H. 2.8 cm., d. 21.9 cm., w. 21.9 cm. Fujita Museum, Osaka.

252. Square plate with design of plum branches in underglaze iron. H. 2.8 cm., d. 22.2 cm., w. 22.2 cm. Fujita Museum, Osaka.

253. Square plate with design of Jittoku (Chinese: Shide) in underglaze iron. H. 2.0 cm., d. 22.1 cm., w. 22.1 cm. Kyoto Folk Art Museum.

254. Square plate with design of monk Kanzan (Chinese: Hanshan) in underglaze iron. H. 2.0 cm., d. 22.1 cm., w. 22.1 cm. Kyoto Folk Art Museum.

255. Square plate with design of Jurōjin in underglaze iron. H. 2.9 cm., d. 21.9 cm., w. 22.9 cm. MOA Museum of Art, Atami, Shizuoka Prefecture.

256. Square plate with design of peony in underglaze iron. H. 3.0 cm., d. 21.9 cm., w. 21.9 cm. Jinzu Shūmeikai, Kyoto.

257. Square plate with design of man watching waterfall in underglaze iron. H. 2.9 cm., d. 21.8 cm., w. 21.8 cm. Courtesy, Museum of Fine Arts, Boston.

258. Square plate with design of Jurōjin in underglaze iron. H. 2.7 cm., d. 22.0 cm., w. 22.1 cm. Brooklyn Museum.

259. Hexagonal plate with design of Jurōjin in underglaze iron. H. 3.0 cm., d. 27.5 cm., w. 27.5 cm. Ōkura Cultural Foundation, Tokyo.

260. Hexagonal plate with design of crane in underglaze iron. H. 3.0 cm., d. 27.5 cm., w. 27.5 cm. Private collection, Japan.

261. Square plate with design of cranes and reeds in

underglaze iron. H. 3.2 cm., d. 22.1 cm., w. 22.0 cm. Private collection, Japan.

262. Square plate with design of iris bridge (*yatsuhashi*) in underglaze iron. H. 2.8 cm., d. 21.7 cm., w. 21.7 cm. Freer Gallery of Art, Smithsonian Institution, Washington, D.C.

263. Square plate with design of plovers over waves in underglaze iron. H. 3.0 cm., d. 21.0 cm., w. 21.0 cm. Cleveland Museum of Art.

264. Square plate with design of Mount Fuji in underglaze iron. H. 3.0 cm., d. 22.0 cm., w. 21.8 cm. Suntory Museum of Art, Tokyo.

265. Lidded bowl with design of cranes and reeds in underglaze iron and cobalt. From a set of ten. H. 7.0 cm., d. 11.7 cm. Kyoto Folk Art Museum.

266. Signature inside foot ring.

267. Lidded bowl with design of spring grasses in underglaze iron and cobalt. From a set of ten. H. 6.5 cm., d. 11.9 cm. Yuki Museum, Osaka.

268. Signature inside foot ring.

269. Lidded bowl with design of pines in underglaze iron and cobalt. D. 11.9 cm. Private collection, Japan.

270. Signature inside foot ring.

271. Bowl with design of pampas grass in underglaze iron and cobalt, and overglaze enamel. H. 6.9 cm., d. 13.1 cm. Kimbell Museum, Fort Worth.

272. Signature inside foot ring.

273. Food dish with design of flowing water and snow-flakes in underglaze iron and cobalt, and overglaze gold. From a set of five. H. 2.4 cm., d. 16.0 cm. Nezu Institute of Fine Arts, Tokyo.

274. Signature underneath rim.

275. Cylindrical food dish with design of crane and reeds in underglaze iron and cobalt. From a set of ten. H. 10.1 cm., d. 6.0 cm. Private collection, Japan.

276. Signature on base.

277. Rectangular dish with design of diadem in overglaze enamels. From a set of five. H. 4.2 cm., d. 9.5 cm., w. 18.9 cm. Fujita Museum, Osaka.

278. Signature on base.

279. Lidded bowl (porcelain) with design of spring grasses in overglaze enamels. H. 6.5 cm., d. 12.0 cm. Private collection, Japan.

280. Signature inside foot ring.

281. Bowl with openwork design of chrysanthemums in overglaze enamels. H. 12.0 cm., d. 19.0 cm. Hatakeyama Memorial Museum, Tokyo.

282. Signature inside foot ring.

283. Bowl with openwork design of maple leaves in overglaze enamels. H. 11.5 cm., d. 26.0 cm. Private collection, Japan.

284. Signature inside foot ring.

285. Bowl with openwork design of wisteria in overglaze enamels. H. 12.0 cm., d. 19.3 cm. Hatakeyama Memorial Museum, Tokyo.

286. Signature inside foot ring.

287. Bowl with openwork design of geese and reeds in overglaze enamels. D. 19.6 cm. Idemitsu Museum, Tokyo.

288. Signature inside foot ring.

289. Food dish with design of chrysanthemums in overglaze enamels. From a set of five. D. approx. 16.0 cm. MOA Museum of Art, Atami, Shizuoka Prefecture.

290. Signature inside foot ring.

291. Food dish with design of maple leaves on the Tatsuta River in overglaze enamels. From a set of five. H. 3.0 cm., d. 18.2 cm. Yamato Bunkakan, Nara.

292. Signature inside foot ring.

293. Food dish with design of peonies in overglaze enamels. Set of five. H. 3.4 cm., d. 17.5 cm. Itsuō Museum, Osaka.

294. Signature inside foot ring.

295. Food dish with design of cedars in overglaze enamels. H. 3.2 cm., d. 18.4 cm. Private collection, Japan.

296. Signature on base.

297. Incense container with design of willow in underglaze iron. Dated Shōtoku era (1711–16). H. 5.3 cm., d. 5.3 cm., w. 6.8 cm. Yamato Bunkakan, Nara.

298. Era mark on base.

299. Incense burner with design of Chinese lion-dog (*shishi*) in underglaze iron. Dated 1715. H. 20.7 cm., d. 13.0 cm., w. 13.2 cm. Private collection, U.S.A.

300. Inscription and signature on side panel.

301. Incense container with design of Chinese lion-dog (*shishi*) in underglaze iron. Dated 1715. H. 7.1 cm., w. 4.7 cm. Montreal Museum of Fine Arts.

302. Signature and seals on opposite side.

303. Charcoal container (*hiire*) with design of *Duluo Yuan Ji* (Chinese poet Sima Guang's eleventh-century essay about his Garden of Self-Enjoyment) in underglaze cobalt. H. 10.8 cm., d. 9.8 cm., w. 9.7 cm. Private collection, Japan.

304. Signature and seals on opposite side.

305. Hand warmer with design of mountain hermitage in underglaze iron. H. 19.2 cm., d. 26.0 cm. Osaka Municipal Museum.

306. Signature and seals on opposite side.

307. Charcoal container (*hiire*) with design of mountain hermitage in underglaze cobalt. H. 6.1 cm., d. 8.0 cm. Freer Gallery of Art, Smithsonian Institution, Washington, D.C.

308. Signature and seals on opposite side.

309. Bowl with design of plum in underglaze iron. Dated Kyōhō era (1716–36). H. approx. 12.0 cm., d. 36.0 cm. Royal Ontario Museum, Toronto.

310. Era mark on base.

311. Bowl with design of *Duluo Yuan Ji* (Chinese poet Sima Guang's eleventh-century essay about his Garden of Self-

Enjoyment) in underglaze iron. Dated Kyōhō era (1716–36). H. 12.5 cm., d. 37.7 cm. Private collection, Japan.

312. Era mark on base.

313. Square plate with design of white lily in overglaze enamels. Dated 1736. H. 3.0 cm., d. 22.1 cm., w. 21.2 cm. Ex-Masaki collection, Tokyo.

314. Signature on verso.

315. Tea bowl with design of rose in overglaze enamels. H. 8.0 cm., d. 13.0 cm. Ex-Bishamondō collection, Kyoto.

316. Inscription and signature on opposite side.

317. Tea bowl with design of moonflowers in overglaze enamels. H. 9.0 cm., d. 13.0 cm. Yamato Bunkakan, Nara.

318. Signature outside of foot ring.

319. Bowl with chestnut design in underglaze enamels. Dimensions unknown. From *Tōsetsu* 71 (1959), cat. no. 5.

320. Signature on base.

321. Dish in the shape of an abalone with design of pine and cherry trees in underglaze enamels. Dated 1737. H. 6.2 cm., d. 24 cm. Private collection, Japan.

322. Signature on side.

323. Foliate bowl with inscribed character *kei* in underglaze enamels. H. 19.5 cm., d. 23.5 cm. Private collection, Japan.

324. Signature on base.

325. Incense container with design of toy top in underglaze and overglaze enamels. H. 5.4 cm., d. 9.6 cm. Freer Gallery of Art, Smithsonian Institution, Washington, D.C.

326. Signature on base.

327. Rectangular plates in the shape of elongated poem cards (*tanzaku*), designs in underglaze enamels. From a set of ten. Dated 1743. H. 2.6 cm., d. 28.5 cm., w. 6.9 cm. Yuki Museum, Osaka.

328. Signature on verso.

329. Square plate with design of orchid and rock in underglaze iron. Painting by Watanabe Soshin. H. 2.6 cm., d. 22.5 cm., w. 22.0 cm. Nezu Institute of Fine Arts, Tokyo.

330. Inscription and signature on verso.

331. Rectangular plate with inscription in underglaze iron. One of a pair. H. 3.0 cm., d. 24.3 cm., w. 21.0 cm. Private collection, Japan.

332. Signature on verso.

333. Teabowl with design of waterfall in underglaze iron. H. 8.0 cm., d. 10.5 cm. Private collection, Japan.

334. Inscription and signature on opposite side.

335. Tea bowl with design of plum branches in underglaze iron. H. 7.8 cm., d. 10.2 cm. Umezawa Memorial Museum, Tokyo.

336. Inscription and signature on opposite side.

337. Charcoal container (*hiire*) with design of mountain hermitage in underglaze iron. H. 11.0 cm., d. 13.2 cm. Private collection, Japan.

338. Inscription and signature on opposite side.

339. Plate in the shape of overlapping poem cards with design of mountain hermitage in underglaze iron. H. 2.5

cm., d. 12.9 cm., w. 18.0 cm. Peabody Museum, Salem.

340. Signature and seals.

341. Rectangular plate with design of mountain hermitage in underglaze iron. From a set of ten. H. 1.8 cm., d. 10.0 cm., w. 23.1 cm. Idemitsu Museum, Tokyo.

342. Edge patterns (different piece).

343. Fan-shaped plate with a design of orchid in underglaze iron. From a set of five. H. 2.5 cm., d. 10.4 cm., w. 24.0 cm. Idemitsu Museum, Tokyo.

344. Edge patterns.

345. Square plate with design of orchid in underglaze iron. From a set of four. H. 2.2 cm., d. 14.6 cm., w. 14.6 cm. Seattle Art Museum.

346. Rectangular plate with design of orchid in underglaze enamel. From a set of five. H. 2.3 cm., d. 9.5 cm., w. 23.6 cm. Idemitsu Museum, Tokyo.

347. Food dish with design of orchids in overglaze enamels. From a set of five. H. 2.3 cm., d. 16.2 cm. Hatakeyama Memorial Museum, Tokyo.

348. Signature on back of rim.

349. Tea bowl with design of plum in underglaze iron. H. 7.2 cm., d. 9.8 cm. Musée Guimet, Paris.

350. Inscription on opposite side and signature on inner wall.

351. Tea bowl with design of spring grasses in underglaze iron and cobalt. H. 6.8 cm., d. 10.0 cm. Museum für Kunst und Gewerbe, Hamburg.

352. Signature outside of foot ring.

353. Confetti bottle (*furidashi*) with Dutch-inspired stripe designs in underglaze enamels. H. 7.0 cm., d. 5.3 cm. Kōzu Museum of Historical Culture, Kyoto.

354. Signature on base.

355. Incense container in tortoise shape with Kōchi-style polychrome glazes. H. 5.0 cm., d. 6.0 cm., w. 7.8 cm. Montreal Museum of Fine Arts.

356. Signature on base.

357. Sauce jar with Cizhou-style designs in underglaze iron. From a set of twenty. H. 5.8 cm., d. 9.7 cm. Kōzu Museum of Historical Culture, Kyoto.

358. Signature on base.

359. Black Raku tea bowl with design of bamboo in underglaze iron. H. 8.1 cm., d. 9.9 cm. Private collection, Japan.

360. Black Raku tea bowl with design of waves in underglaze cobalt. H. 10.4 cm., d. 8.8 cm. Private collection, Japan.

361. "Planed-surface" dish (*kanname zara*) with design of spring grasses in underglaze enamels. From a set of five. H. 2.0 cm., d 12.3 cm, w. 12.3 cm. Private collection, Japan.

362. Signature on base.

363. Tea bowl with design of orchid in underglaze iron and cobalt. H. 7.5 cm., d. 10.0 cm. Tokyo National Museum.

364. Signature outside of foot ring.

365. Square plate with design of Chinese black pine (*maki*) in underglaze enamels. H. 2.3 cm., d. 17.2 cm., w. 17.2 cm. Idemitsu Museum, Tokyo.

366. Rectangular plate with design of mountain hermitage in underglaze iron. From a set of five. H. 2.6 cm., d. 10.9 cm., w. 18.6 cm. Idemitsu Museum, Tokyo.

367. Food dish with design of bamboo in underglaze enamels. D. 9.3 cm. Private collection, Japan.

368. Signature on base.

369. Handled bowl with design of snow-laden bamboo in underglaze iron. H. 18.0 cm., d. 26.6 cm. Tekisui Museum, Ashiya, Hyōgo Prefecture.

370. Signature on base.

371. Handled bowl with design of camellias in overglaze enamels. H. 14.0 cm., d. 18.4 cm. Itsuō Museum, Ikeda.

372. Signature on side panel.

373. Faceted charcoal container (*hiire*) with design of plum branches in underglaze iron. H. 10.1 cm., d. 12.1 cm. Freer Gallery of Art, Smithsonian Institution, Washington, D.C.

374. Signature on base.

375. Charcoal container (*hiire*) with design of willow in underglaze iron. H. 10.4 cm., d. approx. 9.0 cm. Walters Art Gallery, Baltimore.

376. Signature on base.

377. Water jar (*mizusashi*) with design of plum branch in overglaze enamels. H. 20.0 cm., d. 19.4 cm. Private collection, Japan.

378. Signature on base.

379. Spouted bowl with design of chrysanthemums in overglaze enamels. H. 14.0 cm., d. 17.0 cm. Private collection, Japan.

380. Signature on base.

381. Water jar (*mizusashi*) with design of hermitage in snow, in underglaze cobalt and iron. H. 13.8 cm., d. 11.5 cm. Metropolitan Museum of Art, New York. Photo by author.

382. Signature on base. Photo by author.

383. Incense container with design of hermitage in snow, in underglaze cobalt and iron. H. 2.8 cm., d. 9.3 cm., w. 13.0 cm. Montreal Museum of Fine Arts.

384. Signature on base.

385. Stationery box (*suzuribako*) with design of willow and hermitage in underglaze enamels (after sketches depicting Fujiwara no Teika's poems of birds and flowers of the twelve months published in *Kōrin Hyakuzu*, 1815). H. 4.2 cm., d. 21.9 cm., w. 19.5 cm. Metropolitan Museum of Art, New York. Photo by author.

386. Signature on base. Photo by author.

387. Tray for scrolls (*jikubon*) with design of willow and hermitage in underglaze enamels (after sketches depicting Fujiwara no Teika's poems of birds and flowers of the twelve months published in *Kōrin Hyakuzu*, 1815). H. 2.0 cm., d. 32.4 cm., w. 9.5 cm. Private collection, Japan.

388. Signature on base.

389. Brazier (*hibachi*) with design of pines in underglaze iron. H. 20.7 cm., d. 23.7 cm. Zen'yōji, Tokyo.

390. Signature on base.

391. Square plate with designs of pines in underglaze iron. H. 4.5 cm., d. 24.3 cm., w. 24.3 cm. Private collection, Japan.

392. Signature on verso.

393. Food dish with design of thistle in underglaze enamels. From a set of five. H. 2.5 cm., d. 17.2 cm. Private collection, Japan.

394. Signature on base.

395. Hand warmer with design of chrysanthemums in underglaze enamels. H. 16.0 cm., d. 18.5 cm. Private collection, Japan.

396. Signature on base.

397. Hand warmer with design of chrysanthemums in underglaze enamels. H. 16.1 cm., d. 17.2 cm. Private collection, Japan.

398. Signature on base.

399. Tiered food box (*jūbako*) with palmette design in underglaze enamels. Dated Bunka era (1804–18). Dimensions unknown. Private collection, U.S.A.

400. Signature on base.

401. Tiered food box with cloud design in underglaze enamels. H. 14.5 cm., d. 11.3 cm., w. 11.5 cm. Courtesy, Museum of Fine Arts, Boston.

402. Signature on base.

403. Hand warmer with design of chrysanthemums and flowing water in underglaze enamels. H. 19.0 cm., d. 17.8 cm. Osaka Municipal Museum.

404. Inscription and signature on base.

405. Bowl with design of chrysanthemums in underglaze and overglaze enamels. H. 10.5 cm., d. 20.2 cm. Victoria and Albert Museum, London.

406. Signature inside foot ring.

407. Water jar (*mizusashi*) with design of camellia in underglaze enamels. H. 18.0 cm., d. 13.6 cm. Tokyo National Museum.

408. Signature on base.

409. Food dish with design of pine branch in underglaze enamels. From a set of ten. H. 1.0 cm., d. 12.3 cm. Private collection, Japan.

410. Signature on base.

411. Tea bowl with calendar design in underglaze enamels. H. 9.0 cm., d. 10.8 cm. Private collection, Japan.

412. Signature outside foot ring.

413. Spouted bowl with design of chrysanthemums in underglaze cobalt. H. 3.7 cm., d. 13.2. Zen'yōji, Tokyo.

414. Signature inside foot ring.

415. Footed bowl with auspicious designs in overglaze enamels. H. 8.5 cm., d. 17.8 cm. Zen'yōji, Tokyo.

416. Signature inside foot ring.

417. Black Raku water jar (*mizusashi*) with design of pampas

grass. H. 16.1 cm., d. 12.5 cm. Freer Gallery of Art, Smithsonian Institution, Washington, D.C.

418. Signature on side.

419. Foliate bowl with design of cherry blossoms and autumn foliage in overglaze enamels. H. 10.5 cm., d. 12.8 cm. Museum für Kunst und Gewerbe, Hamburg.

420. Signature inside foot ring.

421. Teabowl with design of moonflowers in overglaze enamels. Probably made in 1950s by Yamamoto Nyosen (b. 1916). Dimensions unknown. From *Kenzan* (Tokyo: Atarashii Me Sha, 1960).

422. Signature on opposite side.

423. Rectangular plate with design of autumn foliage on the Tatsuta River in underglaze enamels. H. 3.0 cm., d. 24.3 cm., w. 21.0 cm. Idemitsu Museum, Tokyo.

424. Signature on verso.

425. Priest Kenkō. Hanging scroll, ink on paper. H. 20.0 cm., w. 27.0 cm. Umezawa Memorial Museum, Tokyo.

426. Detail.

427. Eggplants. Hanging scroll, ink on paper. H. 20.0 cm., w. 27.5 cm. Fukuoka Municipal Museum.

428. Detail.

429. Flower Baskets. Hanging scroll, ink and color on paper. H. 110.4 cm., w. 48.6 cm. Fukuoka Municipal Museum.

430. Detail.

431. Maple leaves and chrysanthemums. Hanging scroll, ink and color on paper. H. 130.5 cm., w. 56.5 cm. Tokyo National Museum.

432. Detail.

433. Chrysanthemums. Fan mounted as a hanging scroll, ink and color on paper. H. 18.5 cm., w. 48.4 cm. Private collection, Japan.

434. Detail.

435. Pines in Snow. Fan mounted in a panel, ink and color on paper. H. 21.0 cm., w. 51.0 cm. Freer Gallery of Art, Smithsonian Institution, Washington, D.C.

436. Detail.

437. Lilies and Hollyhocks. Hanging scroll, ink and colors on paper. Dimensions unknown. From Uemura Masao, *Kenzan-Hōitsu* (Tokyo: Takimazawa Mokuhansha, 1940).

438. Detail.

439. Tea Bowl and Pine. Hanging scroll, ink and color on paper. H. 14.5 cm., w. 22.5 cm. Private collection, Japan.

440. Detail.

BIBLIOGRAPHY

Aimi Kōu. "Ogata Kōrin Narabini Ogata Ke no Koto" [Ogata Kōrin and the Ogata Family]. *Shoga Kottō Zasshi* 78 (1915).

————. "Hōitsu ni yotte Tsutaeraretaru Kōrin-Kenzan ga Koto Domo" [Information about Kōrin and Kenzan Transmitted by Hōitsu]. *Nihon Bijutsu Kyokai Hōkoku* 7 (1928).

Brinckmann, Justus. *Kenzan: Beiträge zur Geschichte der japanischen Töpferkunst* [Kenzan: Commentaries on the History of the Japanese Ceramic Art]. Hamburg: Lütcke and Wulff, 1897.

Crawcour, E.S. "Some Observations on Merchants, a Translation of Mitsui Takafusa's Chōnin Kōken Roku." *The Transactions of the Asiatic Society of Japan* third series: 8 (December 1961).

Fukui Rikichirō. "Kōrin kō" [Thoughts on Kōrin]. *Geibun* 6: 6–8, 1915.

————, "Kōhon Kenzan Nempyō" [Tentative Kenzan Chronology]. *Bunka* 9:6 (1942).

Gotoh Museum, ed. *Kenzan no Kaiga* [The Painting of Kenzan]. Tokyo: Gotoh Museum, 1982.

————, *Kenzan no Yakimono* [The Ceramics of Kenzan]. Tokyo: Gotoh Museum, 1987.

Haga Yoshikiyo. "Kyoto Oyakusho Muki Taigai Oboegaki no Rakuyaki, Kyōyaki, Kenzan Shiryō" [Information on Raku Ware, Kyoto Ware, and Kenzan in *Kyoto Oyakusho Muki Taigai Oboegaki*]. *Yakimono Shumi* 6:16 (1941).

Hirotani Kindō, "Kenzan o Meguru Hitobito" [The People Around Kenzan]. *Kobijutsu* 148 (1943).

Idegawa Naoki. Imada ni Nazo o Haramu Sano Kenzan Jiken" [The Still Unresolved Sano Kenzan Incident]. *Geijutsu Shinchō* (July 1983).

Ishida Ichirō. *Itō Jinsai.* Jinbutsu Sōsho series, vol. 30. Tokyo: Yoshikawa Kobunkan, 1960.

Kasuga Junsei. "Kenzan Yaki Yōshi Hakken ni tsuite" [Concerning the Discovery of the Kenzan Kiln Site]. *Tōji* 2:5 (1930).

Kawahara Masahiko. *Kenzan.* Nihon no Bijutsu Series, no. 154. Tokyo: Shibundō, 1979.

Kawakita Kyūdayū (Handeishi). *Kenzan Ikō* [Differing Thoughts on Kenzan]. Tokyo: Yōgei Bijutsu Tōji Bunka Kenkyūsho, 1942.

Kobayashi Taichirō. *Kenzan Kyoto Hen* [Kyoto Kenzan]. Kyoto: Zenkoku Shobō, 1947.

————. *Kōrin to Kenzan* [Kōrin and Kenzan]. *Kobayashi Taichirō Cho Sakushū* [Collected works of Kobayashi Taichirō], vol. 6. Kyoto: Tankōsha, 1962.

Leach, Bernard. *Kenzan and His Tradition.* London: Faber and Faber, 1966.

Mitsuoka Chūsei (Tadanari). *Kenzan.* (Tōji Taikei Series, no. 24. Tokyo: Heibonsha, 1973.

Morse, Edward S. *Catalogue of the Morse Collection of Japanese Pottery.* Cambridge: Riverside Press, 1901. Reprint. Rutland, Vt.: Charles E. Tuttle Co., 1979.

Ninagawa Teiichi. "Tōsei Ninsei no Bunken Hōkoku" [Report on a Document Concerning the Potter Ninsei]. *Chawan* 69 (1936).

Ogata Kenjo (Nami). *Hasu no Mi* [The Seed of the Lotus]. Kamakura: Kamakura Shunjūsha, 1981.

Satō Masahiko. "The Three Styles of Kenzan Ware." In *International Symposium on Japanese Ceramics*, edited by Seattle Art Museum. Tokyo: Kōdansha International, l972.

Shinozaki Genzō. *Sano Kenzan.* Tokyo: Yōgei Bijutsu Tōji Bunka Kenkyūsho, 1942.

————. "Sano Kenzan Monogatari" [The Tale of Sano Kenzan]. *Tōsetsu* 185–189 (1968), 190–191 (1969).

Suzuki Hancha. *Kenzan Tōki Yūhō Densho Kenkyū: Nidai Kenzan Tōki Mippōsho* [Research on Kenzan's Ceramics Techniques: The *Tōki Mippōsho* by Second Generation Kenzan]. Tokyo: Yōgei Bijutsu Tōji Bunka Kenkyūsho, 1942.

————. "Edo Keito Nidai Kenzan Jirōbei" [Jirōbei, Second Kenzan in the Edo Line]. *Tōsetsu* 31 (1955).

————. "Ihachi Kenzan Sakuhin to Tōki Mippōsho" [Work of Ihachi Kenzan and the *Tōki Mippōsho*]. *Tōsetsu* 26–28 (1955).

————. "Godai Kenzan Nishimura Myakuan" [Fifth Generation Kenzan Nishimura Myakuan]. *Tōsetsu* 55–57 (1957), 58, 60, 62 (1958).

————. "Dai Kenzan kara Leach made" [From the First Kenzan to Leach]. *Tōsetsu* 78–80 (1959), 84, 86 (1960), 95, 99, 101, 103, 105 (1961), 108, 112, 114, 115, 117 (1962).

Tamabayashi Haruo. "Kōkan Shinnō to Kenzan" [Prince Kōkan and Kenzan] *Yakimono Shumi* 6:11 (1940).

Tanaka Kisaku. "Shūseidō Ki ni tsuite" [Concerning the *Shūseidō Ki*]. *Gasetsu* 10 (1937).

————. "Konishi Ke Kyūzō Kōrin Kankei Shiryō" [Kōrin Materials Formerly in the Collection of the Konishi Family]. *Bijutsu Kenkyū* 56, 57, 59, 60 (1938).

————. "Shūseidō no Ki" [More on Shūseidō]. *Gasetsu* 17 (1938).

Wilson, Richard L. *Ogata Kenzan 1663-1743.* Ann Arbor, Mich.: University Microfilms International, 1985.

————. "The Sano Kenzan Affair." *Ceramics* 4 (1986).

————. "Kenzan Yakimono Yōshiki o Ou" [Searching for Style in Kenzan Ware]. *Tōyō Tōji* 15–16 (1987).

Yamane Yūzō, *Konishi Ke Kyūzō Kōrin Kankei Shiryō to sono Kenkyū* [Kōrin-Related Materials Formerly in the Konishi Collection and their Research]. Tokyo: Chuō Koron Bijutsu Shuppan, 1962.

———. "Konishi Ke Monjo Chū Kenzan Kenkyū Shiryō" [Kenzan Research Materials in the Konishi Archive]. In Yamato Bunkakan 1963.

———, ed. *Rimpa Kaiga Zenshū* [The Collected Rimpa Paintings]. 5 vols. Tokyo: Nihon Keizai Shinbunsha, 1978–1980.

Yamato Bunkakan, ed. *Ogata Kenzan Jihitsu Tōkō Hitsuyō Narabini Kaisetsu* [The *Tōkō Hitsuyō* with Annotations]. Kyoto: Benridō, 1963.

INDEX

The "weathermark" identifies this book as a production of Weatherhill, Inc., publishers of fine books on Asia and the Pacific. Editorial Supervision: Jeffrey Hunter. Book design and typography: Liz Trovato. Production Manager: Bill Rose. Typesetting: Trufont, Hicksville, New York. Color separations: ISCOA, Arlington, Virginia. Platemaking, printing, and binding: Arcata/Halliday Litho, Plympton, Massachusetts. The typeface used is Centaur.